ADVENTURE CYCLING IN EUROPE

**A Practical Guide to
Low-Cost Bicycle Touring
in 27 Countries**

ADVENTURE CYCLING IN EUROPE

A Practical Guide to Low-Cost Bicycle Touring in 27 Countries

by John Rakowski

 Rodale Press, Emmaus, Pennsylvania

Book Design by Merole Berger
Illustrations by David Bullock

Printed in the United States of America on recycled paper, containing a high percentage of de-inked fiber.

Library of Congress Cataloging in Publication Data

Rakowski, John, 1922—
Adventure cycling in Europe.

Includes index.
1. Bicycle touring—Europe—Guide-books.
2. Europe—Description and travel—1971—
Guide-books.   I. Title.
GV1046.E85R34   914   81-4882

ISBN 0-87857-352-6   hardcover   AACR2
ISBN 0-87857-353-4   paperback

2 4 6 8 10 9 7 5 3 1 hardcover
2 4 6 8 10 9 7 5 3 1 paperback

To Rosemary, an unparalleled touring companion

CONTENTS

Part II: Country-by-Country Descriptions

CONTENTS

Part III: Appendices

x

—ACKNOWLEDGMENTS—

These bicyclists provided help through questionnaire returns and advice:

Carol Allred, Lehi, UT; Patricia Logan, Santa Fe, NM; Jerry Simpson, Jr., Charlotte, NC; Hugh McLachlan, Paris, France; Dave Miller, Massillon, OH; Josh Lehman, Seattle, WA; Clifford Graves, M.D., La Jolla, CA; Ann and Douglas Conklin, Santa Rosa, CA; Rich and Kathi Stafford, Lakewood, CO; George Cole, Blacksburg, VA; Nahum Vishniavsky, Richmond, VA; Gerard van der Veer, Hilversum, Holland; Bert and Dinnie Nieuwenhuis, Hengelo, Holland; Kathy Bales and Rick Stodola, Lower Waterford, VT; Jorma Kaukonen, Mill Valley, CA; Natanael Bjork, Lund, Sweden; Zbigniew Zur, Przemysl, Poland; John Mosley, Van Nuys, CA; Mike Hyman, Seattle, WA; Ken and Jacque Proctor, on world tour; Colin and Veronica Scargill, Bedford, England; Michael and Marcia Horner, Wetherfield, CT; Shelley Longmire, Golden, CO; Hollis Hassenstein, Santa Fe, NM; Leslie Rock, North Platte, NE; Donald Tomlin, M.D., New Canaan, CT; Maurice Upperton, Surrey, England; Tomas Vogl, Immenstaad, West Germany; Margaret Logan, Boston, MA; Judy and Jim Glading, West Hartford, CT; Jim and Gerrie Thorsteinson, Winnipeg, Canada; Robert and Diane Haines, Stanton, NJ; Norman Ford, Boulder, CO; John Williams, Harrisburg, PA; Trudi Weel, Amsterdam, Holland; Jack Lewis, Bristol, England; David Shadovitz, Syosset, NY; Jean and Jim Scheu, Minneapolis, MN; Allen Manthei family, Los Alamos, NM; Jerome Nagel, Denver, CO; Walter Garber, Vienna, Austria; James Donlon, Staten Island, NY; H. Haalboom, Renkum, Holland; Harvey Lyon, Chicago, IL; Venita Plazewski, Madison, WI; Hartley and Jean Alley, Boulder, CO; Greg Smith, Huntsville, New South Wales, Australia; Steve Gordon, New York, NY; Carl Ekholm, Biloxi, MS; Brian and Deb MacDonald, Hamilton, Ontario, Canada; Eusebio Rahona, Madrid, Spain; Dale Petrick, Bentleyville, PA; Carroll and Edith Webber, Greenville, NC; Jennie Yancey, Philadelphia, PA; Morrie Paul, Montreal, Canada; Alan Bubna, Arlington, VA; Robert Woods, Albuquerque, NM; Piet de Jong, Tilburg, Holland; Paul Kluth, Tarzana, CA; Marilyn Schrut, New York, NY.

ADVENTURE CYCLING IN EUROPE

Special thanks for major contributions to:

Lucy Grey, San Bruno, CA; André Everett, Lincoln, NE; Ian Davis, Sydney, Australia; Don Lemmon, Oakmont, PA; Tibor Pollerman, London, England; Douglas Watson, Turkey; William Stagg, APO, West Germany; Walter ten Hoeve, Fort Collins, CO; Tyler Folsom, Seattle, WA; Indy Altersheim, Baar, Switzerland; Dick Phillips, Iceland; Rosemary Smith, Balmain, New South Wales, Australia.

INTRODUCTION

Bike riders, even the most experienced, express anxiety at the thought of being let loose in a foreign country. "How will I be understood?" "Isn't it dangerous?" "I'll be sure to be lost." "What if I'm needed back home?" These and a dozen similar questions come up constantly when I talk to would-be bike tourists.

The concerns are natural and understandable. To many Americans it's still a hostile, or at least an unknown, world out there. Witness the success of the conducted tour, the traveler leaving the security blanket of his commodious bus with trepidation, and scrambling back to it after the lightning circuit of the threatening native quarter.

On the surface, the bicyclist's position is even more precarious. He doesn't have a tour guide who interprets the strange culture, isn't surrounded by fellow travelers who can provide some sort of group succor, and is more often than not in open country, away from even a rustic form of civilization. No wonder the biker's hesitation in taking that foreign tour.

And so he turns to the dozens of bicycling books for guidance and assurance. What do these tell him? Little or nothing, for the most part. The few touring books available deal largely with the domestic scene. They include only a smattering of information about the foreign scene, some almost grudgingly. One refers to extended foreign tours as "for the fanatic fringe"; another suggests that American bikers stick to their own country.

The rest of the bike literature concentrates on the beginner, orientating him to the joys and techniques of the sport, or is technical in nature: repairs, commuting, activism. It's of little help to the biker who aspires to adventure touring in strange lands.

What does one read, then, about foreign touring? A few personal accounts, excellent of their kind, tell of exotic adventures and experiences during long rides. The books have the flavor of being there. Unfortunately, they provide little useful guidance, except between the lines, in such particulars as the condition of roads in given countries, the availability of bike parts, and the kind of places to stay and eat. Besides, they're limited in scope, being the story of one rider, along one route, for a limited time span.

This guide provides more comprehensive information. It tells what to expect overseas, bike-wise, and how to cope with the pretour concerns of security, accommodations and foul weather. It suggests what's important in equipment and what is advertising hype. Stateside bike tourists can find useful hints here, too, as well as encouragement to expand their touring endeavors.

A number of bike tourists contributed data through questionnaires, in personal correspondence, and in face-to-face interviews. The bulk of those riders have traveled all parts of the world and back their statements with years of rich experiences. Those generous people are listed in the Acknowledgments and elsewhere in these pages.

The guide is not a bicycling primer. It won't tell you how to adjust a bike nor of its construction. You won't learn how to get in shape. I expect you're satisfied with your riding techniques; at least, I assume that learning how to increase riding efficiency a bit is not important to you in enjoying a tour. Nor will I elaborate on how much fun a bicycle is, or how cheaply you can travel on it. I assume you've already discovered those advantages of your machine. You're now ready to consider the bicycle as a medium of travel, to take a foreign vacation or an extended tour that you've dreamed about.

Not that I advocate intentional ignorance. By all means, review your basic riding techniques, practice repair and maintenance on your bike to know it well enough to be self-sufficient, and play around with various modifications if that's your thing. Like the anticipation of lovers, those pretour preliminaries are almost as pleasurable for many as riding itself.

xiv

The essential ingredient for bike travel, however, is not the machine but you. A tour is an act of faith — in self-reliance, in a sense of adventure, in the world itself and its inhabitants. Hundreds of bike tourists have started long trips — some across continents or around the world — with just a minimal knowledge of what makes a bicycle go. For them, the locomotion was more important than the logistics.

Specific information soon gets out of date, to be sure. Prices will change, roads improve or deteriorate, and unfriendly governments may close frontiers. Still, the touring principles remain valid, and the listed costs can be extrapolated to inflation rates. The most recent data is better than none.

Perhaps, with more bike tourists on the road, this guide may be upgraded periodically with feedback. Your contributions can make this book grow and they are welcomed. Let me hear from you. Write me c/o *Bicycling* magazine, 33 East Minor Street, Emmaus, PA 18049.

PART I

TECHNIQUES

GETTING
1 READY
FOR
A
STRANGE
LAND

WHY TOUR BY BICYCLE?

"Is there any other way?" countered Josh Lehman when I asked why he used a bike for touring. As a trained geographer, a transportation planner for Seattle, Washington, and an experienced bike tourist and writer, he could well ask the question. The advantages are obvious to anyone who thinks about it even casually: bike touring is economical, self-reliant, healthful and positive, relaxing, dependable, oil and material conserving, enjoyable, life prolonging, social and educational. Some bikers even claim it's aphrodisiacal. You can probably think of yet more reasons to travel by bike.

As against any other mode of travel, except hiking, the act of *going* there contains the meaning, not the fact of having *gotten* there. The steel cocoon of a bus, train or auto imprisons the rider, and it insulates him from the environment. In a large tour bus in Mexico, once, I saw passengers watching TV as the bus snaked its way through the spectacular Sierra Madre Este. The bus paused long enough for me to see the program, an Asian travelogue. The people were oblivious of the outside.

When biking, you don't read, nap or do crossword puzzles to pass the time. The terrain goes by slowly and you take it all in. You're part of the "outside," not isolated in an "inside" envelope. Smells, vistas and sounds prod your nerve endings. Even the touch of the road itself, transmitted through hard tires, and the taste of sweat influence your total sensory experience.

But how do other bike travelers view it?

Brian and Deb MacDonald never bike toured before visiting Europe. On the spur of the moment, they bought bikes and gear in London, and in a couple of days became used to the new routine. They found it the most pleasant travel mode, between slow hiking and expensive motoring. They're sold on biking now.

Lucy Grey writes of the exhilaration of bike travel, and of the human relationships that come from it. She says you meet more natives and on a more meaningful basis when riding a bike.

Ann Conklin claims "independence!"; Tom Fleener, an around-the-world biker, "total experience"; Hollis Hassenstein, "informality"; and Morrie Paul, "flexibility, mobility, freedom."

Jerome Nagel adds to conventional reasons that it's something different to talk about when you get back home. Paul Randall, who rode in Asia, had "a more intimate relationship with people. . . . you're more apt to be invited into a household." Calgary Penn was so taken by a Mexican trip that he became totally committed to the bicycle, and sold his car. Once bitten, a bike tourist is forever convinced.

WHERE TO GO?

Any country in Europe can be interesting. To those who've never been there, a bike tour is an especially exciting introduction. For others, who may have taken a ten-day, organized tour previously, it's a revelation—no rush, no fawning or rude guides, no stuffy buses.

3

Good cycling can be found everywhere. Some places are better than others, naturally, from the viewpoint of road conditions, weather, traffic or terrain. The second part of this guide describes those conditions in some detail.

But because a country isn't quite prepared for the bike tourist in the way of roads or accommodations, doesn't mean that it should be written off arbitrarily. Your machine opens any road to you, even if it doesn't lead along a beaten path of comfort. Camping enables you to sleep and cook almost anywhere. No country in the world lacks a food store, or a grassy field on which to pitch a tent. The wilder it is, the easier a camper can find a spot. Like Neanderthal man, the bicyclist can roam the globe at will.

Read about other touring possibilities, also, in past articles in *Bicycling* or in foreign cycling magazines. See also the publications of the League of American Wheelmen (LAW), the Cyclists' Touring Club (CTC), in England, and the American Youth Hostels (AYH). A few touring descriptions are offered by Bonnie Wong in the "Touring Exchange" she offers at nominal cost of handling, and in some bicycling books that offer foreign tours. Addresses for these, and the other organizations cited in these pages, are listed in the Appendices.

When it comes to a final choice, however, depend more on your interests than on biking conditions, as such. Chances are that the things you'd really like to do in Europe are the same as what you'd do at home, except that you'd want to see the European version of them. If you don't go to the Guggenheim in New York City, for example, you won't enjoy the Louvre. You'd be as bored in an art museum in Paris as you would at home. Probably more so, since they've been collecting art longer there and you'd be seeing more of it. It happens that I go to art museums at home, so I do that overseas, too.

If any tour—prepared or self-made—is to be uniquely yours, initial plans should be only a springboard. Improvise as you go along to suit your pace and tastes. Bicycling harks back to true vagabonding.

BACKGROUND READING

Once you decide on a country, what should you read to anticipate the joys of touring there? Not a "how-to" bicycle book, not even this one. That would be the same as reading an auto owner's manual before driving to Mexico. The best sort of reading has to do more with the country's attractions, its history and culture, and its significance—for want of a better word, its "soul."

4

See and feel it through the eyes of other, discerning travelers, who reacted to it with sensitivity. You'll heighten your ultimate experience if you prepare with this frame of reference. The keen mind and skill of a V. S. Pritchett *(The Offensive Traveller)* or a Paul Theroux *(The Great Railway Bazaar)* will introduce you to the bazaars of Turkey, the streets of Naples, and the fjords of Norway more effectively than the mundane facts of a Fodor guide. A romantic approach? Why not? Isn't bicycling a lot like that, a romance with a responsive vehicle? Those books also help motivate bikers who are uncertain, and convince them to go.

Not that you'd want to arrive there with a singular, prejudiced point of view. You'd simply be alerted to the nuances of the culture. That sort of preparation eases your adjustment to help avoid too many social slips. For that reason, you'll profit also from a bit of background in cultural anthropology, which explains why cultures are different from each other. I list a few books on that subject that I found interesting, including the two mentioned above, in Appendix I.

Some hard facts help, certainly; an almanac or political handbook of the world provides vital statistics. You don't have to study economic or political theory. In a short paragraph, jot down a few names of the country's leaders, the chief products, a thumbnail history, and the ethnic composition of its people. When meeting natives, you won't be embarrassed not knowing the name of the president of their country.

Europeans are keen about world politics. They may be more aware of events in the United States Senate than you are. It has happened to me. I was ashamed to admit that I didn't know the name of Bulgaria's leader and the nature of the Greek Orthodox religion, while the people I met there were familiar with the White House staff. Don't make my mistake.

By all means, read bicycle-related literature to learn about tire changing, maintenance and riding techniques, if you don't know about those things already. Bring a small soft-cover repair book for reference if you must, as you'd bring an auto maintenance manual for a cross-country drive. But just as that auto manual wouldn't help you appreciate the wonders of a Grand Canyon or the Mayan ruins, so the technical bike books won't tell you what it's like to cycle in Europe.

INFORMATION SOURCES

For an overview of any country, the first place to write for information is its national tourist bureau. Although many bureaus respond promptly with standard tourist literature, lists of hotels and campgrounds, and travel regulations, a few take some weeks. Write to them well ahead of time.

Most bureaus won't answer any specific questions you ask. Their bicycling information is generally scant or useless. Except for a very few—Great Britain and the Netherlands are best—they seldom supply as much as an address of a cycling organization, although many will send you a map if you ask for it.

Once you're in the country, though, most tourist offices in cities and towns are helpful with specifics for the region and may have local maps. Location of campgrounds is especially good; the local offices know of smaller camps whose names don't find their way into official government lists.

The problem for a biker, of course, is that the information he gets from local sources is often too late. What he needs, given the bicycle's limited range, is information before he gets well into the interior of the country, where the touring offices are generally situated. He can't easily backtrack to something he may have missed, or change his route abruptly from a schedule, even if it's a loose one.

ADVENTURE CYCLING IN EUROPE

Tourist agents at home have little knowledge that a biker can use. If they've actually visited a given country, their point of view is that of the packaged tour or the Hilton hotel circuit.

A travel guide is a good source for a country's background, requirements for visiting, accommodations, and a thousand other specifics, city by city and region by region. The best of the lot for our purposes is *Let's Go, Europe.* Although it caters to the young, the hitchhikers and those who travel by train and bus, the viewpoint is closest to that of bicyclists. Other guides emphasize more commodious travel, although the *Michelin Green Guide* series is useful in its descriptions of offerings in each country. See Appendix I for information on these and other guides.

It must be kept in mind that most books are somewhat out of date as soon as they're printed. The most recent travel news appears in the travel sections of metropolitan newspapers, such as the Sunday *New York Times*, which offers superlative coverage. Large libraries throughout the United States with 35mm reader-printers have copies of that newspaper in microfilm form. It's worth an afternoon's viewing to look through their recent offerings.

A few biking organizations are excellent information sources. AYH chapters—in New York City or San Diego, for example—will help plan a bike route and make arrangements for an independent tour by a group of riders. The CTC gives the best service in this respect. They'll help with planning a tour and provide data about virtually all European countries in a series of sheets and notes. Those not only describe cycling conditions; they also identify volunteers and cycling clubs that will advise you further. It's a worthwhile organization to join.

LAW is primitive by contrast. Its foreign touring information is nearly nil; it depends more on individual responses of its officers and members than on a formal organization, although its magazine, *American Wheelmen,* does print stories of foreign tours. LAW has no committee that advises on foreign touring, as does CTC.

Cycling organizations within foreign countries may help. They often take a long time to answer letters and some don't respond at all. Those with the foreign equivalent for "cycle touring" in their titles are the most likely to yield something useful. Others with names like *sportif* or *velocipedique* may, depending on which of their members answers you. I list some of those organizations in the descriptions of countries. Enclose an international reply coupon, bought at a post office, with your inquiry.

Look through the reams of travel literature you'll get from all these sources months before leaving, even before deciding where to go. Let them help make up your mind on the destination and route. You'll need that long a lead time for further reading and planning.

USEFUL ASSOCIATIONS

Joining a few organizations allows you to use certain facilities overseas. As a member of the National Campers and Hikers Association, for example, you can buy an international *carnet* card for $4. It gets you a reduced rate in many European campgrounds. In some countries the card is required regardless of the discount feature. The savings from the card will only pay if you'll make much use of it, however. When you camp for a couple of weeks, you may just break even.

For bikers, a better source of the *carnet* is the CTC. A member can buy a card for $1.50, in addition to receiving its bimonthly magazine, *Cycletouring,* and profiting from the best travel advice available in any bicycling organization.

The camping card covers $100 of free, yearly insurance against theft or fire of bike; you also have the option to buy up to $400 more insurance at a cost of 25¢ per $100. That's certainly a bargain today. LAW offers insurance reasonably, also.

For emergency use, it might be a good idea to get an international driver's license, even if you're an autophobe. The American Automobile Association (AAA) will give you one for an application and $3.

A few hospitality organizations print lists of biking members who are willing to meet you and provide a bed or place for a sleeping bag overnight. They ask that you allow yourself to be listed too; that is, to receive guests in your home. Sponsors of three such outfits are: John Mosley and Steve Krueger in the United States, and Leigh Howlett in England. Krueger asks a small fee for his list; the others are free. The international hosts in these lists are few, however, most names being domestic.

A Dutch, non-bike-oriented organization, Travel and Friend (Reis en Vriend), offers a list of contact people throughout the world. Its accent is on Europe. Members, including yourself if you want to join, are not obliged to host the traveler. They merely volunteer to orient you to their country and they suggest local interests and attractions. They may guide you or even put you up, but that's their prerogative. The primary intent of this organization is to improve the relations between people of different nationalities. A donation of about $5 is asked to cover stamps, paperwork and printing of the directory.

Travelers' Directory is a loose United States counterpart of

7

ADVENTURE CYCLING IN EUROPE

Travel and Friend, except that its members do take you into their homes. For the $10-per-year donation you receive a list of international hosts—you'll be listed, too—who supply a place to stay, information and a large measure of friendliness. Each person writes a short description as an introduction that is included in the list. A member also receives a quarterly newsletter, "The Vagabond's Shoes." It informs of economic travel, new fares, finds and trends.

Speakers of the international language, Esperanto, have an association in which members are willing to meet others. There is no commitment to feed or house. The contacts are fraternal and one-world in nature, and much of the exchange is through the mails and in international meetings. If you sympathize with the aims of the organization and are willing to learn the language—which is emphasized—Esperanto can be useful.

Servas International is another organization dedicated to understanding among the world's peoples. Its name is Esperanto for "serve." Through a cooperative, nonprofit system of hosts and travelers in some 70 countries, the 30-year-old program strives to help build world peace. It's not a travel agency or a way of finding a cheap "flop." Rather, Servas emphasizes personal contacts among people of diverse cultures and backgrounds, with the aims of creating good will and of sharing social concerns.

To join Servas, you first submit an application, two letters of reference, a background sketch of your interests and activities, and your purpose in joining the organization. You will then be given an interview with one of its members. The United States has a hundred interviewers in all parts of the country. To offset organizational costs, you'll be asked for a $25 contribution, and a refundable deposit of $15 for a host list (to be returned after your travel). If your political and cultural orientation is in sympathy with that of Servas, this is an excellent way to enrich your bike tour in a foreign country.

The Globetrotters Club prints economic travel information and provides contacts among its thousands of members. Its bimonthly newsletter "Globe" has travel tips and exchanges of news among members. You can advertise free for information and companions there as well as keep abreast of travel bargains. The GT directory lists names and addresses of members from around the world, who offer advice and, possibly, accommodation. If you live near Sunland, California, or London, you can attend meetings and talks about travel.

A great many international youth and world organizations, of varied special interests and too numerous to cite here, might also prove useful. They can be found in *Frommer's Whole World Handbook* and *Let's Go, Europe* (see Appendix I).

8

MAPS

Next to the bicycle itself, a map is the most important item in your baggage. A map can never really contain too much information. The location of a small country lane or a tiny village is always nice to have. That amount of detail, however, will cost you money, weight and bulk. To identify a string of country lanes completely around Great Britain, for example, would take dozens of map sections in the Ordnance Survey, 1:50,000 series. Those cost $3 each, and there are 204 sheets for Britain.

Most bike tourists agree that a reasonable compromise of map scale is between 1:200,000 and 1:500,000. You'd lean to the greater detail of the former scale when the tour is leisurely and circular, and when you'd want to visit all the byways. One inch on that map equals about 3 miles on the ground. A typical map window of a handlebar bag is approximately 8 X 3½ inches. It would show an area of ground 10 X 24 miles when using the 1:200,000 scale, suitable for a day's wandering on country roads.

For an even closer look at the terrain you might choose a 1:100,000 series of map, or even a smaller scale such as 1:50,000. One inch on the latter shows about ¾ mile on the ground. You'd have to buy a few of those more detailed maps for a week's touring, of course.

9

When less concerned with the local attractions, for example when riding on larger, more familiar roads, you can choose a 1:500,000 scale. One inch equals almost 8 miles, or 2½ times that of the 1:200,000 scale. In countries where few secondary roads exist, even a map with a scale as large as 1:800,000 can be suitable. It could actually show all the ridable roads possible. One reliable indication of that is by the legend. Examine it for the surfaces indicated for the smallest roads. If those are dirt or "macadam," you can be almost certain that any other roads that exist are in the same or worse condition. You'd probably not want to ride them, and there'd be no point in buying a more detailed map.

Some maps indicate grades as well as surfaces. A Yugoslav map I used, for instance, symbolizes hills by wedge-shaped darts on the roads. Their direction shows ascent and the number of them tells how steep: one dart for a 10 to 15 percent grade, two for 15 to 20 percent, and three for more. It also shows the location of passes and their elevations. You can plan with that kind of information, either avoiding those roads entirely or accounting for them by riding less those days.

Michelin maps are the standard in Europe, and in other parts of the world, too. Buy them in the United States or Great Britain before leaving for the Continent. You'd want to examine them here before the trip, perhaps to drool a bit over the prospects. You won't save anything by buying them in other countries—quite the contrary. Maps in Scandinavia cost $5 and more, for example. In Britain, Bartholomew maps are a better choice.

The National Geographic series maps are useless for biking. They're beautifully printed, delineate mountain features well without overwhelming other information, and show waterways clearly. But they don't discriminate between classes of roads or code their surfaces. The maps belong on the wall, to be admired as works of art and to inspire the traveler before his trip.

You can save money by getting maps free from national tourist offices. Their quality is uneven. Some are very poor; they show few details, are printed badly, or lack road discrimination. Quite a few can serve, though. Send for them anyhow before you buy.

Maps weigh you down when your route is among a few countries. When you have mail drops, send them ahead. Or do as some bike tourists do: cut off all excess except the legend and a wide swath on both sides of your intended route. I often do that, but not when I want to save the map as a souvenir or for future use.

10

LANGUAGES

Contrary to prevailing American opinion, English is not spoken everywhere. However, in banks, railroad stations, airports, big hotels and fancy restaurants, someone always seems to know it. You may go a week through some Eastern European countries, and even in Portugal and Finland, without hearing a word of English. When you do, it's among the young for the most part. They learn it either formally in school or informally, because they feel it's the language of the future.

Knowing another language or two, or at least enough to say a few "survival" phrases and to read a bit, will certainly enhance the enjoyment of a trip. Learn such phrases as "How far is it to . . .?" "Where is . . .?" and "How much is . . .?" Terms for various foods, water, post office and toilet are necessary daily.

When using the language, ask closed questions ("Is this the way to . . .?") that will elicit yes or no answers. Don't ask the open-ended type that brings long, involved answers. Also point, write things down or draw pictures, play charades, and smile a lot. Your audience may think occasionally that you're an idiot, but you'll get results.

If you have time and inclination, take a formal foreign language course. If not at a school, buy a record course or learn from a book. You may not speak much of it finally, but you'll find your way easier among the shelves of shop goods and make more meaningful contacts with people. Even a modicum of language helps break the ice.

Notwithstanding the growing interest in English, German is more useful today. It's spoken from Spain to Turkey to accommodate the ubiquitous German tourist. German is the second language even in Eastern Europe, especially in the Balkans and Hungary. It would seem that Russian should be useful there, but it's not. Speaking German in Slav countries, except in commercial establishments, is not too smart, though. In some parts of Poland it could be downright dangerous, unless you make it clear you're not German. They haven't forgotten the war.

Where Russian has been taught to the young, they've either forgotten it or have no interest in using it. The young are attracted to English, much as their Western European counterparts, but not many speak it yet.

Learning the basic Cyrillic alphabet of Russian can come in handy in eastern Yugoslavia and Bulgaria. It's needed to decipher local menus and street signs in Serbian and Bulgarian, which use that script. Phrase books in those languages may be printed only in Western characters.

11

TRAINING

I often say that the first week of a long tour serves as training. My listeners are discouraged with that advice, objecting that they would prefer to train beforehand and not waste time en route. Although I sympathize with their concern for a carefree vacation, I still believe that the best way to train for a tour is to be on it.

An active, recreational bicyclist can hone himself into a keener physical condition through daily rides and commuting. Once on a tour, though, the conditions change. At home, he rests between 50-mile rides taken on weekends, and he eats and sleeps in a comfortable home. On the road, he'll be riding those distances for days at a time—with the added burden of a 40-pound load—and he'll have to do without the familiar comforts. That routine will tell after a while. No amount of artificial training situations will get a person as ready for the long haul as will a part of the trip itself.

In addition, regardless of trial runs with camping equipment beforehand, a number of bugs are always left to be worked out. It will take a few days to become accustomed to equipment and routine, especially when traveling with others and having to compromise your methods and tastes to theirs. At the least, the initial strangeness of the foreign scene contributes to tension and consequent fatigue. Even jet lag, an unavoidable accompaniment to east-west plane travel, puts a bike tourist off for the first part of a cycling week.

The above arguments address bikers who've stayed in some kind of shape, of course. They're academic for the person who hasn't been on a bike for months or years. He certainly has to get back in condition first. If a biker can't manage a 6 percent grade at home, he decidedly won't in Spain or Germany either. He had better climb hills for a month or so before he steps onto the plane for Europe, unless he plans to ride only 20-mile days.

The amount and type of training for those who need it is arbitrary. A start of 10 miles a day, working to 50 by the end of a month, might be reasonable for some. Others may find that grueling and would need a different pace or time.

Much is made of graduated daily routines, special diets, and supplements of minerals and vitamins. Those smack of faddism, to me. Nothing substitutes for long sessions in the saddle, as racing great Eddy Merckx dryly put it when asked for the secret of his success. Eddy was known for downing many a beer between races, an abomination to most bike nutritionists, but the habit didn't seem to slow him significantly. You know your own body and how much it can stand. Don't look for a magic routine.

Training for the wholly unconditioned—or simply a normal exercise program, as I prefer to regard it—should include time on the bike to toughen legs and seat, regardless of frequency or set routine. The program should concentrate also on cardiovascular workouts through sprints on the bike itself, in jogging, or in any sustained activity that forces the heart and lungs to work. Weight reduction helps, too. The choice of exercise and pace are a matter of preference and of individual motivation. The important thing is to keep the body responsive and alive by using it daily.

A biker in good physical condition should certainly take a pretrip "mini-tour," with the bike loaded as it will be on the coming tour. That shakedown cruise will help familiarize you with the feel of a weighted bike and will forewarn of any gross problems with packs or balance.

If you're inexperienced in camping but intend to travel that way, practice those techniques at home, too. Refer to Chapter 5 for hints on how to gather those experiences without trauma. Start early to learn cooking techniques; you don't become a cook overnight. Chapter 6 lets you know what you're in for in terms of the skills and equipment needed.

MECHANICAL EXPERTISE

You can either ignore mechanics completely and take the bike to a shop when it needs work, or learn something about it. Either option is viable, although the first will cost you more and will confine your touring to the more civilized parts of the Continent.

If you depend on a bike shop mechanic, he may not have some of the specialized tools needed for your bike. That can happen even in remote parts of Western Europe, and certainly in all of the east. You'd need to take those tools with you in those areas. An obvious example is a freewheel remover, which is different for each make of freewheel. Check with your local mechanic for his advice as to what you should take for your particular bike.

In Turkey, parts of the Mediterranean, and Eastern Europe, bike shops may lack replacement parts for your make of bike, unless it has French or Italian threads. Or you could be a day's ride from a large city where the shops are usually situated. It's wiser to learn a few things about the bike if you go to those parts of Europe.

Local AYH chapters in the United States and a growing number of colleges teach bike mechanics. Some excellent books can teach you the rudiments, too. Take sections of your bike apart and put them together again, for practice and to build confidence in your ability. I've always held that if you can read, you can repair your bike.

13

Lest this discussion of mechanics deter you from leaving home, I can assure you that breakdowns are fairly rare. The bicycle is a very reliable machine, at least one which has a good basic construction.

In almost two decades of touring outside of the United States, much of it in remote places like Afghanistan or the interior of Romania, I've never had any mechanical trouble I couldn't handle. To illustrate, I made a 5,600-mile loop of northern Europe in 1979, starting in the Netherlands and through Scandinavia, Eastern Europe, Austria and northern France. I was subjected to rain, gritty roads and hard climbs, and I rode through many unpopulated or rustic areas. My only mechanical needs were the replacement of a handlebar shifter handle and two broken spokes, and I repacked my wheel bearings at midtour, a normal maintenance procedure at 3,000 miles. I replaced tires at 3,000 miles, normal again. Using lower pressure and heavier sidewalls, I had no flats at all. If that seems unusual, in 1974 I rode from Portugal to Iran with no flats either, nor with any mechanical problems.

I'm not especially mechanically inclined, but I've learned enough about the bike to maintain it and be prepared for emergencies. You can do the same, if need be. In most of Europe, though, that need is minimal.

2 HOW TO GET THERE

PAPERWORK, VISAS, INOCULATIONS

Regulations change often; check with either the airlines or consulates for the latest information for entrance requirements. In general, the farther north and west the country is in Europe, the less it demands of you. Most customs officials and police in Western Europe wave you through borders, some without even looking at your passport.

A passport is necessary, nevertheless, except in a few countries of the Americas. Apply for it in person at a county clerk's office, at selected post offices, or passport agencies of the Department of State in a number of cities. Take along a birth certificate that has a raised seal and filing date affixed, your Social Security number, two recent photos 2 X 2 inches, a $10 check (personal will do), and $3 in cash. If you have an expired passport, it will save you bringing the birth certificate. Allow three weeks to get the passport, although it usually takes less time. Once you get it, immediately record its number somewhere else—address book, health card—for reference in case of loss.

For Eastern Europe, visas are needed. In some countries you must exchange your money for their currency prior to entrance, at a fixed amount per day of visa. Check on this, too, since changes do occur. Hungary, for example, switched to an open system in 1979 from its former policy of prepayment.

If you're passing through an Eastern European country that doesn't especially interest you, here's a tactic that saves you the prepayment. Instead of a normal visa, apply for a 48-hour transit visa. It allows you to pass through the country without exchanging money officially. You can cycle north-south through Czechoslovakia, for example, or chop a corner out of any other of the Eastern Bloc countries in two days easily enough. Whatever money you'd need while in the country may be exchanged on the open market, without the restrictions and unfavorable exchange rates of state banks. Or you can cycle as far as you can for most of the 48 hours and take a train or bus the rest of the way. Forty-eight hours is meant literally, starting with the exact time your papers are stamped at the border.

Definitely secure all visas before leaving home. They're usually cheaper in your own country and you'll avoid any chance of delays or complications at borders. Visas aren't issued at most borders in any case, only in an embassy or consulate at a major city of another country. All kinds of things can go wrong there: the staff may be preparing for a state visit of one of their leaders and have no time for you; you may be asked for payment in an exact denomination of cash, which you may not have with you; or you may arrive in the city during a long holiday period.

Allow a few weeks of processing for each one, when applying. A visa usually takes a week, but it could take much longer. It's simple to get one: some multiple application forms, a few head-and-shoulders photos and a fee in the vicinity of $10. Write to the embassy or consulate of the country that you're interested in for the forms. Addresses are listed in Appendix L. Make a few extra photos, while you're at it. They may be useful later for in-country use or if you decide to visit an adjoining country that also requires a visa.

15

Note how long the visa is valid, and work that into your tour schedule. Some visas must be used within a given amount of time from the day they're issued. If you are cycling a few months before reaching the destination, the visa may expire before use. Consider also the possible need of renewing the visa at midtour, and the method and place convenient for that renewal. It may be issued in the capital only, and you wouldn't want to be in some remote part of the country when it nears the renewal date.

Europe requires no inoculations, ordinarily. On rare occasions, an outbreak of some disease will make a shot necessary. Check on the current situation. You'd take no risk getting one in most of Europe anyhow, if needed. If you're nervous about a chance of danger in a backward region, get the shot at home before leaving.

The United States asks for a smallpox vaccination of a returnee if he visits a country that had an outbreak of that disease within 14 days. Since it's unpredictable when that might happen, I find it's worth the precaution to keep a smallpox certificate current. It could save bother and delay during a trip.

That immunization, and any others you receive, must be recorded in an International Certificate of Vaccination. It's available from the passport agency, your local health department, or from the Super-intendent of Documents, Government Post Office, Washington, DC 20402 for 50¢. The certificate must be signed by a physician and validated with an approved stamp.

An excellent organization to join is the International Association for Medical Assistance to Travellers (IAMAT). It costs nothing. The association of English-speaking doctors throughout the world offers the traveler consistent medical service and charges. A free booklet lists member doctors, the fees charged, and general advice on health. Other useful information is also offered, such as world climate charts, for which the nonprofit organization asks for a voluntary donation.

TRANSPORTATION

Your travel agent knows all about air and ocean transporta-tion. Go to him first to establish a base price. Budget guides suggest ways to save money, especially for youths and students. Some of the associations I mentioned in Chapter 1 enumerate up-to-date savings possibilities in their bulletins. What many sources often don't mention is that married couples and people in their retirement years are also often eligible for discounts on boats and trains in some countries. The savings, where known, are pointed out in Part II.

16

Proof of marriage is usually not asked for, and unwed couples can take advantage of these savings also. If you're traveling as a couple and your passports are inspected, insist that you are indeed married and that your wife has retained her maiden name. You won't be challenged.

BIKE TRANSPORTATION

International airlines carry bikes as one of the two allowed pieces of luggage without cost. Ask the airline first, though, before buying the ticket. A further precaution is to have "free bike" and the pertinent airline regulation written on your ticket. I feel skepti-cal of the current knowledge of ticket clerks; the last time I flew to Europe I made doubly sure by writing to National Airlines for a copy of their latest policy. I went to the airport armed with the central office's response. Sure enough, the clerk tried to charge me some $40 for the bike. Without a word, I handed him the letter. "Boy, you sure come prepared, don't you?" he said. It pays to invest a stamp and a short letter to avoid this possible problem.

One aspect of bike transport should be pointed out, no matter the policy. When an airline gives you a choice of packing it in a bike box or taking it on the plane unboxed, always choose the box. Pick the largest one they allow. You can stow most of your bulky camping equipment in it—sleeping bag, tent, pad—and provide an extra measure of safety for the bike at the same time.

Place enough of your heavy items, such as bike tools, in the box to make up the 70 pounds that's usually allowed per piece of luggage. You'd not be able to take along all that excess equipment otherwise, without paying extra for the weight, if you sent the bike unboxed.

If you now still have many separate packs or panniers, lash them together with rope or several shock cords into a solid package. Put that into an ordinary plastic garbage bag and wrap a couple of shock cords around that again. The airline allows two pieces of baggage, never mind the esthetics. They'll charge you for each piece over two, if the packs are separate.

When you're ready to return home, you'll have less chance of finding a box. Icelandic provides boxes at Luxembourg, Glasgow and London, if you request them ahead of time. To carry a box from a bike shop in the city—if you can find one—to a distant airport is nearly impossible without help from someone with a car.

17

Happily, by the time you complete the tour, some of what you've originally brought with you—food, clothes, inexpensive camping items, spares—will have been used up, or you can consider them worn out and expendable. Your load will be somewhat lighter.

Send the bike as is, when you must, and pack all the rest into the same compact package as before. Save the original garbage bag for this purpose. Like the bike box, it might be hard to find in some countries.

Don't hesitate to use the airline's scales to insure that the package doesn't exceed the maximum allowed of 70 pounds. If it does, remove the heaviest, small items and put them in your pockets or in the under-seat bag you'll be allowed to carry on board as hand luggage. A pair of front panniers held together by a shock cord will be just small enough to comply with the size limit. Wear as many extra clothes as you can stand, in addition. Also consider the worth of what you're bringing back. If to replace an item would cost less per pound than what you'd be charged for it as overweight, simply throw it away. It's not worth bringing back.

TAKING BUSES AND TRAINS

European countries are more liberal than the United States in transporting bikes on trains and buses. They can usually be put on as is, stripped of bottles and pump. On long train rides, with a baggage car transfer at a major city, your bicycle may arrive later than you. Avoid that by either sending the bike ahead a day or more, or take the journey by stages and transfer the bike personally at each delay point. Talk to the railway people ahead of time to determine any potential problems. One practice there that's common is a requirement to bring the bike to the baggage room a couple of hours before train departure. Bus lines don't usually ask this.

Morrie Paul and a friend leapfrogged their bikes by train a dozen times during a European trip. They sent the bikes ahead to a small town from a major city and spent a couple of days visiting on foot in the city. When they arrived at the town, their vehicles were waiting for them.

There's ordinarily a small or moderate charge on trains, seldom on buses, and usually not on ferries and steamers. You might have to place the bike on yourself, which is better for its safety. Water transport is the easiest of all. You just wheel it on the boat, packs and all, and secure it to something with a shock cord.

18 ORGANIZED TOURS, AN ALTERNATIVE

Joining a group tour may appeal to you as a way of breaking into foreign touring. The number of commercial organizations grows yearly; over 30 were listed for the United States in the April 1980 issue of *Bicycling.* Even more organized tours exist in Britain and the rest of Europe.

Many of those organizations have tours overseas. Prices vary greatly—$30 a day and upward, exclusive of transportation—and so do riding styles. You can travel comfortably on an International Bicycling Touring Society (IBTS) tour, with motor support and hotel stays, or rough it on an AYH camping trip. Tours last from a week to four months. You can easily find something to fit your budget and riding preference. A list of organized tour outfits that go to Europe appears in Appendix F.

When your time is limited and your pocketbook not, that's a good way to tour. An experienced leader will smooth the way and insure that all necessary details are arranged. You need only bring your passport and visa, if needed, and get your packed bike to the rendezvous. The anxieties of organization will be relieved and you'll be in the reassuring company of others during the tour.

That company may not be to your liking, unfortunately. It'll be a grab bag, and you'll have no choice of companions. But you can presume somewhat what kind of people to expect from the offerings of the organization and the mode of travel. IBTS people tend to be mature, urbane and professional, while AYH groups are younger and bouncy.

WHAT TO BRING WITH YOU

3

BIKE: BRING, BUY THERE, OR RENT?

The only assurance of having the bicycle you want is to bring it with you. The extra effort of packing it is more than compensated for by the time and frustration you'll save in trying to get a suitable one in the host country. Contrary to expectations, the kind of foreign bike you see in American stores isn't readily found on the floor of a bike shop overseas. The bike you saw at home was an export model made especially for Americans.

There's nothing wrong with the quality of a European model, of course, but it'll probably be a road-racing type with features undesirable for touring: a limited range of gears, a short, stiff frame, and a narrow, hard plastic seat. The components can be replaced, but that entails extra money and time, and depends on their availability. Or the bike you'll be offered will be a utility type, with upright handlebars, three speeds or one, wide tires, and a wire basket up front. Besides the bike itself, it'll be more difficult to buy bike accessories you'd want: panniers, carriers and tools.

The fact is, there are predominantly two contrasting types of Continental bicyclists: the shopper or commuter on the workhorse, and the *sportif* rider who is, or emulates, the road racer. The bikes sold in shops cater to one or the other.

The notable exception to the above is in England, which is more conscious of bike touring than any other country in the world. Should your trip be there, or nearby on the Continent, you might consider buying among a wide range of English bikes and accessories. If you do decide to buy a bike in Europe, whether in England or elsewhere, bring the broken-in saddle from your old bicycle and have the price adjusted. You'll suffer on the new saddle otherwise.

The other objection to buying a bike overseas is losing time in looking for a suitable one. It's a factor often overlooked by those who want to save a bit of the cost of a bike. You'll pay for a hotel or hostel—often more expensive in big cities—and transportation around town while you shop. You'll stay a day or two longer than you calculated; the $30 you save on the cost of a bike will be soon eaten up.

Renting a bicycle is fairly common in northwestern Europe. Except in England, it has serious shortcomings for the bike tourist, the chief one being the quality of bike you'd get. It's usually the utility type, passable for casual riding in flat country but too heavy to pedal in hills. Maintenance of it will probably have been sloppy. Bikes rented from train stations are usually in the worst condition.

The location of the place that you rent from—the train station or bike shop—circumscribes the nature of your tour. You can ride only a certain distance and then must return to the rental facility. You'd be wedded to the rail route or confined to one country's border. Having to lug your packs between rental stations is also unappealing.

Still, if your intention is to ride minimally and only as a convenience in getting around from a base of hostel or hotel, renting might well suit you. Bring your panniers with you, in that case—you need to carry your clothes in something anyhow—and a few basic tools. Rental agencies are indicated, where available, with the countries in Part II.

21

SPARE BIKE PARTS

The safest practice is to bring spares with you, unless you're absolutely sure that they're available where you go. From personal experience, I can say that there are no spares to be had for 10-speeds anywhere in Eastern Europe, in Turkey, and outside of the larger cities in a goodly portion of the rest of Europe. Again, England is the notable exception.

That broad statement of availability must be qualified: the bike parts that have to thread on or fit to your particular bike—the spindles, freewheels, chainrings—can't be found everywhere. Fortunately, most of those parts need replacement infrequently, and they seldom break down. Some last 10,000 miles or longer. Other replacement parts, those needing no specific size or fit such as chains, cables and derailleurs, are more universal in Europe, although still scarce in Eastern Europe.

What I carry with me are a pair of wheel spindles (ever since one sheared in India), a derailleur cable and another for brakes (back), a pair of brake shoes, a dozen spokes in the exact size for my bike, a few metal valves, both Schrader and Presta, and an assortment of nuts and bearings. On very long trips, I also bring two or three of the smaller freewheel cogs, which need replacement more often than the larger ones. I like to send extra tires ahead to mail drops, when I can.

The most common tires in Europe are the 700c series. England and Sweden sell 27 X 1¼-inch tires everywhere. You can get the latter also in some bike shops in large cities in a few other countries. If you intend to bike with that size, it's wiser to bring extras or have them sent to mail drops. One emergency tire between two people is always a good precaution, in any case. Tubes with Presta valves, rather than Schraders, are commonly sold in Europe. Bring a pump with a Presta adapter.

Sew-ups are a poor choice, unless you're riding with a very light load and are certain you'll not be subjected to any rough road surfaces. I've not heard of a single long-distance tourist who has used them.

Tyler Folsom, who rode around the world in 1976–78, carries an old piece of sew-up tire and a sew-up needle and thread to make repairs on 27 X 1¼-inch tires. He sews a patch inside the sidewall of a gashed tire. It's strong enough to ride a couple hundred miles. Tyler also carries freewheel parts—hairsprings and pawls—after having had many freewheel problems on his long trip. I've never had trouble with my Sun Tour, myself.

A bell is useful in Europe to signal the many pedestrians and bike riders on paths and along the road. In many countries it's the law. Any simple one will do, even a toy bike's Mickey Mouse, which I have.

You might pad your handlebars with either a commercial Grab On type or a homemade affair of a strip-on Ensolite pad. Long riding days will make your palms sore otherwise. It goes without saying that the other end will get sore, too, unless you go with a well-worn saddle. I find that plastic saddles, no matter how scientifically designed for just *my* rump, eventually bring discomfort. I use only a leather one. Some people swear by plastic, though—to each his own.

A white light in front and a yellow or red in back is required in most countries for night riding. A blinking rear lamp is good safety practice. If you seldom ride after dark, don't buy anything elaborate as a front light; a flashlight and holder will do.

TOOLS

You will need for tire changing, a patch kit, pump (Zefal high pressure is best), irons, and a pressure gauge. As tools, Phillips (usually) and regular screwdrivers (I prefer a combination, ratchet type that works on a torque principle without a conventional blade or handle); pliers; a small adjustable wrench (a 4-inch fits the largest nut on a bike, other than the headset lock nut); a hex key set (only sizes needed on your bike); and a freewheel remover. Odds and ends, like a small length of copper wire, some electrical and surgical tape, a cleaning brush (old toothbrush or small paintbrush), and oil. All those suffice for the usual trip up to a few thousand miles.

Beyond that, specialized tools are sometimes needed for regreasing bearings and replacing worn components. Among those are a chain removal tool, a pair of cone wrenches (to get at the wheels), a crank extractor set and a bottom bracket set (to regrease bottom bracket at about 6,000 miles). Only a long-distance biker who performs that kind of maintenance a few times during a trip carries those. They can be forgotten by the ordinary tourist in Europe. See Chapter 1, in the section on Mechanical Expertise, for more discussion of this point.

A superfluous, heavy tool carried by many bikers is a large adjustable wrench. Its purpose would be to remove the freewheel when a broken spoke has to be replaced on that side of the wheel. But you can safely ride a few miles with a broken spoke to any gas station and borrow the tool. Save a half-pound or more of extra weight, unless you want to double the wrench as a hammer for tent stakes or to use it as an emergency weapon.

CAMPING AND RAIN GEAR

Within reason, the weight and bulk of tent, sleeping bag, panniers, cooking gear and other camping paraphernalia is not all that crucial. A potential weight savings of as much as 10 pounds for those articles can usually be achieved by buying super-lightweight equipment. But most of us can reduce that much weight in our own bodies far more economically and with dividends in health. That may be too much to ask, and there are those who'd rather spend extra money on light materials. Still, if you're willing to pedal 10 extra pounds of body, you shouldn't mind 10 extra pounds of equipment.

I'm not too concerned with weight, as such. I choose a lighter item if all other factors are equal, but will opt for more convenience or durability at a cost of additional ounces, or even pounds.

Most of the push to sell lightweight equipment comes from a spillover of backpackers' criteria to that of cyclists. It follows naturally, since virtually one small group of manufacturers makes and sells the same camping items, rainwear and cooking gear to bikers as to hikers. And, of course, the latter were buying those things first.

What this means to the bike tourist is that he ought to be skeptical of manufacturers' claims, especially with equipment that serves both bikers and backpackers. What you pay for in special features may not be of use to you as a biker. Contrariwise, the features you need may be missing. Review the periodic evaluations in *Bicycling* and talk to fellow cyclists about the suitability and performance of particular items that you're interested in buying.

Examples of poor design for bicycling purposes are many. Rain gear lacks reinforcement at backside and knees, where bikers stress rain pants; anorak jacket styles don't allow movement for stretched arms, and you have to buy a larger size; hoods hamper the view of a bicyclist when he turns his head.

I use Gore-Tex material for my rain gear. I feel it's the only effective material to keep you dry and reasonably free of inside condensation, in spite of a tendency to leak at the seams if not carefully sealed. And yet I was stung with a pair of Gore-Tex gloves that were inadequate for bike use, although they were sold as such. They soon leaked at the palms and thumb/index finger seam, although they received only a normal amount of wear against handlebars. They should have been reinforced with heavy water-proof material at those points.

24

Bike panniers feature lightweight material, more useful to backpackers than to cyclists. Bikers are in greater need of bags that are waterproof and durable. A profusion of zippers that soon snag, and which admit much of the rain that seems to enter all bags, is a common design weakness. No manufacturer has yet made flaps substantially longer or tighter over zippers to bar water, for example. Nor have many provided easier access for seam sealing, the lack of which is another major source of leaks. Pannier makers all admit their bags leak and suggest that everything be put in plastic. As for durability, I've not yet had a bag that didn't wear a hole where it contacted the bike frame.

EQUIPMENT REQUIREMENTS

My preference in a back pannier is one which has a drawstring opening for its main compartment, with a flap that covers it as well. Such a design is drier, since the pannier is covered with a double layer of material, and it hasn't a zipper that can fail. Two product examples with a drawstring design are the American Kirtland GT model and the British Karrimor.

The size of panniers should approximately match your travel

WHAT TO BRING WITH YOU

style and space needs. If camping with full cooking complement and a load of 40 pounds or more, you should use both front and back panniers, and possibly a handlebar bag. The back panniers are usually described with a term like "grand touring" and have a volume of 2,000 cubic inches or more. Fronts have less capacity, about 1,000 cubic inches.

A handlebar bag holds about 600 cubic inches or less. It's primarily a convenience, holding a camera, notebook, map and odds and ends that you'd want to find in a hurry. In all, the 3,500-plus cubic inches of bags offer enough baggage space for the needs of the longest trip.

For shorter tours, when you're doing light cooking as in a hostel or if your needs are simply more Spartan, you can substitute smaller rear panniers—those with 1,500 or less cubic inches—and skip the handlebar bag. And with the lightest loads, use only small panniers in the rear. Those can be the same ones you'd ordinarily use up front; they're usually interchangeable.

Saddlebags are another option for stowing gear. The ones sold in the United States are ordinarily a kind of handlebar bag attached to the rear of the saddle. The English version is a roomier container, complete with a backboard arrangement and provisions for storage of tent, sleeping bag and clothes. It holds everything that would usually be strapped on the rear carrier.

I never use either kind of saddlebag, since it commits a load almost entirely to the rear wheel. Better to use front panniers instead, which afford more flexibility of load distribution. Saddlebags could take the place of rear panniers, of course, but that isn't a common practice. When so used, they would shift the weight of the load higher on the carrier, a bad idea.

In sleeping bags I prefer a synthetic to a down type. The Polarguard Berkshire, sold by EMS in the United States, is a good design and is economical. A down bag is lighter, but the synthetic stays warmer if the bag gets moist. The latter's bulk feels more comfortable to me, too, even if it takes more room on the bike than a down. And the Polarguard's fill doesn't shift in the bag. Down often does, causing cold spots.

I use two tents, depending on where I go. Both are made by R.E.I. One is made entirely of mosquito netting, for warm-weather use and in areas of high humidity. The other, a two-person Ascent, is better for colder weather. I like it for its room and the projecting eaves, which allow door and window to be left open in the rain, letting in air. Both tents have flies and are quite waterproof. When I travel alone or want privacy, I often use a 1¼-pound bivy sac of Gore-Tex instead of a tent.

PACKING AND BALANCING THE LOAD

The emphasis I put on front panniers is for the best of reasons—to balance and distribute the load more evenly over the wheels. The weight of baggage should approach being equal front and back, and it should sit low on the bike for stability. That's impossible to accomplish without using front panniers.

Advice to balance the load evenly is almost a ritual in magazine articles and books. But I'm always puzzled how the authors would have that done. Their illustrations consistently show a tall mound on the rear carrier, with just a handlebar bag up front. And they hardly ever mention the use of front panniers, other than in connection with mammoth loads or as an option.

A handlebar bag doesn't do it. Its capacity is too small to shift significant weight from back to front, and the bag sits too high on the bike. In my opinion, it's a poor buy and should be regarded as a luxury rather than a necessity. Buy front panniers rather than a handlebar bag.

Packing and balancing the load is an exercise in logic and organization. Put related objects together in 1- or 2-quart plastic bags—socks in one, cold-weather gloves and thermal underwear in another, spare parts in a third, for example. Store each bag in the same spot within the pannier all of the time. The insides of your panniers soon become chaotic if articles are tossed inside helter-skelter. I've seen bikers dump all the contents on the grass in frustration when searching for a loose stove part or an extra pen. Before leaving home, organize the bags and make a master list of contents, if necessary, to jog your memory.

Balance the load by placing heavier items close to an imaginary line drawn through the wheel hubs. That means in the bottom of bags, close to the wheel line. Equalize the weight, first front and back and then left and right, within the panniers. Weigh each bag to help attain this. Some heavy items may be used often and it may not be practical to keep them in the bottom, but the general principle should be followed.

The problem arises when, as will happen, some things are added or taken out en route—food staples or a sweater to wear—and one side gets heavier than the other. The resulting imbalance causes the bike to wobble or shake, and handling becomes difficult.

You don't have to play any complicated musical chairs to rebalance the gear. A half-pound of notebook or a bag of tools changed from one side to the other will do it. Remember that every shifted pound makes 2 pounds of difference between the two sides.

Another cause of imbalance is loose packing. When the con-

26

tents of a pannier bounce around, so does your control. Pack things snugly. Items kept on top of the carrier—sleeping bag and tent, usually—should also be tightly secured with shock cords or nylon straps to keep them from moving about. I once lost a sleeping bag that jiggled loose from under too-long cords.

Don't let things dangle from the sides or end of the bike, either. Although hanging cups and pans may make your bike resemble a Gypsy wagon and so enhance your romantic image, they could easily catch on to something that you pass and give you a sharp jolt back to reality.

Holding the weight of panniers should be a pair of reliable racks. Pick those carefully. If they break on the road—I've had the legs of three Pletscher carriers snap during long trips—there's little you can do to jerry-build them. Steel ones can possibly be patch-welded locally. You might find another rack in a bike shop. It'll be at least a nuisance and a layover; you'll not be able to ride with the broken ones. Saving $10 to buy the cheapest rack is false economy. Get a solid one like Blackburn's. I used mine—front and back—for over 22,000 touring miles; they still show no sign of fatigue.

Bike tourists sometimes carry baggage on their backs in rucksacks, or even huge backpacks. I wonder why—if they can't afford panniers, if they're hikers temporarily on bikes, or if they have some misguided belief that they're doing the right thing. Manufacturers abet the use of day packs on bikes by advertising it—another example of the wrong criteria applied to bikers.

It's not the right thing to do: it strains the back and is dangerous, making the rider top-heavy and restricting his ability to turn his head. Baggage belongs on the bike. It makes as much sense to strap it on your back as it would to do so when riding in a car.

27

CLOTHES AND PERSONAL ARTICLES

There's little reason to be self-conscious about wearing the same clothes day after day on tour. You have no one to impress except your companions, and they're in the same position as you. A woman biker who has just one blouse and skirt for evening wear can be comforted by the thought that only her hubby knows it's her only dress outfit. Her other audience changes daily.

Carry as many clothes as you deem necessary to insure cleanliness, given a delay in the daily washing of what's worn. I bring three each of underwear and socks, and one each of riding shorts, light dress trousers, jeans for riding, sweat shirt, dress shirt, nonbulky sweater, and a sneaker type of biking shoe. I often take a pair of light, suede dress shoes, but I use them so infrequently that each time I swear I'll never bring them again.

Ordinarily, a nylon shell or two suffice to foil a chilly wind, but when expecting a stretch of cold weather I add a set of thermal underwear (Damart is good), a balaclava and gloves. I don't wear a hat or gloves otherwise.

You don't have to try to look like a biker, although the specialized clothing manufacturers would make you think so. Brightly colored jerseys may be advertised to have a safety advantage, but a red windbreaker or orange sweat shirt is as attention getting and is considerably cheaper.

Any shorts you find comfortable would do, but chamois-lined ones do seem easier on the rump for me. The British idea of wearing plus-fours or plus-twos—a kind of old-fashioned golf trousers that stop just below the knee—and long stockings is probably the most sensible for biking. Those kinds of pants are nearly impossible to find in the United States. Nor do they reflect the racer image Americans prefer.

28

Fabrics should be easily washable. Clothes that can be thrown into any washing machine—a limited option in Europe, where laundromats are scarce—and that can be hand washed often and in any kind of soap—a more common practice—are better than some of the more expensive, specialized bike clothes that need careful treatment.

The stiff, leather biking shoes that are the standard for bike racers are all wrong for bike touring. They wear out fast when walking; a bike tourist does a lot of that. With cleats, they're impossible off the bike. My foot has never slipped from a pedal while using the sneaker type of bike shoes. I don't see the need of the extra thrust that cleats would give me, either.

The things that some bikers bring along on a tour strains the imagination: Ray Reese carried a teddy bear on his Guinness-record-setting ride around the world. Considering that he carried no tent and pared his add-on weight to a minimum, that mascot was obviously important to him. The Japanese Takafumi Ogasawara brought a prized butterfly collection on his around-the-world ride. The psychological lift of a valued object offsets its weight and bulk, apparently.

On a more practical level, you might want to use electrical appliances—razors, coffee cup heater, radios. A line of small, light convertors is available in hardware and electronics stores. They allow the use of 110-volt gadgets in the European 220 system.

A score of equipment lists are printed in bicycling books and articles, to advise the novice on what to bring. Their common element is disagreement: one will admonish the tourist to bring only essentials, never anything that can't double for another use; another urges him to seek comfort first, even at the expense of weight and bulk. Without any excuses I include a typical list of mine in Appendix B.

COMPANIONS

Those traveling alone have the greatest freedom. They also despair. The Japanese Minoru Ueda said he sat down along a desolate road in the American West and cried. Reese considered giving up his trip because of loneliness, and Ian Hibell wrote that he started talking to his bike as he rode. And so, most bike tourists eventually seek companions.

Not only is there sociability with a group, but costs per person are cheaper: accommodations, food and even transportation in some cases. Sharing use of tent and cooking gear means less weight for each person to carry, too.

29

What's the best size for a group? Two riders need a great degree of compatibility to succeed. They must share a strong common goal, be highly motivated, and have a sympathetic understanding of human frailties. At least one must be a saint; inevitable frictions build between the best of friends in time.

Shopping and cooking for two is a bit awkward, although it's better than for the solitary biker. Most store packages hold more than what a pair can finish in a day. Both riders are also involved daily in a kitchen routine, a chore that usually needs a cook and a helper. The advantage with more people is that the others get days off from those chores.

A group larger than three becomes unwieldly. The odds are higher that someone will have a mishap. Should a biker get lost or held up by bike trouble or sickness, everyone's schedule is affected. The efficacy of group economy is also lost beyond three or four. A group of five is often obliged to pay for two camping sites, the limit usually being set for four occupants, and cabins or huts in the campgrounds of many countries contain four beds. Whereas three riders may still be invited to be guests at a private home, a larger number rarely gets that break.

ADVENTURE CYCLING IN EUROPE

Cooking for four or more is hardly cheaper per person than for three. The usual food packages—a carton of eggs (ten, in many countries), a liter or quart of milk, a loaf of bread, 250 grams of butter—are about right for the daily needs of three hungry bike tourists. A 3- or 4-quart pot, good sizes for carrying on a bike, and an 8- or 9-inch frying pan hold just enough for three diners.

All these arguments make a group of three optimal for bike touring. It's a truism that there's only one conversation possible with three. That favors concentration and unanimity; four at a table can talk at cross-purposes. With a pair of riders, if one gets mad at the other all conversation stops. With three, one of a disgruntled pair can speak to the third rider. That's certainly more civilized, and the neutral person may further serve as a referee to patch things up. Life can be more amenable.

It all sounds pat and ideal. But generalizations are hypothetical. No matter the number of people, the success of a group effort is finally unpredictable. Some luck is needed as well as an undefinable chemical affinity among the members. The only sure way to predict compatibility is by a trial ride of a few days. Take that test before leaving, if you can, or the tour itself may turn out to be a trial.

30   Given some common purpose, the relationship still needs work. Before starting, the group should agree on a general route, pace, schedule, food preferences, and points of interest. Don't leave it to be worked out later. When I organize a tour, I like to set those things down on paper, as so many specific points to discuss. Once agreement is reached, the final outline serves as a kind of informal "contract." In any later disagreement, it helps to be able to refer to the initial group plan for arbitration.

Sharing housekeeping tasks, food costs and talk entails responsibility, constant effort and some compromise. Tempers should be kept in check or sublimated. Happily, the physical release of bicycling itself helps relieve tensions. So does the natural glamour of a foreign setting, a conversation piece for even the most sour moments. Appetites aren't as finicky either, when one depletes his calorie reserve by the end of the riding day.

It's important to allow personal time for each member. Privacy is harder to find in such concentration of group activity, but it must be. For me, it's been the most crucial factor for a successful tour with any number of companions.

I make no formal demands that any member team up with others during the day. They can choose partners if and when the mood suits them. The simple thing to do is to agree on a place to meet for lunch or to shop and let each rider get there however he or she wishes. Some persons need time to take pictures, have quiet interludes for solitary contemplation, or the privacy to write notes. If they're imposed on by more volatile members, they eventually become resentful and trouble begins.

Don't feel obligated to have a group sing, a BS session, or some kind of togetherness each evening, either. Let those things spring from a felt need, not a format. A discussion of the next day's destination or a decision for a rest day can be decided with clean dispatch. Vote on it. Or, if the general principles were agreed on before the tour, those can be cited.

Mixed groups of men and women add more dimension to interpersonal relations. A woman's presence often opens doors of hospitality. A man and woman are more apt to be invited into homes than two men. Perhaps people feel safer with the woman's presence, or they might be interested in learning her viewpoint as a bike traveler. Or maybe they feel sympathy. The sight of a "helpless" woman shivering in a cold rain seems to wrench an emotional response from an onlooker. On my around-the-U.S.A. trip I always had Maureen Bonness, hair wet and lips purple, stand just behind me when I knocked to ask permission to camp on someone's property. The reaction was usually predictable.

I've always noted a civilizing effect, or at least an improvement in the quality of conversation and of personal hygiene, with women in my group tours. There was less use of superfluous swear words and more effort for expression. I'm not sure what would be the effect of a male joining an all-woman group; I've never experienced it. I'd be interested in hearing the result of such a situation from someone who's been in it.

31

4 WHAT TO EXPECT THERE

CULTURAL SHOCK

Much has been written of the trauma of foreign travel, and with good reason. When you step off the plane or boat into another country, you become almost instantly disoriented.

The very look of everything is different. Whether you're in the Middle East or France, the architecture is unfamiliar, the people talk in a gibberish, and sometimes—in Italy, for example—the very air is heavy with pungent smells, unfamiliar music and a clammy humidity.

More than the initial sensations, you soon realize that customs are even stranger: merchants in the street may grasp your arm to pull you into their stores "just to take a look, not to buy," people will stare at you intensely for no reason you can think of, and you may have to squat over a hole in a Bulgarian toilet instead of sitting down.

The longer you're in a country, the more differences you discover, some readily seen and others not so immediate. You'll note that personal space is more intimately seen in southern parts of Europe. If you ask an Italian for directions he may clasp your arm familiarly and put his face in yours when he advises you. He's not "pushy"—it's his way of being friendly. Turkish cafe customers will sit at your table without preamble, even if other tables are empty. They'll immediately engage you in conversation or look over your shoulder while you write notes. Anything that happens in public in those parts is considered open to public scrutiny and participation, and you're fair game.

Religion may play a much more important part in the lives of many foreigners. Dress in Moslem areas—in the Balkans and Turkey—is not just a matter of taste; it's an injunction. Lack of decorum is an affront to the strictly orthodox. That you're a Westerner and wear different clothes will be tolerated—you're an infidel, after all—but shorts on men and halters on women will be frowned on. I believe that much of the rock throwing I experienced in eastern Turkey was caused by my riding in shorts, never mind the heat.

The psychological shock of the unfamiliar sometimes drives the traveler to eagerly seek reminders of home: English newspapers, hamburgers, fish and chips, fellow Americans or Britons. Better to try communicating with the natives and to learn something of their culture, if the trip is to have some meaning. With knowledge comes greater appreciation of what's seen; doors will be opened to new experiences. Besides, it's only polite to conform to the values of a host country.

"Most anxiety when traveling overseas is caused by problems at home," as was pointed out by Paul Kluth. He wrote me: "Anxiety comes in letters from the family—gasoline prices, hot water heater problems, increasing taxes, student busing, difficulties raising teenage daughters with an absent father, and a lawn that keeps growing. When the radiator hoses ruptured on my wife's car, I foresaw the sickness of surviving in a mad, sick civilization. The pressures are right in our home towns."

Americans find occasional antagonism even in the friendliest of countries. You'll be challenged on policies that the nationals don't agree with. At home you may also disagree with those policies, possibly, but overseas you somehow feel you must champion them. It's human; your loyalty is being tested. Don't get sucked into an argument, though. There'd be little point to it. The challenger wouldn't change his mind, and if your reaction is indignant enough it would only confirm his belief in the jingoism of Americans.

In spite of all efforts to be objective and fair, a traveler may still hold a residual cultural prejudice. I've experienced that often enough. I'd meet and talk with relish with an educated Pole about world affairs, only to squirm later at what I perceived to be his primitive slurping of soup at a restaurant.

Each time something like that happened, I resolved to temper my attitude thereafter, only to fall into another culture-bound trap the next time. I try now to reserve judgment; one man's slurping may be another's gusto. It takes patience to learn and enter another's world. That's what travel is all about.

SAFETY

Bike safety overseas is directly correlated with two factors: the experience the country has with motorized travel, and the number of bicyclists on the road. The happiest combination is in the Low Countries along the North Sea. In Belgium, the Netherlands and Denmark most drivers are skillful, polite and safety conscious. The great numbers of bicyclists everywhere insure attention from motorists, most of whom are bikers themselves. A biker's right to the road is assumed.

As an extra bonus, the area has the best network of bikepaths in Europe. Though one feels very safe when sharing roads with cars, the separate bikeways add an extra pleasure of complete relaxation to bike touring.

The next best circumstance is in an undeveloped country, one that has reasonably surfaced roads but few cars. Turkey comes to mind immediately, as do Yugoslavia and Greece along their minor roads.

In countries off the beaten path, such as Finland and northern Norway, traffic is tolerable most of the year. But the road surfaces and cycling conditions may be inferior. In northern Finland I had to cycle slowly for most of a whole day in gravel, on a main highway, pursued by hordes of tenacious mosquitoes. The road had no cars, however.

The worst is a country that has suddenly discovered the car. Poland is a good example. Until a few years ago, most roads held hay wagons and motor scooters. Then the Polish Fiat, Serena, and other auto plants were constructed. They spewed out thousands of cars to consumer-oriented Poles. Emotionally, and with little skill and much abandon, the drivers took to the roads. On a trip I made there in 1979, cycling on main highways was touch and go with impatient drivers on the way to resorts. Even smaller roads had a share of local hot-rodders zipping past me.

How to remain safe? The same way as at home. Driving defensively, keeping off the main roads where possible, avoiding rush hours, and never cycling after dark are my guidelines. I also find the eyeglass type of rearview mirror essential. Its immediate information is the best aid to safety.

There are times when you can't avoid unfavorable conditions. You may get caught in a fog or heavy rain and drivers will have a hard time seeing you. Or you'd have to negotiate a long, unlighted tunnel and meet drivers who'd not expect bikers there. Norway has dozens of such tunnels. You'd certainly need a blinking light in those, and a lot of caution. When I went through them, I stopped and hugged the wall each time I heard a car coming.

Anyone who bicycles at night on a highway is crazy. Like others, I've acted crazily at times, usually because I was determined to reach a destination. If you must bike after dark, at least use the

34

high-intensity, blinking yellow light sold by a few makers in the United States. I don't even trust that; I get off the road, well onto the shoulder, every time I see the light of a car behind me.

I must be extremely lucky. I've had only a couple of minor brushes with motor vehicles and a few near-misses. It's not because I've been especially careful. By nature I'm usually preoccupied and forgetful. I find it impossible to concentrate on the road every minute of the day. Once I rode blithely into a ditch in broad daylight. That was in Afghanistan and I think I was probably a bit tetched with the sun. But I do have nightmares just before a trip, in which I ride off mountain roads into the void, so I believe that unconsciously I must be seriously concerned with safety.

PERSONAL SECURITY

Europe is safe. It doesn't compare to any West Asian or South American country in the way of danger. It's safer than the United States by far.

The worst that can happen is that your bike may be stolen, a risk you take anywhere. But if you don't leave it out overnight unlocked—it's senseless to encourage a would-be thief—you'll be secure in that, too.

Chain the bike at night, of course, and take your gear into the tent. For further peace of mind, hang a battery-operated security alarm on your bike. Get one that sets off with any slight movement. Radio Shack sells one for about $25, with battery, which is very light and has a volume of over 110 decibels, enough to wake the dead. What happens then is problematic; it either scares off the thief, lets you confront him, or drives you deeper into the womblike safety of your sleeping bag.

Eastern Europe seems the most secure area to me. Although there is some petty pilfering in the cities, people generally respect personal possessions. Their sense of larceny is directed more to public property and cheating the state, rather than the individual. I don't know why. It may be because of an emphasis on the worth of individual freedom, cherished by the populace because of its relative scarcity. Or the Communist emphasis on puritan morality may be bearing fruit.

I lean to an explanation having to do with the backwardness of the region and a harking back to a simpler and more honest age, especially among the older peasants. Whatever the reason, I feel safe there in my person and in possessions, whether I camp for the

35

night in the open, leave my bike unattended in a village or town during the day, or walk the streets of a capital at two in the morning. I'd not dare do that in a typical American city.

But the world situation changes very suddenly and unpredictably, in a political sense. When I took my around-the-world ride in 1974, the friendliest Asians were Iranians. I was constantly invited to homes and could have spent a year in that country as a guest. Almost overnight, the government and attitude changed. Now it's seemingly one of the more dangerous countries, at least for Americans.

What about a weapon? Don't you really need one in a threatening country? I'm asked that question fairly regularly, the last time by a man who intended to tour North America. He anticipated problems with "maniac truck drivers and assorted hoodlums."

I say no. I sincerely hope my advice doesn't leave someone defenseless some night, facing a couple of psychopaths alone. But I'm a peaceful man and believe in the basic goodness of man. Even if you had a weapon, it would only increase the chances of real violence. The classic case I remember is that of a few Europeans with pistols who were approached one night in some West Asian country by a group of natives bearing rifles. The travelers panicked and started firing. The Moslems fired back, naturally. All the Europeans were killed. They didn't realize that most nomads in that region carry arms as part of a long tradition. They meant no harm; they were just curious.

A traveler can't get across borders with a weapon unless he smuggles it, anyhow. If it's detected, it leads to trouble or at least confiscation. The most formidable weapon I've ever carried was a slingshot. It helped even the odds against rock-throwing kids in eastern Turkey; those shepherds were very accurate.

In some instances a supposed danger is more a matter of bombast between governments than antagonism from ordinary citizens. I was in Turkey during its invasion of Cyprus, with the supposed aftermath of ill feeling toward Americans. Except for a lot of nationalistic fervor and macho strutting, I received no threats nor was I treated badly at that time. Later, in eastern Turkey, nomads and teenagers threw stones. But that was the normal attitude of Kurds of that region to any strangers, even to Turks, and before Cyprus. It had nothing to do with that crisis.

Other times, the press plays up minor incidents to sell copy. I happened to be cycling through Mexico in 1975 when American newspapers all along the border told of stormy encounters with unfriendly Mexicans. The tension started when President Echeverria raised gas prices for camper-tourists and was lambasted by the United States for that act.

Again, I was treated well. Possibly, the harassment was directed more at affluent trailerites, while my modest transportation and way of life didn't irritate the natives. I believe, though, that the thunder was loudest within the newspapers. When a street crime happened in El Paso, Texas, it hardly merited a mention on the back page. But just across the border an incident involving an American was reported as a pogrom.

Absolutely safe travel, that consumer-oriented mode with all the creature comforts that is so lauded by the travel industry, is not what I seek anyhow. Venita Plazewski, who rode with Tyler Folsom around the world, put it this way: "After all, we have no assurance that we'll see the light of tomorrow even when we go to sleep in our very own beds. Sometimes we must follow our spirit and it must be free. Many of us have a great concern about security; it's possible that we hold too fast to that illusive quality."

A possibility of some danger—at least of unexpected encounters, of a poised breath at a sharp turn of the road—is what makes bike touring electric. The traveler in a conducted tour is soon jaded, but never I. Let others be herded through the Casbahs on their "adventure holidays." I'll take mine clean, on my own.

37

HANDLING MONEY

There's no satisfactory substitute for traveler's checks. A letter of credit to a bank along the route was the practice in Jules Verne's day but not today, not unless you're afraid of losing traveler's checks and of the subsequent wait for replacements.

A credit letter is still used. It's issued by a home bank against a foreign one, which will issue you the money on presentation of the letter and a positive identification. You pay a service charge and your money is tied up just as with traveler's checks, but you do have the assurance that if the letter is stolen, you definitely won't be out money. If you lose traveler's checks you're obliged to report it within a short grace period, or be subject to penalty. That might be a bit difficult when you're out in the wilderness and can't speak the language. Still, a letter of credit doesn't serve well. It can only be used in large cities with international banks, and you get all of your money in a lump sum—unless you take it in traveler's checks.

Barclays/Visa issues its own traveler's checks free. Sometimes, unlimited amounts of traveler's checks of other companies are sold at a fixed special fee, usually in the spring in the United States.

ADVENTURE CYCLING IN EUROPE

Some travelers like to buy checks in the currency of the country they'll visit, as a hedge against the further deflation of their own currency. Unless you live in New York or London, though, it will take time and your local bank or travel agent will charge a handling fee, possibly canceling any financial advantage gained. An interesting article on handling money in this manner appeared in the *New York Times* Travel Section, September 30, 1979. It may be looked up in 35mm reader-printers in most good-size United States libraries.

Avoid cashing checks intermittently, one or two at a time, in those countries that charge a flat fee for the exchange service. If you're with someone, take turns cashing a large sum of money for both of you and save on the fee. Try to time those exchanges with your visits to large cities where American Express or other traveler's checks offices are situated. They'll not charge for cashing their own checks, as a rule. Pick up a pamphlet that lists current overseas offices at any Amex office.

Cashing traveler's checks can be a hassle in backward areas and even in large cities. The American Express office in Istanbul, I found, wouldn't cash that company's checks, although they would sell them. And at a bank in the medium-size city of Silistra, Romania, I waited an hour while bank officials searched through regulations and money specimen books to determine if they could cash an Amex check. Only my threat to call the bank's central office in Bucharest induced them. They were more afraid of censure from that office than of making a regulatory mistake.

Carrying a lot of cash is sheer madness. Still, it pays to bring some with you. The amount depends on your confidence to hold onto it safely. The cash brings better exchanges in those countries where a black market flourishes and where it's relatively safe to indulge in that generally illegal practice. Check carefully with the backpack-carrying, travel-wise young Europeans who are found all over the world; they're always on top of that kind of information. The cash, in small denominations of $1 and $5, is also handy for minor spending when you are about to leave a country and don't want to change a check of a large denomination.

You may be likely to get robbed—your purse snatched or pocket picked—if you don't watch your money carefully, especially in large cities of countries that know poverty. Once, on a street of Casablanca, a young boy tried to interest me in coming with him to a shop. He grasped my wrist and pulled gently to urge me. Suddenly he ran. I realized that he had removed my watch, undoing the leather strap as he held me lightly. I never felt it. That region has had centuries of practice on tourists in that highly perfected art. Young purse snatchers in Rome or flim-flam money changers in Turkey will soon part you from your money if you let them.

Many travelers rely for security on either a money belt or a bag suspended from a drawstring around the neck and under the shirt. I don't like either of those expedients because of the awkwardness and constriction while riding. But I do hold my valuables in such a bag around my neck when I get off the bike. When I ride, I carry the bag in the front handlebar bag where I can see it.

You can hide money in a deeper part of a pack where it would be more secure, but then it's too inconvenient to get to. The bulk of your money should be hidden, in any case. Any measure you take to safeguard money has to become a fixed habit. Put it away immediately each time; a moment's inattention can cause grief.

When leaving a country and converting its money to that of a new country, only bills will be accepted. Coins, which won't be, should be spent before reaching the border.

If you run out of money and have to get more from home, it's possible to have it cabled in care of an American Express office or a bank. It will take a few days and cost you handling and cable fees.

A better expedient is to get an American Express card before leaving home. It and a personal check are good for drawing up to $800 in Amex checks and $200 in cash, depending on where you are. The card costs $35 a year, but it may be worth the peace of mind. **39**

Other credit cards can get you money advanced, too, but American Express is the best known and will present the least problems. Wilfred Cresswell, an Englishman who rode around the world 1976–77, found that his Barclay card was of little use in Eastern Europe. But he said he was never refused money anywhere with an Amex card, which he also carried.

Paying for bills by credit cards, however, is not a good idea. They're only accepted in the more expensive shops and would be an uneconomical way to travel.

CUTTING COSTS

Citing actual costs in a guidebook is a chancy proposition. They're outdated very soon, unless yearly revisions are made. But an indication of price is needed by the traveler anyhow, commodity to commodity and country to country. A verbal comparison, such as "Swedish campgrounds cost about twice as much as French," is too diffuse and lacks a common base.

ADVENTURE CYCLING IN EUROPE

And so, unless otherwise indicated, I provide estimated costs for each country in 1981, or those reported reliably at the time of writing in 1980. The reader may make a mental adjustment to allow for the lapse of time to the reading of it. Count on a 10 to 15 percent rise in prices per year on the average, at least.

This approximation will result in some error, what with varying changes in currency values and rates of inflation in each European nation, but it's the only way I know to give a feel of what it costs to tour overseas. To simplify matters, I give those costs only in dollars, rather than in original currency.

What you'll spend daily—other than for transportation—depends largely on your travel style. One based on camping and cooking costs the least—a minimum of about $7 a day in 1981 in southern countries like Portugal or Turkey, when using formal campgrounds some of the time and camping in the open the rest—to twice as much in Switzerland or Norway under the same conditions.

Those costs are only for eating, hygiene and sleeping. Shopping, carousing, visiting museums and such will be extra.

The sky is the limit when using hotels. Even with the cheapest in southern Europe, you'll spend $18 daily when sharing a double with a partner. It can be three times as much in Scandinavia. You'll not be able to cook in hotels and would have to eat at least one meal in a restaurant. Your spending will be even higher if those meals are lavish. The cost of a hostel vacation is somewhere in between hotels and camping.

You have a somewhat different problem in the matter of costs in Eastern Europe. There, a minimum amount has to be exchanged per day of visa. If you don't spend it all, they won't reconvert it.

That daily $12 or $15 you'll be obliged to change may be more than you would spend conventionally, and you'll have zlotys or kopecs to burn. It's better to use that excess for restaurant eating than for hotels. The quality and variety of food in groceries is inferior to that in the West, and you'll eat better meat and produce in moderately priced restaurants. Besides, you'll be able to enjoy sampling the native dishes.

It's evident that learning to sleep on the ground can easily save you half the cost of any bike tour. Your outlay for tent, sleeping bag and other equipment will be no more than the cost of the motels you'd use otherwise during a two-week vacation. From then on you have a free ride, except for the nominal cost of campgrounds. More about camping in the next chapter.

Most of the daily expenses should go for food, to my way of thinking. Skimping on it, in amount or quality, harms the tour. You soon tire physically and psychologically with inferior rations. You can save, however, without compromise of basic nutrition or taste, by cooking your own meals and wise shopping.

Other ways to save on a trip are in air fares, various travel discounts for groups and the elderly within certain countries, travel with a companion to share costs of food and lodging, a bike maintenance program to prevent the need of repairs, and avoidance of high-cost tourist traps. I won't discuss most of those. You can use your common sense or read specific travel suggestions in a guide like *Let's Go,. Europe,* or in some of the budget travel newsletters mentioned in Appendices C and E.

Some or even all of the costs of a long tour can be alleviated by working overseas. Frommer's *Whole World Handbook* covers the various possibilities best, although other sources pay some attention to it.

In general, there are two major disadvantages to this option: you need a lot of extra free time for the entire trip, and the only kind of job you'd be able to find would be illegal. Most countries won't give you a work permit. The menial job you'd find illegally might barely feed you for the time that you'd be working.

Another source of money is through a special skill you may have. Lloyd Sumner gave talks about his computer-aided art as he rode around the world. Ian Hibell presents slide shows of his travels to help keep himself more or less permanently on the road. Takafumi Ogasawara took advantage of the publicity he got in Germany about his around-the-world journey to set up a newsstand in Nuremberg and make some quick cash.

Some few write about their travels. Don't count on that; it's too uncertain. If you have something to say and sell an occasional story, apply it to the next tour; don't expect it to support you as you go along.

It remains that saving is the only real alternative. Its corollary, happily, is that while you're on that trip you may actually spend less money than if you stayed home. It depends on where you go. If to Hungary or Turkey, for example, a long stay can even absorb the cost of transportation, in this respect. Should you be between jobs or on a teaching sabbatical, your trip may cost you no more than keeping an apartment in a city, never mind the eating.

EMERGENCIES

You're subject to fate when traveling overseas. Something serious may happen to you, or one of your family may get sick. There will be no way to get in touch immediately. That uncertainty

41

is an understandable concern that each of us has to bear some time in life. For, unless face to face with loved ones continually, something can happen as well while you're in your own country, en route during a vacation or during an extended business trip.

True, you can keep in daily touch by phone at home. That can be done overseas only at high cost, although a wire or phone call at regular intervals might be worth it for the peace of mind.

About the only certain way to prepare for an emergency is to plan your whereabouts carefully, day by day. The logistics are formidable; you'd need to reserve and abide by specific stopovers each night and to designate the exact route between them. Not only is that difficult without detailed knowledge of the country, but all chances for spontaneity during a trip would be lost.

A kind of compromise entails preplanning of roads or general sectors of a country and an approximate schedule before leaving. Accommodations can be left flexible. The schedule can be updated by ordinary mail, or a wire if it changes radically. In an emergency, your family can telephone the State Department at home, informing them approximately where you are and asking them to get in touch with you. (Phone 202-632-9461 or 202-632-3015 in the U.S.; 202-655-4000 after hours.) Those authorities can then call the United States consul in the foreign country, who will ask police there to look for you along the designated road. Your position can be determined by your schedule. The police should have an easy task of this; they'll need to look for a bicyclist laden with packs on a stretch of 100 miles of road at most. What with the speed of electronics, it shouldn't take too long to dispatch the searchers.

What happens when they do find you is something else. You'll need to get to an airport, sometimes remote from where you'd be, and return in time to do some good at home. A cousin of mine was notified immediately in Poland of her father's death—she was not on a bike tour and was staying with relatives in a known place—but she didn't manage to return in time for the funeral. It happened that she was visiting a nearby city, out of touch for the day. She lost two more days getting to Warsaw from that village and then to her home. At bottom, your contact with home while overseas is minimal. You'll have to come in terms with that, if you're ever to leave the country.

Having to get in touch with home isn't the only kind of emergency, of course. You may get sick. I've never had a major illness on a long tour, luckily. I'm not worried about it, trusting to the good nature of people everywhere.

Ordinary health insurance covers you. Carry its card with you. Blue Cross/Blue Shield in the United States provides an Overseas

42

WHAT TO EXPECT THERE

Claim Form and instructions for making claims. In general, you need an itemized bill and a completed form for each provider of services, whether hospital, doctor or pharmacy.

Europe offers excellent medical treatment and you'll get good care. Most of it has liberal, socialized services that include foreigners. You'll find the costs a fraction of what you'd pay at home, and sometimes it's free. For a list of English-speaking doctors in foreign countries, send for IAMAT's booklet (see Appendix C).

You may have a mechanical breakdown, away from a population center, and that could be an emergency situation. In my experience, the more isolated I was, the more likely that someone came to my rescue. As at home, the lone biker holding a wheel in the air in the middle of a desert gets more response from a car than the same biker in the midst of a populated area.

The worst thing that ever happened to my bike was a smashed front wheel in Romania. Without the benefit of a word of Romanian, I was taken by a few villagers to the home/factory of an ironmonger. He jotted an address and some directions on a piece of paper and hailed a car on the highway, keeping my bike safe for me. The driver took me to a bike shop in Bucharest where I bought a new rim and tire. On my return to the village benefactor, I was helped with the wheel (all the spokes were too long, and needed filing down), given a dinner and a bed. There was no question in the minds of the villagers; I had an accident there, and they assumed responsibility for me.

There's only a slight chance of being lost in Europe, but it may happen on occasion. It's not an emergency unless you let yourself think so. You can always ask someone for the direction to the nearest large city to become reoriented. Still, there are those travelers who aren't comfortable unless they're always in control of route planning, each mile of the way.

I have a fairly good sense of direction, but I don't keep conscious track of where I am. I do note certain navigational indicators, in passing. The sun is the most obvious. Allowing for its travel by time of day, you can easily tell east and west. In its absence, note the flow of streams and the lines of mountain ridges relative to your travel, and keep track of the prevailing wind direction. Those can be related to your map or to the direction you started with.

Sometimes, man-made indicators tell you the direction. When you know, for example, that a TV station is situated only in a nearby city, all TV antennas will point to it as to a north star. Bringing a compass is a good precaution.

Once as I was leaving northern Hungary for Vienna, Austria, I sensed I was on the wrong road. I saw an unusual number of cars with Czechoslovak and Polish plates. Those Eastern Bloc drivers can't be heading for Austria, I reasoned, since it's difficult for them to get permission to go to the Western Bloc countries. I realized I must have taken a wrong fork in the road, which proved to be the case when I retraced my way.

A rider may become separated from the group and so be considered lost. An agreed-on route and daily destination helps keep everyone in tow. A chalk mark message left on the highway will keep the others informed of your whereabouts, when you take a side trip. When I'm riding apart from a group and stop in a cafe, I make a point of leaving the bike in full view of the highway so that those following can see it.

During periods of national unrest, rely on your consulate for guidance. Your local passport office or the State Department has a current list of countries the government considers dangerous for Americans. Keep the consulate's phone number in some handy place—written into your passport or the International Certificate of Vaccination Card. See Appendix L for phone numbers of consulates in European countries.

The United States consul—and I imagine the Canadian and British, too—can do only so much for citizens who are traveling abroad. They replace lost or stolen passports, help find appropriate medical services, and advise those in trouble with the law. They won't lend money, take the place of tourist bureaus, or provide legal services. Consuls suggest that you become familiar with and obey the local laws, especially those dealing with drugs and currency.

44

HASSLES

Western Europe presents no problems at its borders. You may be examined more closely in crossing between the mutually suspicious Greeks and Turks, but otherwise you spend no more than a few minutes at borders of any of the rest of the Western Bloc.

Eastern Europe may be difficult, depending on where you are. Its attitude toward bikers is inconsistent, even within the same country. The first time I came to Czechoslovakia, I was searched carefully, right to the contents of my toilet kit. The customs maid even massaged my toothpaste tube for imagined contraband. The second time, a bored official scanned my papers and waved a finger imperceptibly for me to pass on. Tibor Pollerman gives good advice for entering those countries: don't go to the head of the line at airports, since the first few people always seem to have their luggage searched.

WHAT TO EXPECT THERE

Border people in that part of the world can be adamant about a minor infraction of rules. I once forgot I had half of a water bottle of leftover Polish vodka, besides what I was allowed in an unopened bottle that I declared. The guard smelled it out, and I had to endure a long lecture about trying to sneak out more than I was entitled to. Then he sifted through the rest of my baggage, obviously as a punishment.

Another incident, in Bulgaria, began when a military guard at a checkpoint near Turkey misread my passport. With a weak command of English, he concluded that the city of issue, Philadelphia, and the city of my birth, New York, should have been the same (issue and birth had the same meaning in his English dictionary). He concluded that he tripped me up in my forged document, and that I must be a spy. Only the arrival of his superior officer, after a couple hours of detention, saved me from who-knows-what.

On both occasions, I may have made a mistake by communicating with my examiners in Polish—Bulgarian is close enough to make sense. After those experiences I spoke only English at any border where the guards didn't smile and make a friendly fuss, both in Europe and elsewhere in the world. When they realized they'd have a hard time communicating, they spent less time hassling me.

Reports of state surveillance of foreigners within Eastern European countries is much exaggerated in the U.S. press. Newsmen, businessmen and American officials may be watched, for all I know, but the ordinary tourists I've talked to have never noted it.

It should be easy enough to tell if you're spied upon when traveling by bicycle. Your high mobility makes it practically impossible for someone to follow you without you knowing it. To check on your movements once off the bike, the whole population would have to be mobilized into a spy network. Through friends and relatives in Poland, at least, I know that simply isn't the case.

Not that there aren't the village snoops or the neighborhood monitors in cities, who keep an eye out for "unsocial" behavior. They watch their fellow comrades mostly, and are distrusted and held in contempt by those neighbors. The attitude of the ordinary citizen to a foreigner is no different nor less tolerant than anywhere else in the world.

Some open police activity in a few of those countries may irritate. I was stopped six times in two days by Hungarian Auxiliary Police in 1979. They hardly said a word other than to ask for my passport. Except for losing a few minutes of time, nothing else came of the checks. Only hitchhikers and bicyclists seemed to be stopped. The German biker with whom I was riding at the time said it was common and probably the easiest way that those minor officials could fill a daily quota of investigations.

While in Iran in 1974 I experienced a considerably more serious incident. I was taken into custody while strolling on a street and led to a police station. I spent the next couple of hours being shuttled from one station to another by Savak agents—the family I stayed with in that city identified them as such—without knowing why. I believe it may have been my picture taking in the market, but I never knew for sure. I was finally dumped in the outskirts of the city to find my way back on my own.

I don't remember reading in the American press about police surveillance in Iran at that time. Later, of course, it developed that it was fairly common. Asia is more Byzantine in its spying than Europe.

Regardless of where you are, one caution has to be observed. Never take pictures near military installations, strategic terrain such as at borders, or even bridges, in some countries. The military of all nations are nervous about people who look closely into their backyards and at their destructive toys. I was stopped in Yugoslavia once by an officer in a car as I photographed the Danube. Across the river was Romania. What saved me real trouble was that both sides had only pastoral fields and some sheep, and that the officer was in a hurry to get somewhere.

Throughout the world the past attitude toward "hippie" travelers has largely ameliorated. The former practice of forcing haircuts on long-haired young, as in Greece and Morocco in the 1970s, is past. Still, anyone who looks different from the usual tourist is more apt to get attention.

An unkempt biker is doubly suspicious. The fact that he carries his house and pots with him reminds officials of Gypsies, a group that remains harassed in most of the world. You'll sometimes be asked for proof of means. That usually takes the form of showing an air ticket out of the country or a few hundred dollars in traveler's checks. Eastern Europe has a benign and automatic check of means, of course, through its practice of requiring prepaid exchange of currency.

The minor nuisance of loose dogs is less of a problem throughout Europe than in the United States. The only place they've chased me consistently was in Turkey, where they run loose and often in packs. Since those poor beasts are routinely abused by Moslems, getting off the bike and threatening them often sends them scurrying away. I've even charged dogs, making gurgling noises, half for effect and half in anger at their harassment.

5 WHERE TO SLEEP

TRAVEL STYLE

Bike touring styles differ in comfort. On one end is the Cadillac set, groups like the International Bicycling Touring Society. They cushion the way with sag wagons and dress for dinner. At the other extreme are the Ian Hibells, who slog their bikes through mud or sand and cook lonely, one-ingredient meals over a Primus.

You can tour either way or in between. The easier you make it for yourself, however, the more you limit the route. Conveniences and facilities aren't found everywhere; if you insist on a ready bed, served meals and motor support, you'll have to settle on cycling only in developed areas. At the least, it'll cost you a bundle. Most of us have to be prepared for the other alternative—to bring your own house and make a lot of meals.

Camping, either completely for economic reasons or partly to provide for emergencies when housing can't be found, has a price, too. You have to work harder to lug the extra weight, you must stop sooner to set up camp, and you need to learn additional skills. Those may exact too high a price on your time and effort. In that case, the options are to stick to civilized countries or take organized tours.

Hostels may seem a middle ground, but you may find their locations limited, the curfews restrictive, and the crowds not to your liking. Although they offer an advantage of a cheap stay in a city, that advantage diminishes in the countryside. Their cost in some countries is also quite high relative to a camping option.

You'll probably find a mix of styles the most satisfactory. Whether for an economic reason, a break from routine, or to be with people for a change, the options give you more flexibility in route and schedule.

HOTELS

I'm not a hotel goer during cycle trips, except infrequently, and so have few useful words of wisdom. I simply choose the **47** cheapest room, as long as it's clean and there's a bath somewhere in the building. A cheap room is hard to find in Europe nowadays. A December 30, 1979, article in the *New York Times* on the availability of double rooms for about $25 came up with relatively few in major cities: none in Stockholm and Vienna, a few in Paris, and a number in Madrid, although most during the off-season.

Hotel rooms seem an awkward option for the biker. Hardly any have a place to store a bicycle. Some tell you to leave it outside. If they let you lock it to something in the lobby, you're still obliged to carry all your baggage to your room for safety. That's probably up a few flights of stairs, since your cheap hotel likely has no elevator. Most places are reluctant to let you bring a bike inside at all, let alone take it into the room.

Bed and breakfast (B&B) homes in Great Britain and the Republic of Ireland are safe for storing a bike and are much cozier than hotels. They cost from $11 to $15, including breakfast. Your total daily expenses would be lower than for hotels but higher than for camping. The owners of those private homes are real people, not the formal and distant managers of hotels.

Many private homes in other countries offer something comparable to the B&Bs. Where known, I indicate them in Part II. I've had little personal experience with those *zimmer* and pensions, but I have passed home-made signs that advertised private rooms all over Europe. The houses always looked charming and inviting. Bikers who've stayed in them had nothing but praise, and those rooms do cost less than even the cheapest hotels.

YMCAs are another possibility, though they have limited offerings; they're situated in cities and accept men only, for the most part. But in a few countries—Finland, Germany, Italy—a few allow men and women in "tourist hostels." Send for their free directory.

Arguments for and against these indoor modes are obvious: you carry very little weight on the bike except for clothes and a few sundries, but you're tied to a route that offers those formal accommodations. You're also dependent on restaurants, unless you intend to eat nothing but cheese, cold cuts, bread and fruit. Indoor stays are pleasant as an occasional break rather than a constant fare, to my taste.

48

YOUTH HOSTELS

Somewhere between hotels and camping, youth hostels are a good compromise when an ample supply of them exists. Unfortunately, it doesn't in most countries. Neither their number nor location is always convenient for the bicyclist. Usually he must zigzag or take an arbitrary route when he depends on hostels alone for sleeping.

Often, hostels are full by the time the biker arrives, unless he starts riding at the crack of dawn to beat the inevitable crowds. My experience has been that houseparents in Europe seldom make a distinction between travelers who bike in and those who use trains or who hitchhike. They don't save spaces for latecoming bikers. I've often been turned away, even on cold rainy evenings. No hostel has ever let me roll out a bag on the floor, though there was always space for at least that. Sadly, the hostel movement has deteriorated from its original premise that its users would get there under their own power. Now, only a small percentage of people do so.

At a few hostels in resort areas I've met guests who were entrenched semipermanently on a cheap summer vacation. In a Swedish hostel, a Norwegian man told me that he has been coming for two-week stays for years. The houseparents exercised their option of allowing a guest to stay longer than the official limit of three days. They may have preferred to avoid the uncertainty of new arrivals or the extra bit of processing work. Or the favored visitor could have been a crony.

49

Hostels are often on the outskirts of cities, or a few miles from public transportation. On a bike, you have an advantage in that. If one hostel is full, you might be able to get to another easily, whereas the hitchhiker would get discouraged and go to a hotel instead.

Your keenest competitors for hostel space are those young train or bus travelers, or hitchhikers and backpackers, not the motorized crowds. The young are more likely to travel on the cheap than the older, more affluent motorists. Whatever hampers those quasi-backpackers in getting to a hostel helps you. Since most travel guides cater to them, look for the negative information in those guides—the hard-to-get-to places and those to which no public transportation exists or is expensive—and choose them over the more accessible ones.

The cost of hosteling is higher than commercial camping, especially when a group is involved. Each person pays the same at a hostel. The cost of a campground site is shared, and each person pays less as the group gets larger.

A hostel does have decided advantages: it saves the bother of carrying a tent; there are almost always other people for companionship; and it may include a members' meeting room and a kitchen. Of course, it's always more pleasant to be indoors looking out when it rains.

Hostels in Britain, Germany, Belgium and Scandinavia offer family rooms for married couples and their children. The interpretation of a family is often loose enough to include unmarried couples, although a few houseparents are still straitlaced about it. In contrast, Moslem countries keep the sexes far apart. Spain even has separate hostels for men and women.

A hostel's kitchen might have gas burners and an assortment of pots. Utensils are limited, though, and you should bring your own. Some—in Austria, Hungary, most of Spain—have no kitchens. Cooking is a problem then. You might have to cook out in a field somewhere or eat in a restaurant. I've seen people put butane stoves on meeting room tables to make meals, but houseparents ordinarily forbid that. It hardly is worthwhile to use hostels without cooking facilities, except in cities where hotels are expensive.

Many youth hostels allow camping on the grounds, the cost of which is less than an inside cot. You still enjoy cooking and washing privileges. That's often an even happier arrangement than staying indoors, where a curfew closes the door of the dormitory and restricts your evening freedom. The frenetic energies of a roomful of young students also may keep you awake.

50

CAMPING

You may already be an experienced camper, having slept and cooked in the open enough to feel confident in handling a foreign tour. In that case, you might skip this part. The remarks are meant for bikers who never had to set up camp and cook. Those travelers may be fully confident that they can endure the extra rigors of camping. They just need some advice and experience before plunging into the foreign scene.

The way to start is not all at once. I've witnessed dozens of bikers arriving at camps with brand-new gear, only to flounder into late evening with unfamiliar routines: erecting a tent in a suitable site, firing a tricky stove, and cooking outdoors for the first time. Those techniques should be mastered one at a time. Their total effect after a day's ride is devastating on the beginner. He may just decide to chuck it in, disgusted.

Practice before starting a tour in earnest. Start with loading your gear. You don't have to go on tour for this; simply pack all you've got, following the principles in Chapter 3, in the section on Camping and Rain Gear under the heading Packing and Balancing the Load, and take a ride for a few hours in the countryside. Pick a route with a variety of directions, riding conditions and terrain. Ride on a somewhat windy day to undergo the effects of crosswinds, too. Don't complicate matters with rain, extreme heat or cold. The object is to learn, not to see how tough you are.

Any effect of improper loading on the handling of the bike will show up. You'll discover shimmy or crabbed tracking, and you'll soon get the feel of a loaded bike. It may be a good idea to repeat the ride in traffic and in hills to experience those conditions, too.

When you get back from your orientation ride, and after making those needed adjustments to balance the load, set up a kitchen in your backyard. Don't run into the house for a wood platform for the stove or a handy gadget. Use the available material on your bike. You needn't cook anything. Just get the stove started and simmer some water to demonstrate that you can control the flame.

Cook a complete meal another day. Ride on the loaded bike to a nearby park, or anywhere that water is available. Make a simple supper, but do it from scratch—no freeze-dried or packaged meals. Cook basically, under the conditions found in places where stores may carry only a few staples. That would be the worst case you'd find overseas.

Prepare a spaghetti and meatball dish, for example, or liver and onions and a side dish of rice. Wash up, but don't use the park's hot water faucet. Heat it yourself. Again, it's best to practice under the worst conditions likely to be met, as along a stream. **51**

Cooking is not something learned in one trial, or even a few. It needs time to build confidence. But you should at least become familiar with its mechanics before attempting the first camping tour. An introduction to cooking is presented in the next chapter.

It also takes a bit to get your body accustomed to sleeping on hard ground. A couple of overnights in your backyard helps, but you might need a week to feel comfortable. The campsite along the road may not contain the same cushion as your lawn grass, and it may be hard to avoid rocks or tree roots. On the other hand, those adverse conditions will probably be balanced by your readiness for sleep after a long day in the saddle.

Try, even if you don't master, every technique needed on a tour. Include an overnight in the rain to make it complete. The idea is to keep all conditions constant and to introduce just one new variable at a time to concentrate on it fully.

Now, take a weekend ride for a shakedown cruise, using all the new-found skills. You'll be in familiar territory in case anything goes seriously wrong. That tour should point out any lack of equipment or methods. Do that with one or more bike tourists if you wish, to get the hang of group sharing. Going alone might be better, though, to test your self-sufficiency. After this trial, you're basically ready for the longer tour.

FINDING A FREE SITE

To book ahead at a hotel or hostel limits your options. Even the use of formal campgrounds cramps your style; you're dependent on their existence along the road. But a tent in the open can be pitched almost anywhere, giving you flexibility in schedule and route. It's the surest way to remove the anxiety of finding a place to sleep.

A free site can be found in a variety of places. The conventional advice is to get permission from someone to use it. Do that if you can find a person to ask, certainly, to avoid the possibility of an embarrassing confrontation later. In much of the world, it's not easy to find that someone, though. You may be miles from a house or no one may be about. Sometimes you're turned down initially, only to be accepted after a bit of conversation. I never hurry away from a friendly talk.

If there's a question in my mind about using a site, I look for public land. River banks, beaches, any place on a desert, a spot along a railroad, and national parks or forests almost certainly are public or usable. Even when close to towns, you may be able to camp in a park or picnic grounds. Check with the local police. They might even suggest a place. If they do, they'll look out for you, too.

In sheep and goat country, look for droppings. When you see them in a field, you can be fairly sure the land is used publicly. Those animals aren't penned; where they go, so can you. You might have to brush the camping area a little, but the grass won't be overgrown when sheep are around, in any case.

You'll have a peaceful night at a cemetery; no one exercises a proprietary right there, as sometimes happens in the United States. Cemeteries are clean, quiet and grassy, and the smell of flowers is pleasant. Sometimes a mausoleum with a roofed porch can be used in case of rain, but I generally make camp away from the graves.

Rest parks are a good choice, too, even if "no camping" signs are posted. When they are, eat first but don't set up a tent until dark. If a law officer comes along, he won't jeopardize your safety by making you ride somewhere else at night. All rest stops are legal for camping and are exceptionally pleasant in Norway and Sweden. *Allemansratten,* "everyman's right," is the law of the land there. That allows you freedom of access, even to private land. The only restrictions are on immediate grounds around private homes, and on land under tillage.

The problem with free sites is water. Seldom do any of them have it and you must cart it in, unless you can beg some from a motor camper also there. If you've asked to camp on private property you can get water there, also, but out in the boondocks you must search for it. You then take a chance on a contaminated source, unless there's snow runoff in a high mountain area or you happen on a small stream in completely uninhabited country. Even then a dead animal upstream could pollute it. The water can be boiled or treated, of course. Time and extra fuel will be spent on that, diminishing the attraction of the site.

COMMERCIAL CAMPGROUNDS

Good water and adequate washrooms are found in formal campgrounds. Their washrooms are overwhelmingly superior to those in hostels and in many of the cheaper hotels, in fact.

Choose a site not too far from the washroom. At dishwashing time you'll want to be close to it to draw its hot water. Better campgrounds have separate cookrooms and dishwashing rooms. Many have comfortable dining rooms as well. At poorer ones, you might find primitive plumbing, or hot water may be available at certain hours only. At some camps sinks may lack stoppers so it's a good idea to carry one, or a soft ball.

Once you choose your site at the campground, establish your piece of turf. Delineate it in some definite manner—a clothesline between trees on one side of your space, the bikes parked on the other, and a couple of tents end to end at the back. If you don't, campers will walk through your area indiscriminately, tripping on guy lines and upsetting your stove. You haven't the bulk of a car or trailer to hold them back.

European campgrounds, unlike those in the United States, don't have formal site designations. They squeeze in customers as long as they come in. It's dog eat dog. Some motorized campers, in addition to taking a king-size space with car and trailer, claim even more territory by erecting a perimeter of a commercial folding fence. You must be firm in holding onto your space; you've paid as much for it as they.

Another peril in formal campgrounds is a giant tour bus checking in for the night. It brings a hundred passengers at one swoop. They double the camp's inhabitants and strain the facilities. If you see one of those monsters turning in, grab soap and towel and rush for the bathroom immediately. In a half-hour all the hot water will be

53

used up and not replaced until they leave. Camps are great places to meet natives, especially in Eastern Europe, where contact with them is otherwise fleeting.

Private campgrounds, as against state-run, offer some stock of groceries, from a few basic necessities to a supermarket. A cafeteria is often on the premises, where one can linger over a drink and write letters. Some have recreation halls, but those are generally full of running kids or a blaring TV.

Prices vary greatly in campgrounds. The most expensive in Norway charge about $6 for two people. You can often get a break in price at a private camp. I ask for a discount, arguing that I use less space than a motorized vehicle, do less damage to grass, and don't make use of all the services—playground, utility hookups, dumping facilities. Sometimes I offer to take space that would be inaccessible to a motor camper, in a patch of trees or along a fence. Even if it doesn't work, the argument will plant a seed with the manager to consider bikers in a special use category. You get a discount with a camping *carnet,* too. Check Chapter 1, in the section on Useful Associations.

Stop in campgrounds even in off-seasons, when they're officially closed. The water may be turned off, but the grass is there and occasionally there is an overhead shelter. Check with someone first. I've never been turned away by a caretaker. They've even opened washrooms for me.

6 WHAT AND WHERE TO EAT

STOMACH PROBLEMS AND WATER

Before I rode my bike around the world I had to make a basic decision: either I would eat in restaurants or I would play it safe and cook everything myself. The first course would almost certainly lead to some diarrhea; the second would keep me healthy but frustrated, since I would miss the experience of native foods at the source.

A dilemma, and I agonized for some time, but it was neatly solved for me. While still thinking about it, my partner and I split up just as we entered Eastern Europe. The stove we were using up to that time was his. He cooked during the rest of his tour. I couldn't find another stove east of Trieste and was destined to eat in restaurants. The die was cast. So were the contents of my stomach for the next year or so; I had frequent diarrhea the rest of the trip.

You have much the same kind of decision to make, but I hope without the same fate. Although the north and west of Europe are as safe or safer than home, Mediterranean areas and the southeast have primitive hygiene, poor refrigeration and suspect water. Even in Poland, ordinarily trouble free, I once drank holy water at a miraculous shrine at the insistence of my cousin; he guaranteed me of its uplifting effects. As a consequence, I passed the night getting out of bed and running to the outside latrine.

Some stomach upset is probably unavoidable. All accounts of long trips mention its eventual occurrence. Mexican visitors to the United States, for example, complain of getting *turistas*. The best one can do is cut down on its frequency and harshness, and learn to live with it.

Carter and West, authors of *Keeping Your Family Healthy Overseas*, state flatly that most contaminated food is due to unsanitary handling and not the food itself. Hands unwashed after going to the toilet can easily introduce fecal matter. So can flies.

Before eating in a restaurant, note the condition of the kitchen and see if there's soap in the toilet. Don't be upset with a kitchen that looks crude. Many parts of Europe don't have American chrome and plastic. The cleanliness of the kitchen is what counts. If you must eat in a suspect restaurant, avoid foods that are handled with fingers—the raw salads, bread and cold items—and concentrate on the cooked foods that are ladled or picked up with a fork.

Avoid also foods that spoil easily or that are kept, refrigerated or not, for a long time. Custards, mayonnaise-based salads, chicken and fish are prime examples. Rather than drink natural milk in backward countries, use the powdered kind. When buying canned goods, watch out for those from which air rushes out with a pop when punctured. In many parts of the world regulations are lax and storage may be overlong. I've found that to be the case in Turkey, for example.

Although never a danger in Western Europe, the practice of eating rare beef should be avoided in the rest of the Continent. There's some chance of tapeworm. Eggs shouldn't be eaten raw when salmonella is pervasive in the area. That's also rare in Europe, but it can occur in southern climates. Pork should always be cooked thoroughly anywhere, of course, to avoid trichinosis.

56

Water is by far the worst culprit for stomach troubles, however. Carter and West advise as the safest course that contaminated water be filtered first and then boiled 20 minutes. The United States Health Service says 10 minutes of boiling. Other sources say that the minimum time is 5 minutes at sea level plus a minute per each 1,000 feet of elevation.

Iodine, in the tablet form called Globaline, can be added for purification (one per quart, let stand 15 minutes). It tastes bad, and most people prefer Halazone tablets, of chlorine (one per 16-ounce water bottle for 30 minutes). Tyler Folsom recommends carrying three bottles on the bike, each with successive stages of time for purification. That way you never run out. Mask the taste with Kool-Aid or powdered juices.

Ever since my experiences during the world trip, I've paid special attention to safe water sources and proper treatment. I'll never travel without a stove again, if only to boil water.

Tea and coffee made from well-boiled water are always safe, although to drink from cups or glasses that are rinsed in untreated water is a common mistake. Better to pour the drink into your cup or water bottle. Ice cubes can also be unsafe; I never use them unless I know the source.

Soft drinks from capped bottles are all right, though you may be shocked at the things you might see in them. Turn a Coke bottle upside down and hold it against the light in Asia and you might see something resembling the snow in an old-fashioned glass paperweight, as the sediment settles slowly and ominously. The beverage may be safe, but the sight will certainly shake you.

I've found beer the safest and most satisfying liquid to drink at the end of a riding day. Most of Europe makes excellent beer. Its cost is usually less than coffee and no more than a soft drink.

The fruit and vegetables that you buy on stands and eat casually should be treated first if without a peel and if at all suspect. Carter and West suggest washing in a weak, nonammoniac detergent and then rinsing in safe water. They claim that soaking in either bleach (a solution of 1 teaspoon to ½ gallon water for 15 minutes) or potassium permanganate, the older recommendation, has not been proved to be any safer than detergent. The latter is more readily available by bikers, too, and can double as a laundry and dish soap.

Though water and food may be kept pure, a sloppy dishwashing technique can easily generate diarrhea. Food left to deteriorate in the grooves of pots and lids introduces active bacteria into the next meal. The best practice is to wash two separate times. Run a knife into all recesses of utensils and scrub well with a stiff nylon brush. Follow by copious rinses to remove soap, then with a final scalding rinse to sanitize. Let dishes air-dry upside down, rather than wipe with a towel that may itself be dirty.

57

What if the tummies come, in spite of all precautions? Lomotil or Entero-Viaforme tablets or liquid paregoric, according to printed directions (or doctors' recommendation with paregoric), will relax stomach muscles and reduce the severity of cramps. In Iran I ate a small bit of opium, equivalent to the size of a matchhead, with some success. You'll still have to go through the cycle, however, so it's best to take time off from riding and relax until the bout is over and you feel better.

A thoroughly grim and unappetizing subject, but it's better to be prepared for the worst rather than be caught naive and susceptible.

NATIVE FOOD

It wouldn't be surprising if the bike tourist stayed away completely from native food after reading of all the preceding perils. Those risks are minor in Europe, and the most that would ordinarily occur could be some slight upset. It would be a pity to miss the pleasures of native dishes to avoid some discomfort.

Mealtimes vary, country by country, and to buy meals may cause a scheduling problem. By the time you arrive at the restaurant for a midday meal the food or the hour for it may be gone. You'll have to be content with snacks and coffee instead. The missed meal may have even been the main one of the day. In some countries the evening meal is the light one, like the American lunch. It's often eaten late, just before bedtime.

Vacation periods complicate matters, too. During summer in France all the cafes in a small town may be closed, the owners gone for a few weeks to the seashore or mountains. Careful inquiry, though, might reveal another cafe, somewhere in a back street, that volunteers to stay open for the benefit of the locals who remain in town.

Eating out is expensive in Europe, but a traveler can get a fair taste of the country's food by occasionally and judiciously sampling dishes in moderately priced restaurants, while he cooks the bulk of his meals. The place in which to eat depends a lot on your budget. I avoid those with an "international cuisine," which in essence includes chops, steaks and nondescript dishes.

58 A native restaurant that caters to middle class families is a good choice. Walk through, and if you hear a majority of the customers talking in a language other than that of the country you're in, walk out again. Or consult a native you've befriended for advice.

European restaurants post menus in their windows and you can shop around without having to enter. In the less urbane areas, you can ask to enter the kitchen and look in the pots. That's more likely the farther south and east you find yourself. In Turkey I made a regular practice of it, smelling and inspecting each offering.

COOKING

Cooking for yourself isn't as exciting as smelling in pots of native cafes (can that meat be reindeer?). It'll cost you less, though. You'll have satisfaction in the extra degree of self-sufficiency, too. You needn't depend on finding open cafes and you can ride into any wilderness, given that you bring enough provisions to last.

Cooking takes time. If that's more important than money and if you'd rather not be bothered with the extra chores at the end of a cycling day, by all means plan your trip around routes that will contain eating places. You'll not have to carry the extra gear, either.

However, since you may opt for boiling your water anyhow, the stove and pot needed for that might as well serve as the basis for making emergency meals when needed. You can keep a small supply of dried soups or a couple of cups of rice, the weight and bulk of which are minimal. Put them in the bottom of the pannier until needed, just as a first-aid kit or spare bike parts.

A regular cooking regimen—a hot meal each evening and maybe in the morning, too—can range from convenience foods to near-gourmet dining. Prepackaged, ready-for-stove meals aren't available everywhere and they cost more, but they do save time and fuss. There's little need to discuss their preparation since the techniques are simplicity itself: pop the can of spaghetti or meat stew into the pot and heat until warm.

The quality of those fast meals is something else. Their texture is soggy; they're overcooked or tasteless. Not wishing to offend a bland palate, the manufacturers hardly ever add spices or exotics. You can improve those meals by adding intelligent amounts of condiments, and you can pick brands and dishes that still retain some texture of the original ingredients. Try the prospects at home to preview what you're in for. In any case, you'll have a hearty road appetite going for you to help you stomach those foods.

Cooking from scratch is not complicated, but it does need concentration. At least a minimal kitchen must be carried. Besides the stove and pot, you'll need a few utensils, staples and cleaning accessories. A metal bottle of spare fuel for the stove can be carried in a water bottle cage on the underside of the down tube, near the bottom bracket where it won't do any damage if some leaks out.

59

Shopping must be a planned affair, one that involves planning and consultation with your partners. Unlike the choice offered in a cafe, once the decision for a dish is made, everyone eats the same thing.

Buying goods on the foreign scene can be frustrating. Although many foods are similar internationally, a lot of the familiar things aren't there and others may not be recognized. A riding companion of mine once bought a can of pimiento instead of peppers, based on a misleading picture on the label.

Don't be shy to ask for the smaller portions of eggs, butter and meat that you'd need for just two or three riders. The supermarkets —Europe is full of them—may turn you down, but owners of small shops are cooperative. In Norway they even split a standard kilo (2-pound) bag of sugar for us.

No European store will bag your groceries. They expect you to bring a sack with you, although some sell shopping bags. In Scandinavia those are generally large plastic ones. Save them. They're useful for wrapping your cooking gear in related groups and to keep things dry. A nylon net bag is handy for shopping, too.

It can double for hanging food by a rope from a tree overnight, safe from varmints.

Shop hours must be watched, since neighboring countries and even those shops in the same country may differ in practices. Some shops close in the middle of the day for a siesta. Others stay open through lunchtime but finish business at four in the afternoon. Hours may change by district and by village or city. Inquire carefully about schedules.

A source of water is crucial. If it's not at the camping site, it'll have to be brought in from the first available habitation, public pump or stream. Watch the source, as mentioned previously.

To carry water you'll need a container. Best are the folding plastic types holding from a few quarts to gallons. About 2½ gallons should be enough for the whole evening, including a quick wash of hands, face and teeth for two to three people. You can do with a smaller one, but the difference in weight and bulk is insignificant.

Make camp at least 1½ hours before dark. Cooking is hectic enough after a hard day in the saddle without the added disadvantage of darkness. Cyclists need the extra time, anyhow, to check and maintain their vehicles. If you're with a group, choose a cooking spot somewhat away from the tents and from where the fun and games are going on. You can do without the kibitzing and roughhouse.

You have, effectively, two choices of stove type overseas: butane and kerosene. White gas is unavailable, and alcohol is inefficient and expensive. Not all butane fuel is available either, but the C-200 cartridge is fairly universal except in Eastern Europe. Bring extras with you there.

A butane stove is clean and convenient, with no priming needed, but its effectiveness is lost as temperatures drop. At freezing, it won't burn at all. In cold weather, a good tactic is to keep the stove overnight in a corner of your sleeping bag to warm it for morning use.

Kerosene is common and cheap. Its usual smell is obnoxious to many people, but a refined type has little odor. It's called white *fotogen* in Scandinavian countries and is sold in bulk at gas stations, as well as in liter containers. The word for kerosene is paraffin in Great Britain.

How to cook is not the province of this guide. Learn that from a friend or spouse, or a backpacker's type of cookbook. There are many good ones on the market. Try mine.

Here are some cooking hints, though. Concentrate on meals that can be made mostly in one pot. Meat and vegetables can be sautéed in it to start, then the stock and rest of the ingredients can be cooked together. It'll save you extra pots to carry and wash, and once all is on the fire you can relax. Wash but don't peel potatoes and vegetables. You'll get vitamins, minerals and roughage from the peels, and you'll save work.

Bring an assortment of spices in 35mm film canisters made of plastic. A large number of them take little room, and weigh next to nothing, yet they enable you to greatly vary the taste of otherwise ordinary dishes. Carry condiments, sugar, peanut butter and other staples in the reusable plastic tubes that are sold in backpacking stores. They're neat, light and unbreakable. The tubes are unobtainable in Europe, except in England, so bring them from home. I fascinated Eastern Europeans when I filled those tubes from the bottom with jam or coffee. They'd never seen anything like it.

DIET AND NUTRITION

Make a special effort to seek out a variety of foods. That one practice will almost assure you of good nutrition. Include representatives from each of the four groups that nutritionists recommend you eat each day: fish, meat and legumes; milk products; fruit and vegetables; and grain products.

Don't neglect greens and fresh vegetables because of danger of diarrhea. Wash them (use the method described earlier in this chapter) and have no fear. Their absence in your diet will do more harm than the occasional stomach upset you may get.

61

A lone biker cooking for himself is especially prone to eat repeated meals of limited fare. He may find it easier, for example, to buy ground meat or a chop and cook rice daily than to shop for varied ingredients. Or the large amount that he must buy at a time will take a few days to finish.

Milk or milk products may be omitted where scarce or unpasteurized. Powdered milk can be substituted. You don't have to drink it; use the powder in soups and sauces or add it to coffee or tea. Cheese is a concentrated milk protein, also. Europe is renowned for the variety and quality of its cheeses.

When traveling any length of time and in regions of shortages of fresh foods, as in northern Scandinavia or Eastern Europe, take a multiple vitamin tablet daily. It's good insurance. Women should take iron supplements, also.

7 HOW TO KEEP WELL, CLEAN AND HAPPY

HYGIENE

The most pronounced material difference between the United States and the rest of the world is in quality of plumbing. If you're a chauvinist about toilets, you'll be unhappy out of the States. You won't find the domestic splendor of chrome, ceramic tile and tempered glass, except in small pockets of urbanized Scandinavia. There the plumbing competes for looks and efficiency with home.

The rest of Europe is shamelessly satisfied with old-fashioned pull-cord water closets, exposed and loud pipes, and unimaginative white instead of decorator pastel. At worst, you may have to use an open hole in a tile floor, North African style, with giant steel footsteps showing you where to place your feet.

Keeping clean may be a problem if you camp in the open a lot. It's possible to wash yourself and clothes in streams and rivers when in remote areas, given warm weather. You can use public bathhouses where they exist. Most of the time, though, you'll likely follow a Spartan regime and check into formal accommodations for a good wash.

Many camp managers will let you use the shower without camping—they're usually pay showers anyhow—and you can often negotiate at motels or YMCAs to pay for a wash only. In Italy and the shore areas of other countries, consider showering at a swimming pool or beach instead of the hotel or campground. The price you pay may be comparable, and you'll have the pleasure of a swim, too.

My decision to use a formal accommodation, instead of open

camping, is often dictated by need of a bath. Happy is the time when I'm lucky enough to stay with a host, soak luxuriously in a tub, and get the use of a washing machine!

MAIL

Next to keeping reasonably clean and slaking immediate animal appetites, mail affects morale most. Without an occasional letter, and especially when things aren't going exactly right anyhow, you imagine all kinds of dire happenings at home. No amount of logic alleviates your anxiety if an expected letter doesn't show. Are they in a hospital? Dead? The possibility that a letter can be misplaced or late is discounted; something must be terribly wrong.

That the feeling is illogical is borne out by the opposite reaction when you do get a letter. Obviously, the news is days old; something could have gone very wrong indeed since it was written. But the letter brings an immediate smile to your face. Everything's all right. The sudden relief is just as irrational, although palpably real to you. And so, receiving mail is a serious matter.

After years of frustration in trying to outguess post offices, I now conclude that the only effective insurance for getting mail is simply to allow a lot of time for it to arrive. After careful calculation of a reasonable number of days, I'll double them. That's the lead time I plan to supply people at home for a given mail drop. Since the news will be old anyhow, a few extra days will make little difference compared to drawing a blank at the mail window. **63**

Why letters should take so long in transit is beyond me. I calculated 10 to 14 days for letters in Eastern Europe during my 1979 trip. That was reasonable, I thought, based on experience from a previous trip. But I didn't receive a single letter in the East using that lead time. Leaving forwarding addresses in post offices was futile, too. I didn't get letters until well after I returned home.

Mail to Eastern Europe took as long as 25 days to arrive and never less than 20. Even in efficient Scandinavia, mail time was closer to 10 days than the week I allowed. My traveling companion got her letters from Australia faster than I did from the United States. It made no sense.

Your first precaution in receiving mail is to have it addressed well. Inform your friends to send letters to "Surname, J; Poste Restante, Main Post Office 1; City; Country." Don't have them write "Mr. John Surname." An unlettered clerk may file the latter name under "M" for Mister, or "J" for John. In many parts of the world the surname is written first. You can't assume a Yugoslav clerk to know that John or Mr. is not a family name. Srb is a fairly common surname in that country, after all, so why shouldn't there be a Mr?

Poste Restante is the international term for General Delivery. Post offices have a special window for it, but that may be combined with other services such as packages or postal savings, as in Poland, or be handled at an office outside of the general post office itself.

Letters are sometimes sent to the wrong post office branch or are bounced around from office to office of cavernous old buildings. You may find yourself shuttling among buildings, never sure which one is really supposed to have your letter—a very Kafkaesque experience. At the least, you'll wait in interminable lines. To be fair, these experiences are not common throughout Europe and are most likely in the more bureaucratic parts of the Eastern Bloc.

Problems occur more frequently in large towns or cities, which contain a number of important post office branches and in which bureaucracy is well entrenched. As a rule, it's best to select a small to medium-size town for a mail drop. Don't pick a village. Hours there are usually limited to a few, and you might have to wait an extra day if the office closes in the early afternoon.

64

The amount of time that a post office will hold mail varies, although it's seldom less than ten days. An instruction to "hold until 10 June," or whatever date you think would be safe, may help keep the letter there until you claim it.

Better than the post office by far is mail addressed to American Express or other traveler's checks offices. Those offer a limited number of pickup points; they're only in the largest cities. Still, use them when you can. Your local representative should have international offices. Those in tourist areas usually have lines in front of their mail windows, but the wait is worth trading for the uncertainties of the post office. Amex holds mail 30 days for customers. Show one of their checks or a card and you're considered a customer.

Some Amex offices will honor only cards. They may charge for mail pickup if you have only their checks. They always charge to forward mail to another city, as do some post offices, as in Sweden and Austria, for example.

Although it's a limited option, mail addressed to a personal contact at a private home is the very best way. There's never any confusion and you don't have to go to midcity daily to check for mail. If you've arranged with a bank for getting money or if you contact an organization, those may be used also. Hostels everywhere will hold mail for you, but make sure they're still operating or haven't changed addresses. That might mean writing beforehand to see if you can use them. The same thing goes for hotels, those in which you'll make reservations.

Aerograms aren't widely available in Eastern Europe. Neither are the onionskin paper and light envelopes that allow a few pages to meet the minimum postage for a letter. Buy those in Western Europe.

When sending letters home, don't drop them into mailboxes. Those must be emptied infrequently because my letters took a month or longer to arrive when I used them. Leave letters only at post offices. In Asia it's wise to insist that stamps be cancelled in your presence; they've been stolen off letters. I've never heard of that happening anywhere in Europe, but it may be possible in Turkey.

To receive a package anywhere overseas is difficult. No postal authority at home can predict accurately how long it would take to get there. A traveler is reluctant to wait for a package with that kind of uncertainty. If mailed too early, the package may be sent back. There's no telling how long it would be kept.

Mailing to the other places mentioned above is better to avoid frustration. Have the package mailed long before you expect to get there and have it held for you. An American consulate or embassy will hold it, too, although they don't like it and don't advertise the fact. They're more gracious about it in Eastern Europe and Asia.

Sending a package home from Eastern Europe can be a nightmare. Long lines, forms, and the need of sewed sacks or scarce boxes must be dealt with, and you may be unpleasantly surprised to pay a heavy duty on certain items. You'll be shunted from line to line and office to office before you satisfy all requirements. As a foreigner, you'll usually not be able to use offices in small towns or villages where lines are smaller. They'll tell you to go to the city. A native, if you meet one, can send your package easier.

My first experience of that sort was mailing a souvenir wall plate from Romania. It cost me next to nothing, about 75¢ in a village craft shop. I wrapped it well with a lot of padding in a cardboard box that took me a whole afternoon to find. After being directed to the wrong lines and the wrong post office in the adjoining big city, I finally reached the right man.

"Open it up," he said. All my careful wrapping and tying would have to be redone. "Fill out those forms," he said next. Instructions for the host of papers were in Romanian, Russian and French. Fortunately, I could read the latter. Once over that hurdle, I was

65

told that my box wasn't secure enough; I had to pack it in a wooden box. I had none and even had trouble finding the cardboard, I told the man.

They searched through the building and found a wooden box. We packed and nailed, while stolid customers stood behind me. Those stoics must have been used to it. The last bad news was a customs fee, many times what I paid for the plate. As it turned out, the plate arrived home broken.

In all, it was an interesting experience—as good a way to waste a day as any other—but I wouldn't want to repeat it. Since then I try to avoid mailing packages there. I take them with me out of the country to mail in Western Europe.

MEETING PEOPLE

Imagine the scene in a Turkish village when a foreign car or camper drives into the market square. Local activity stops and the peddlers run to the vehicle with their wares in the hope of an inflated sale. Sharpsters narrow their eyes with speculation and saunter over, some tricks in mind.

Contrast that with you as a bike tourist, coasting into the same market. Although eyes will turn to look at your unfamiliar appearance, you won't be thought of automatically as a lucrative sales prospect or a pigeon. You might be overcharged a little, if you don't have the going price in mind, but not by much. The shrewd peasant mind instinctively recognizes enterprise, the same need of ready wit and adaptation to circumstances that he must also possess to get by. The trickster comes to you not so much with larceny in his heart—though he won't turn down a chance to pick up a bit of change if you relax completely—but with a professional's respect for your hustle.

You'll be the exotic one, and they'll be interested. They'll want to know where you came from and where you'll go next. "Why?" will be a familiar question. Trying to explain, however clumsily, will ingratiate you with your audience.

People will come to you spontaneously wherever you travel. But it's far better to make a deliberate effort to encourage that, especially if you're on a long tour and will stay in the area for a while. Advertise your presence. Attach a plaque to your bike with a map and something like "Tour of Bulgaria." A U.S. flag will indicate your national source. It may attract a few argumentative types who'll want to debate you, but that's also part of the excitement of foreign encounters.

HOW TO KEEP WELL, CLEAN AND HAPPY

"Wobbling" Wally Watts, the around-the-world unicyclist of 1976–77, had a unique idea. He asked the mayor of his home town, Edmonton, Canada, to write an open letter of introduction to foreign mayors. Wally presented copies of the letter, with souvenir medallions of the Canada Games, in each village and town he visited. The letter didn't exactly elicit enthusiasm in a sophisticated Western Europe, but it drew favorable responses farther east and south, where officialdom in any form gets a respectful reading. He was often bedded in a mayor's home, or something equivalent, as a reward for this piece of ingenuity.

Don't rush through a community if you want to meet someone. People may be shy or reserved; give them a chance to gather nerve to talk to you. Help them along, in fact. My favorite ploy is to ask the hesitant for directions, even if I know those well enough. It's a good icebreaker. Everyone wants to help a stranger. A conversation follows naturally.

Those with a bent and taste for publicity can make that work. Reporters are seldom in the street waiting conveniently for your arrival. A visit to their office helps them discover a story. Newspapers in small cities and in towns are especially favorable. Their usual story excitement is the local fete or a new contract at the shoe factory.

Carry a few copies of 5 X 7-inch photos of yourself riding the bike for those papers which are too small to have a photographer or a camera. Most reporters will prefer to write their own stories, but you might bring copies of a short release for those occasions when either time or language difficulties make an interview awkward. The story the paper runs on you will help make contacts. I've had people stop me on the road and invite me to their homes because they read about my trip.

But nothing compares to the certainty of a prearranged visit with a native of the country, someone who will acquaint you with local customs, suggest places to go, and explain the significance of what you're seeing. How to get those names? The various organizations mentioned in Chapter 1, in the section on Useful Associations, and those listed in the Appendices will sometimes suggest them. You can also join professional or fraternal organizations, or special interest groups with international ties, such as engineering or psychological societies, the Rotary International, or the Masons.

Names can be gleaned through some homework: by scanning past bicycling magazines for open invitations from residents of foreign countries; by doing the reverse, that is, writing to foreign publications to announce your trip and solicit invitations; through correspondence with pen pals, as in Esperanto magazines; and through cycling and business acquaintances with foreign ties who might furnish you with names.

Do these tactics work? They often have for me. Once a multinational correspondence is established, it's amazing how contacts spread like a chain letter. Your experience of the trip expands, too.

DIVERSIONS
SEX

Take it with you. Like bike parts, it's difficult to find in other parts of the world.

RADIO

I don't bring a radio with me on tour, preferring to let nature make its own music. Part of bike touring, for me, is freedom from hearing blatant commercials and the Muzak pablum that's fed us everywhere. Still, some might like to get more immersed in the sounds of a foreign country, and a radio is the easiest way to do that.

You might consider buying a combination of a radio with a cassette recorder. The sounds of the country—the markets, cafes, casual singing or instrument playing in the streets—can be taped, and it can be used for note taking. The recorder can be placed in a handlebar bag or suspended in a special case from the top tube, where it will be convenient for use during cycling. A remote mike can be strung from it to your pocket. When a thought occurs to you or if you see something interesting en route, it's there to take a verbal note with no need to stop.

KEEPING A TRIP RECORD

A diary and photographs keep the trip fresh in your mind long after it's over. For me, note taking is not only a record; it's also a discipline that extends and sharpens senses. Writing and photographing help me organize and make significant the events of the day or month, and they identify further elements for observation and study.

Your approach need not be all that formal, but you should take notes somewhat systematically anyhow. Don't be self-conscious about the effect they'll have on posterity. Write as if composing a letter to a friend. In fact, many tourists do that quite literally. Tyler Folsom wrote hundreds of letters in the place of notes and had a meaningful record afterward. I take notes as a thought occurs to me, right on the road. I stop the bike and jot them down, otherwise the thought may be gone forever. A recorder can be used instead, or as an adjunct.

Besides daily occurrences, conversations and sights, you should record such mundane items as prices, the kind of vegetation and terrain you passed through, the weather, what you ate, and the way the people dressed. It will all have more meaning later when you reflect on it.

Photos will supplement and enrich your trip record. No matter how graphically you describe a scene, it can't match the visual reproduction. And, of course, you'd want a set of slides to show your friends or bike club members.

I like a 35mm, split-rangefinder camera. A single lens reflex of mine once fell apart, shaken loose by rough roads. The rangefinder model I've used since has stood up to a number of long trips without even minor problems. I carry two of those cameras, in fact, one for color and the other for black and white. With a tripod—yes, I carry a small light one—the combined weight is about 3½ pounds, the same as the reflex camera I used previously.

I always bring all the film I intend to use for the entire trip. **69** Sometimes that comes to dozens of rolls. In spite of the customs restrictions of some countries, which limit film to a few rolls, I've never been challenged. Not only is film more expensive in Europe, but it's hard to find what you want. You may be able to buy only an off-brand of color and have trouble processing it. Even black and white film may be scarce. During our trip in Scandinavia, Rosemary Smith could buy only outdated film for her black and white, 110-size camera.

I've always felt nervous about passing through security checks at airports with all that film, and have insisted on examination of it by eye instead of X rays. I read recently about an instance in which X rays in the USSR fogged a professional photographer's entire assignment, in spite of assurances by security agents that it wouldn't. The exposure they used was much greater than the standard dosage. If you're apprehensive about that kind of possibility, as I am, don't pass the film through the machine. Or store it in special, lead-lined plastic that can be bought from Kodak.

DRUGS AND DRINK

You've no doubt heard enough about the tough laws dealing with the use and smuggling of drugs, and you're amply warned. I can attest to the horror stories from observation at the scene, and from some of the people who dealt in that illegal business. Those were near-professionals who knew the chances they took but were still bent on making a killing.

Should you have a cute idea of stuffing plastic bags full of some exotic in your double-butted tubes, forget it. It's known to the customs agents already. My bike has never been searched in those places, but I'm sure it would be likely to. One search is all it takes.

Use of drugs is tolerated more in the north and west than in the south and east. Eastern Europe is behind the rest of the Continent in drug use, but marijuana is becoming more common. An influx of foreign travelers is introducing it. The authorities are disturbed and don't take kindly to either users or smugglers.

Drinking is the socially accepted way of losing your senses in Eastern Europe and Scandinavia. The harder stuff—vodka, aquavit, spiritus, slivovic—is the common drink and is dirt cheap compared to our prices. Polish vodka actually costs less ounce for ounce, in liquid form, than coffee.

Wine, naturally, is the more popular drink farther west and south. It's expensive, if vintage, for the budget biker. A lot of good, moderately priced wine is common throughout the region, though. A cheaper table wine is a good partial substitute for bottled water in areas of bad water.

70

Beer is excellent in all of Europe; only Poland, Romania and Bulgaria make beer inferior to America's. Beer is generally cheaper than coffee or soft drinks overseas.

The atmosphere in a public drinking place in Europe is different from a bar in the United States. A British pub is a family place, where entertainment comes primarily from the occupants, not the TV tube. In Poland it'll be much the same, with food dominating; a bar-restaurant is the rule there. In Czechoslovakia a bar-buffet emphasizes food, too, with beer. Alcohol takes a rear seat to coffee in Italy's bars. France's bistros are the traditional places to sit at tables and socialize. No barstools there.

PERSONAL SHOPPING

The cardinal rule once you cross into Turkey is to settle all prices and to get the exact services you agreed upon, before paying. In Istanbul a friend and I were disarmed by the broad grin of a friendly taxi driver and didn't ask about the fare. He stunned us with an absurd price at the end of a short ride. No amount of reasoning moved him. He considered it a point of honor to stand pat at the price, and was ready to sit there all day if necessary. At other times, whenever I negotiated beforehand, I was never asked for more money at the end of the service.

The practice of bargaining varies throughout Europe. In the Communist Bloc, prices are fixed by the state. The cost of an article is printed right on the wrapper and is uniform for the whole country. But any private dealings you have with citizens for services are negotiated. In the Mediterranean countries, prices are semifixed and it's possible to haggle, except in department stores. The rest of Europe has fixed prices.

It hardly pays to bargain for inexpensive items and small amounts of food. Those have a going price that can be learned soon enough. If someone asks for a much greater amount, just walk away and buy from another stand. But if you buy a luxury, especially a crafted one, you can normally discuss it.

Bargaining is as much a social art as a business transaction. Even if you have no taste for it—most Americans are uncomfortable with the idea—you should still experience it once. It's much like gambling or drugs; it grips some people almost emotionally. Who knows? You might become addicted, too.

A quick overview of the fixed prices asked in department stores for the same item gives you a financial anchor point. The help of a native friend is best, but only for advice. He can give you some idea of the going price and at what bid to start. But he shouldn't participate. Bargaining is a one-on-one contest.

Start by establishing rapport with the merchant. That's extremely important in a transaction that comes closer to intimacy between strangers than any other human activity. Proud Turkish merchants, sitting cross-legged on a stack of rugs, won't even talk to you if you show any sign of antagonism or disdain.

Be friendly and show casual interest in what you want. But not too casual—you want the merchant to know you'd buy, yet you're not eager. Don't ever degrade the product. It will be insulting to him. Why would he carry inferior goods if he's a sound businessman?

The rest follows naturally: a price stated; a counteroffer; tea and social talk; counter-counteroffer; more tea, and so on. You may succeed in knocking the price down to department store level or lower. He may throw in additional items to appease you. You may meet his price but choose a better-made companion piece instead of the original.

You'll enjoy an hour or longer of cheap entertainment, in any case. And you'll have a lesson in psychology and interpersonal relations, even if you pay more than you intended. It's really a lot of fun.

HOW TO
8 HANDLE TERRAIN AND WEATHER

DAILY RIDING REGIMEN

"How fast can you go on that thing?" is the usual question I'm asked by nonbikers when the subject of pace comes up.

"Too fast, unfortunately," is my usual answer.

The response is partly a put-down to those who don't appreciate the value of bike touring—their base is the car trip, which has the object of hurrying and getting that unpleasantness over with—and partly a sad truth I realize about myself. For, sooner or later, I get caught up in a fever of "let's see how far I can go today."

In that affliction I find myself slogging along fixedly—curiously, it happens mostly in the rain—and I resist any stops. I put off looking for a camping spot, or even taking a coffee break. It might be that I feel that if I settle down comfortably somewhere, I'll call it a day.

Why I do it is a mystery. The mood doesn't last more than a couple of hours and I feel foolish afterward. I realize then that my hypnotic compulsion produced nothing in the way of enjoyment of the ride. If you ever catch the same disease, pinch yourself to slow down.

A bike tour should never be allowed to become a mad ride. For that you don't have to leave home. You can just pedal around the block a few hundred or thousand times.

My usual overseas pace averages 40 miles a day. That is, 1,200 miles in a calendar month. The daily range is greater, naturally, so that on a somewhat compulsive day in an uninteresting flat farmland I might ride 100 miles, and in scenic mountains not more than 20. I find my pace decreasing with the years; I tell myself it's not so much from diminishing ability as from an increasing realization that I miss too much with speed. Ideally, given time and means, I'd like to ride even less miles, and only two days out of three, spending more time in investigating my surroundings.

Obviously, each person has special areas of interest, and I'm not advocating a particular style of touring. Some people like to ride directly to their destination without any delays. To others, the act of rambling contains the significance of the ride. I fall into the latter category. I spend a lot of hours on the road, with frequent stops for photos, cafe breaks, conversations, note taking and just general loafing.

Companions may compromise one's natural preferences, unless each person rides alone and meets the others at the end of the day. That sort of thing should be discussed and agreed upon before the tour. It's surprising how often it isn't, even between friends who've cycled together long, but casually, previously.

The only practice I try to impose on fellow travelers is an early morning start. It saves daylight for an earlier stop in the afternoon while stores are still open. It's certainly more pleasant, also, to make camp, eat, and get cleaned up while it's still light.

ROAD CONDITIONS 73

Roads in Europe vary in quality from excellent to terrible. You may be on a smooth, lightly traveled road one day and a rutted, truck-filled one the next. Even in advanced industrial nations I've experienced rough surfaces, impossibly steep grading, and poor banking. My worst roads were in the Balkans, with those in Romania the most primitive.

Main highways offer the best engineering. Because they do, they draw the heavy through traffic, motorized campers, weekenders and trucks. Holidays and weekends are worst. Southern France is so glutted by beach seekers, for example, that churches have no masses Sunday morning, offering them on Saturday night instead; daylight hours are devoted to motoring.

The attractions along those fast roads are aimed at the tourist crowds—tacky curio shops, playlands and McDonald's-like fast food shops. Avoid those main roads when you can. If you find yourself unavoidably on one during a holiday or weekend, take a day off or ride early in the morning before traffic builds up.

Avoid cycling during July and August in those choked areas also. The bulk of Europe takes its vacations those months. You'll find whole towns abandoned then. If you can work your schedule to visit just before or after the high season, you'll have a more pleasant trip.

ADVENTURE CYCLING IN EUROPE

For a glimpse at authentic native life, and less traffic, you're better off on secondary or even tertiary roads, those which are not inviting to the comfort seekers. Unfortunately, the byways will take you away from hotels, commercial campgrounds and hostels. Those amenities are situated mostly where the bulk of motor traffic rides. On the other hand, the local cafes and inns you do come across will be more pleasant. Some will hardly be identified, since most natives know of them and few outsiders drop in.

You'll be likely thrown more on your own resources and may have to come equipped to camp in the open. In case you go into complete wilderness—forest areas shown on your maps and an absence of towns will alert you to that—add another couple of days' worth of emergency food. You might not be near grocery stores.

By avoiding main roads, the route you choose will no doubt be longer. Distances between cities are greater by 50 percent or more on alternate roads. Work that into your calculations for cross-country mileage and schedule.

Cycling may be harder, also. Whereas main roads are cut through walls of rock or are tunneled in mountains, to improve grading or to avoid winding climbs, secondary roads follow the contours of the land. But don't dismiss the latter just because of the work. They may offer dividends in scenery and unspoiled communities.

The condition of the lesser roads might be inferior to the paved superhighways, but that depends on where you are. Maps will indicate road surfaces as asphalt, macadam, gravel or dirt. Even the smallest roads in the West are likely to be asphalted. They're usually not in more backward countries and in mountainous regions. Poor countries can't afford to cut a road and maintain an asphalt surface in mountains and areas of harsh winters.

Macadam is crushed rock with a cover of some kind of bituminous layer. It offers a smooth base for a comfortable ride when it's in good shape. Often it's not. When I rode in Romania, macadam roads were full of potholes. In sections, the surface was gone entirely, leaving deep ruts through crushed stone and down to the earth and rocky subsoil. I was forced to thread my way among small boulders to keep from cracking an axle. In dry weather the roads were dusty, and in rain impossibly muddy. I had to chisel caked mud from between tires and mudguards with a screwdriver.

Packed gravel with a clayey earth binder that hardens in the sun makes a firm road, even in rain. It can be much superior to macadam. Loose gravel is bad news, as is soft earth. The worst is sand. In areas close to the sea it's wiser to keep to paved roads entirely. Even in sections of those, sand often drifts across the highway.

When you know you'll be on rough roads, choose tougher touring tires of a lower pressure and heavier sidewalls. Michelin 50s are a good standby. Pay extra attention to heavy-duty pannier racks, such as those welded directly to seatstays, or the models that attach to seatstay lugs. Perform maintenance frequently and check your bike nightly for looseness and any signs of problems.

It's best to avoid riding through big cities entirely, unless they have something you especially want to see. Not only is traffic heavy, but many European cities are cobbled or have tire-catching streetcar tracks (ride at right angles to cross those, not parallel to them). If you must ride into the city, do so at slack times. If caught in traffic, sit it out at the nearest cafe. At least ride slowly and carefully; don't be tempted to hurry and get out of the traffic. Better yet, reroute to another road.

HILLS AND GEARING

It's possible to avoid hills altogether by carefully laying a route around them or by cycling in flat country like the Netherlands and Denmark. Railroad tracks or rivers can be followed for more level routes. You can ride a train to a higher altitude and then coast down. Roads that run at right angles to the direction of rivers can also be avoided.

There's nothing wrong with cheating hills; cycling doesn't have to be a bout of masochism to be enjoyed. Still, a lot is missed by evading a few climbs. There are those—myself included—who maintain that it's worth a tough grade to enjoy the arrival at the top. Tom Fleener, an around-the-world biker in 1977–78, likens it to combat with a worthy opponent: he struggles to get to the top, held back by the mountain's gravity; he conquers the summit, and then succumbs to the mountain's gripping pull on the way down.

Other bikers have described it also in similar, euphoric terms. Hard climbs hold a fascination, much as Himalayan ascents for a Hillary. I think that exuberance is actually a physiological process. Some of the by-products of oxygen depletion must affect thought and sensory processes in the brain and cause a high. It should be investigated.

But, induced visions aside, I'm personally past the stage when I want to show how strong I am going up hills. At a younger age, when the grade was too much for me, I used to make the excuse that I preferred walking up a hill once in a while to see the scenery, rather than tarnish my macho self-image. Now I use a triple chainwheel, with the lowest gear I can get. What's to prove?

Which lowest gear that should be depends on your condition and what you're carrying. Don't worry about displaying weakness with a big cog on your freewheel. Only a technically minded biker will know that your gear is super-low. The unsophisticated, who will be your most adoring public, will only be more impressed by three chainwheels in front and a monster freewheel in back.

Even other bike trappings, unrelated to movement of the bike, fascinate the uninitiated. In northern Norway, a pair of boys inspected my loaded bike with excitement. What was it that so impressed them? It was the two water bottles and a metal one below holding fuel. They finally met a three-bottle bicyclist!

My present gear has a 27-inch low development. (For those not familiar with the concept of "developments," it refers to a numbering system that derives from a ratio of the number of teeth in the front chainwheel to that in the back freewheel. The lower the number, the lower the gear. Gears on bikes can go as low as 21 inches and as high as 112. What you usually find on bikes in a store range from mid 30s to 96. To get either a greater range or lower gears, you have to ask for modification of chainring and freewheel, and possibly pay more for it.) I'd drop down to even a lower one, except that I've got the lowest possible in the Sugino Mighty Tour system. I would have to buy a whole new drive train to go below 27. I use that gear only a small portion of riding time, on the steeper grades in hilly areas, but it saves me effort. Even with that low I still grind chainwheel teeth into fishhooks before their time. I should get a lower gear, obviously.

Many riders get along nicely with higher gears than mine, using lows in the 30s. They might be carrying lighter loads—25 pounds perhaps instead of my usual 50—and so don't need the help. Some have younger or stronger legs and hill climbing may offer them a major part of their bicycling kicks.

If you find it tough going up hills, try a few riding tactics. Zigzagging, or riding in S-curves, is one way of reducing a difficult grade. It's effective, but it can be dangerous on roads with more than very light traffic. Your control of the bike is not as positive, what with the effort and the lower, imbalanced speed. Vision is also hampered by curves and by the crest of the hill ahead. Oncoming traffic may not see you easily, and a truck may be on you in the middle of the road before you know it. I don't recommend this tactic except when there's a long unobstructed view from both front and back.

Another way to cope with a series of choppy hills involves a

76

strategy. When approaching a descent, resist the temptation to coast. Instead, accelerate and gain the greatest speed you can before entering the downgrade. Keep cranking in the highest gear until you lose the pedal. Lower your profile to minimize wind resistance. You're now riding as fast as is possible.

When you reach the level part before the next hill, try the pedal occasionally. As soon as you feel a response, start pedaling hard again to maintain your speed. As you enter the next ascent, shift down fast by large steps to hold onto your speed, keeping an even cranking cadence. An ability to shift rapidly and smoothly is necessary. You may have to practice that some before attaining proficiency.

With luck, you'll make the crest of the next hill before having to shift to the lowest gears. You'll have at least collected compound interest on your pedaling investment in a sharp gain of momentum and altitude.

This roller-coaster technique should be used only on a series of short hills that have no curves or crossroads, from which cars can surprise you. The road surfaces should be free of rocks and potholes that could cause a fall. The technique is dangerous on long hills, where a buildup of speed would be excessive.

On long hills, safety should be the first concern. Start to coast slowly, pump your brakes often and sit up to help slow the bike by presenting more of your body surface for wind resistance. Watch curves with soft shoulders. You can spill easily while banking in gravel or loose dirt.

Take rests at the top of hills rather than before you climb, not so much for physiological as psychological reasons. Facing a long climb after a pleasant stretch on the grass and a light snack is discouraging. Conversely, the most exhilarating and deserving time for a break is after the cycling effort. The view from the heights is a bonus.

When all else fails in negotiating a hill, you may have to get off the bike and push. Well, you can always tell yourself that you'd rather walk for a change and enjoy the scenery, can't you?

PLANNING FOR SEASONS

It makes sense to tour a country when its weather is most likely to be best. Tourist office information will give some hint of that, although unfavorable aspects may be glossed over. For example, an average daily temperature in a desert country may be cited to convince you that the area is temperate; the awful fact may be that days are extremely hot and nights freezing. The same with rain. The annual rainfall may sound reasonable, but it could be evenly distributed as a fine spray the entire time you'll be there.

Look for other measures—average afternoon temperatures, month by month, or inches of rain by month—and check with additional, impartial sources like the *National Geographic Picture Atlas of Our World* (Washington, D.C.: National Geographic Soc., 1979) and the *Hammond Almanac* (Maplewood, N.J.: Hammond, Inc., 1979) for a more complete picture.

When you take a long tour that includes a number of countries, during a whole summer perhaps, your problem becomes more complicated. Neighboring countries may differ appreciably in weather. This is not as true of Europe as of Asia, unless you travel north and south, from Scandinavia to Sicily, for example. You'd then need to plan your route according to season.

The planning can be aided by a systematic tabling of rain and temperature ranges by month and by country. Because you might lack specific data for many of the cities within an area, your table can provide only a broad picture. To illustrate the principle, look at the table on pages 80–81. It shows one of the route options that I considered for my around-the-world trip.

The table contains data for the tentative months of arrival in major cities. Selected data for adjoining months are supplied, too, to indicate trends or abrupt changes in weather. For instance, it can be seen that temperatures would stay fairly constant at the start of this trip. In contrast, temperatures drop dramatically during fall in West Asia. I'd have to arrive in Kabul well before November, when nights would be near freezing.

The rainfall information is significant, too. In October the monsoon is still at Lahore and Calcutta. It's gone during the next two months, when the previous high temperatures drop also. That would be the best time to visit. Then later in Central America, I'd want to cycle before May, when the rainy season starts.

The table shown was the result of manipulating the schedule to take advantage of the weather. Complete data for all months was first sifted to see trends along the route. If it were impossible to find a fit, a reverse route or a layover somewhere might have resulted in a better plan.

Your situation may not be as global, but the plan will be useful nevertheless. You'd be forewarned of which clothes and rain gear to bring and what to send ahead. The pace may have to be slowed for a siege of hot days. Conversely, you'd want to speed up if you knew that you had to arrive somewhere before bad weather comes.

Wind data isn't as systematically available as temperature and rain. Winds are much more variable and unpredictable, to start with, even if there is a prevailing direction. World wide, winds blow west-northwest in the northern hemisphere, but that's a matter of statistical majority and not necessarily your situation. You might be there during a week when minority winds are blowing in the opposite direction.

If everything else is equal and you have flexibility to choose any month for a tour, select June. There's less traffic then and it has the longest days of the year. That's no small advantage. It gives you more time for cycling or setting up camp.

RAIN, COLD, HEAT AND WIND

Inevitably, some bad weather will catch you during any trip of more than a few days. Unless you're satisfied to while away a lot of time indoors, you'd better be prepared physically and psychologically to ride under any weather conditions.

I don't think I'm a masochist, but I often enjoy riding in some rain. I certainly prefer that to lying in a cramped tent all day. I avoid a heavy downpour, with its hampered visibility and puddles that hide dangerous road surfaces, but I often find a light shower delightful.

79

When it's warm, I strip down to minimal decency and make myself one with the elements. The sensations are basic: the rain cools and washes my skin, the wet smell of plowed earth or cut grass permeates the air, and the lack of shadows allows colors to be seen in a new light.

Those who see rain less quixotically can use adequate rain gear. Gore-Tex material, although expensive, will keep you dry and not gather any significant condensation within the garment. You must remember, though, that if you sweat without wearing a rainsuit when riding hard, you'll still sweat while wearing it. Don't blame the rain gear. It will make you warmer, of course, and you should shed some clothes.

Keeping feet dry seems an insurmountable problem. The best solution in cold rain is to use low rubber shoe covers and overlapping rain pants. Covers split easily if not taken on and off carefully. They also deteriorate rapidly if carried outside your pack, exposed to light. Put them in plastic and keep them inside your pack.

The covers can be protected from tearing on toe clips if the latter are leather covered. Covers do tear on the rattrap parts of pedals, but that will be only on the underside. Water won't spread very rapidly through the rubber soles of your biking sneakers, unless immersed completely in water, and your feet should remain reasonably dry.

Your feet will sweat within the rubber, and after a time you

Average High and Low Temperatures and Days Rain

	Feb.	Mar.	Apr.	May	June	July	Aug.	Sept.
Lisbon	58 47; 8*	61 49; 10						
Seville	62 44; 9	67 48; 9						
Casablanca	64 46; 8	67 49; 8						
Valencia		63 47; 5	67 51; 5					
Barcelona		61 47; 7	64 51; 8					
Marseilles			59 41; 10	65 46; 10				
Nice			64 49; 7	69 56; 8				
Milan			66 46; 6	72 54; 9				
Vienna				66 50; 9	71 56; 9			
Budapest				72 52; 9	78 57; 8			
Belgrade				74 53; 9	79 58; 9			
Sofia					76 54; 9	82 57; 7		
Bucharest					81 58; 9	86 61; 7		
Istanbul					77 60; 4	81 66; 3	81 66; 3	
Ankara						86 59; 1	87 59; 1	
Teheran							97 71; 1	90 64; 1
Kabul								
Lahore								
Delhi								
Calcutta								
Bangkok								
Perth								
Sydney								
Panama								
Honduras								
Guatemala								
Mexico City								

*Average high for day during the month; average low; average number of days rain during month. Boldface data is at the time of scheduled arrival.

HOW TO HANDLE TERRAIN AND WEATHER

may be wet anyhow. To cope with that problem, a shoe cover of the "breathable" Gore-Tex has recently been introduced. It costs a prohibitive $35. You'd have to wear out six of the cheaper rubber covers to make up that price. It's doubtful if the Gore-Tex version would have that long a life. One way to alleviate sweating with

Oct.	Nov.	Dec.	Jan.	Feb.	Mar.	Apr.	May
76 53; 1							
73 42; 1	62 33; 2						
95 59; 1	**83 47; 0**						
93 65; 1	**84 52; 0**						
89 74; 6	**84 64; 1**	79 55; 0					
	87 72; 5	**87 68; 1**	89 68; 1				
			85 63; 14	85 63; 3			
			78 65; 13	**78 65; 13**	76 63; 14		
				89 71; 2	**90 72; 1**	90 74; 6	87 74; 15
				80 57; 1	**84 58; 1**	84 58; 1	90 74; 14
				81 57; 3	82 58; 5		84 10; 15
				75 47; 9	77 51; 14		78 54; 17

rubber is to take occasional breaks, removing rubbers and shoes for an airing.

The usual advice to place everything in plastic during rain is sound. If your handlebar bag features a plastic window for the map, that will probably leak also. Place the map within an additional Zip-Loc bag, the plastic envelope that seals with thumbnail pressure.

Using mudguards (fenders) is also wise. Their chief asset is to keep dirty water and mud from being thrown back onto the chain, crankset and bottom bracket area. They keep you and your panniers cleaner, too.

Common sense and preference tells you what to wear to keep warm: a number of light layers of clothing—I sometimes wear my complete wardrobe—a nylon windbreaker, a wool cap and winter gloves.

The only precaution I take in heat is to increase my water intake and slow down. I avoid cycling in midafternoon, lazing in a cafe or under a tree instead. In the Mediterranean countries it's a good time to visit old, thick-walled churches and museums, which are surprisingly cool in the hottest weather.

82

Strong winds can't be avoided as hills can, but the effects may be somewhat minimized. Small roads are best to take on those days. Their narrowness means more chance for such natural windscreens as patches of woods and houses to take effect. Those screens are close to secondary roads, whereas main roads are cleared widely on both sides and offer less protection.

Strangely, mountains are your best friends on windy days. When you climb, you're sheltered from the full force of the wind by the crest up ahead. Once you reach the top, and the gust of wind, gravity is with you on the way down. Also, the random nature of hills diverts winds so that their direction is more varied.

As a general rule you will encounter the least wind right after sunrise. By midafternoon, you will feel the wind pick up, most noticeably if you are traveling in flat country with little protection from trees, such as in Denmark or the Netherlands near the sea. You might find that cycling in these areas in the middle of the afternoon is as tough as fighting the hills. When you are riding against the wind, it is relentless.

9 THE BICYCLE AND ITS RIDERS

WHAT KIND OF BIKE?

Bike tourists have used every kind of machine to make epic trips. A score of whom I know rode from a few thousand miles to around the world on heavy 1- or 3-speeds. Their wheels were 26 X 1⅜ inches, the packs cumbersome affairs of canvas or leather, and the handlebars upright.

They were not, necessarily, old-timers or pioneers in bike travel. Heinz Stucke rode around the world in 1971, as did Wilfred Cresswell in 1977, and Dervla Murphy made her epic Ireland-to-India trip a few years earlier; all rode 3-speeds. I rode with Thomas Vogl in 1979 for a bit in Hungary; he was returning to Germany from a round trip to Turkey with a 1-speed.

I've met scores of other naive travelers on long tours who used both simple machines and elaborate 10-speeds, all trustful and without the faintest feeling of dread for what they were attempting. What they had in common was that act of faith in themselves and in the bike, to which I referred in the Introduction. They chose the bicycle because they considered it the most reliable means of travel other than walking.

Their faith was well justified. Consider, for example, that unlike a car or even a motorcycle, you can push a disabled bicycle for miles to a place of repair. If it's too far to walk, the bike can be thrown on top of a bus or bullock cart easily. You never run out of fuel. And the simplest technology—the village blacksmith, welder or mechanic—can usually fix what would break on a bike, at least well enough to get you to civilization. It continually amazes me, therefore, that there's so much apprehension about touring in a foreign country, and that people go through all that trauma in selecting and outfitting a bike.

Most any bicycle would do, really. The differences among them are minuscule for purposes of accomplishing travel. You'd get greater

83

efficiency and more comfort in one compared to another, to be sure. But you have a basic machine that is a light year more trustworthy than any other means of transportation.

It's true that I've chosen my bike with some care. I'm on it more than the occasional tourist. What would be minor advantages to her or him—a longer wheelbase, a kinder fork angle, small-flange hubs, and well-worn, leather saddle—mean more to me in the aggregate. Those features provide me, relatively, with the feel of a favorite easy chair instead of one at the kitchen table.

I now ride a Nishiki Grand Touring 15-speed, which has those more comfortable features for my long rides. The bike is also outfitted with components and accessories I've found to have added durability or dependability: a Sun Tour 13–16–20–26–34 freewheel and Sun Tour VGT derailleur (I've never had that steel workhorse fail yet); Blackburn front and rear racks, the latter bolted to the seatstays; a set of Kirtland panniers fore and aft; and, usually, Michelin 50 tires, the heavier but stronger 27 X 1¼-inch standbys for rougher roads. And, last but not least, an Avocet triple, with 28/47/52 chainwheels to make the way easier for an aging body that finds hills increasingly steeper than they used to make them.

84

MAINTENANCE

No matter the kind of bicycle you ride, it needs proper care to perform dependably. At home you're apt to do that periodically. You take shorter rides, in favorable weather and over good roads, and bike maintenance can be casual. In contrast, the tourist's bike is subjected to greater stresses, with heavy loads and under weather and road conditions that can't easily be avoided.

The big difference between the two kinds of use, in a word, is dirt. Rainwater, mud or road dust will introduce earth, grit and sand into the exposed and moving parts of the tourist's bike—into chainring, freewheel, chain and derailleur. The task is to get it all out before it does lasting harm.

Each evening you should pick out accumulated dirt and wipe off excess crud with a brush or screwdriver and a rag. Then reoil the chain lightly. Put a drop each at the point where the pivot pin passes through the inner link, one on each side, for a total of 232 drops in a 116-link chain. If that seems finicky, remember that the important "stretch" wear is there at the rollers, not on the surface of a chain.

The freewheel and chainring need not be oiled; more than sufficient oil from the chain will be thrown off onto them. The derailleur needs no oil at this time either.

THE BICYCLE AND ITS RIDERS

When the whole gear system seems heavy with foreign material, clean it with solvent and a brush. The timing of that depends on how adverse the conditions have been. It could be anywhere from a couple of hundred miles to a thousand.

Do that right on the bike without removing any components. Just slip the chain off the chainring to let it hang, and pass it a few times through a can of solvent, brushing as you move along. Be sure to change the solvent as it becomes dirty. Brush and wipe the other components. Let all air-dry and then reoil. Don't be fastidious about the type of solvent to use, whether gas, diesel or turpentine. Any kind of wash is better than none, and to wait until a proper solvent is available may do more harm than using second best.

On a trip longer than a few weeks, you can clean more thoroughly, while laying over somewhere for a couple of days. Remove the chain and components, steep them in turpentine or kerosene and clean well. Let drip and dry. Soak the chain in heated oil and drip overnight.

Once the chain gets appreciable wear, replace it the first chance you get. It's the weakest link in your drive system, and, happily, the cheapest and easiest bike part to find in Europe. Don't wait because you have another $2 worth of wear left. A sloppy chain could cost you $20 worth of wear on freewheel or chainring later on.

The overhead cost of a replacement is a minor expenditure, anyhow, compared to the air transportation and other investment in the tour. I'm not even as concerned with the cost of components as I am with finding them. Unless spares are carried, or you're in a country that sells a full line of components, you can get stuck.

I replace a chain and tires each 3,000 miles or more often, and those freewheel cogs that show wear at 6,000 miles. As pointed out above, wear is variable depending on weather. Hard use, a lot of hill climbing, for example, can aggravate wear, too. On a wet Scandinavian trip in mountains a chain wore in just 1,000 miles. On the other hand, I used one chain all the way from Athens to India on another trip, what with the absence of severe conditions.

I seldom clean the rest of the bike. I don't give the bike a name or talk to it, either, and I don't take any special pride in its sleek looks or wonderful efficiency. It has no sentimental value for me; no need to get sloppy about it. I just expect it to be faithful and reliable, which it will be with adequate care.

A group of bikers can share the use of maintenance items and tools. Even better is to duplicate many of the bike components. Ian Hibell did that with two companions during his South American ride. It saved carrying extra tools and spares, and it simplified maintenance.

A thorough discussion of maintenance procedures can be found in any basic book. These are the points I consider most important for the tourist.

THE WOMAN BICYCLIST

Cycling is one activity in which a woman is nearly equal in strength, and even superior in endurance, to a man. She need not fear that she won't be able to keep up. Most women I've cycled with, those that were in some kind of basic shape, were less tired at the end of the day than I, and certainly in better humor.

As David Smith, M.D., argued in a *Bicycling* article (November 1978), a woman's smaller size presents less wind resistance, a gram of her muscle produces as much work as a male's, most of her body muscle is in the legs (the male's larger shoulder muscles don't aid bicycling in the least), and her aerobic capacity decreases less with age than a man's. Her disadvantage in having more body fat in relation to muscle works against her mostly on hills, but she can offset that by outfitting her bike with somewhat lower gears.

86

Then why, if she can ride as well as a man, are there so few women bike tourists? There were a few classic long tours taken by the adventurous—the around-the-world trip of Louise Sutherland, and the Ireland-to-India ride of Dervla Murphy are the best known. Still, those were the handful of outstanding exceptions, and the sight of women tourists overseas is an oddity. Or stateside, for that matter. And those few women who do tour usually do so with a man.

The reason is twofold: social and psychological. In spite of women's lib and a looser social structure, today's women are still exercising less than men. Their presence on bikes—unless they're eccentric senior citizens or the quite young—is in the minority. You hardly ever see a woman commuter, for example, and few who shop by bicycle, at least in the United States. The typical woman, more than a man, is also influenced unduly by a society that has emphasized the auto as serious transportation, and which regards the bike as a plaything.

Women do ride casually in cycling clubs, partly because it's a fun thing and is social, but also because they're with a group of men who, they feel, make riding safe. They need not fear the unpredictables of mechanical breakdowns and the harassment from macho types.

Repairing and maintaining a bike is not by nature the exclusive province of men, though. Only past tradition, schooling, and lack of

THE BICYCLE AND ITS RIDERS

opportunity for women accounts for male mechanics. If you're a woman who claims she's all thumbs, you can take a course in bike repair. Or you can simply consult a good repair book and practice on your own bike. If you can follow a recipe, you can make sense of repair instructions. A lack of familiarity with mechanics shouldn't be the excuse to stay away from a bike tour.

Physical danger is another matter. In Europe a woman is completely safe in the northern and eastern regions. She can ride without challenges or threats in any of the Nordic or Slav states, even into the most primitive regions of Norway or Romania. In the Communist countries, in fact, the emphasis on equal opportunity of the sexes—women can work as laborers and I've seen women hauling fertilizer on bikes—brings an equal reaction to a man or woman on a bike. That vehicle is regarded as a reasonable transportation vehicle for anyone.

Unfortunately, the Mediterranean countries—Spain, southern France, Italy, Greece and Turkey—still have a tradition of the demure and susceptible female and the hot masculine pursuer. A female is liable to passes, catcalls and possible intimidation.

When June Clifton rode with our group in Spain, whistles and hoots followed her everywhere. Once, an ardent suitor even scratched hopefully on her tent wall at night. In Scandinavia, in contrast, male heads turned no more at the sight of the equally attractive Rosemary Smith on her bike than at me. The northern temperament is reserved.

The possibility of a serious threat, however, is slight anywhere in Europe, except in Turkey. It's rare to hear of a woman's rape or robbery, while on a bike. Not that the Latin doesn't hope to score with a long-legged American, but a sharp put-down usually cows the most ardent Italian or Spaniard. The advances are mostly a nuisance.

Turkey is more serious, though. There, the lone female must put aside the strong convictions she may have about being due equality with a male; she simply won't be treated equally, and she had better accede to the local mores. Those demand a man as a "protector."

A Turk won't be necessarily deterred by a male escort—any Western woman seems to be regarded as fair game, attached or not—but he'll respect the man's position, if not the woman's. Rather than approach her directly, he will try to strike a deal with the escort for her favors. If the man refuses—I assume he would—the Turk shrugs philosophically, usually. But if the woman is alone, he'll persist in badgering her and perhaps will try to force himself on her.

I remember a Canadian man and French woman in Van, Turkey, who were traveling together and considered themselves a common-law, married couple. They spent an hour bargaining with a young Kurd for a kilim rug and got an especially good price. The friendly merchant then took them to dinner and guided them around town. At bedtime the Kurd asked that the woman stay with him over-night, and was hurt when she became upset. He pointed out to the man that he acted in good faith, pleasing the man and woman both, and was owed a favor in turn. He considered the man had the privilege of granting that favor, of course.

Turkey along the Aegean Sea is not all that bad. The attitude there is similar to the Latins'. Inland, though, there is real danger even when a group of women camp and ride together. Women should avoid camping in the open, riding after dark, and provoca-tive dress or manners, whether with men or not. Appearances are easily misconstrued by impressionable Turks, young and old.

At the end of the nineteenth century, the bicycle freed women from hoops, long skirts, and a life confined to the home parlor and "feminine" activities. It took them out into the open air, put color in their cheeks and adventure in their hearts.

In the century since then, the egalitarian bike was soon replaced by the tyrannical auto. Subtly, the supposed freedom of choice promised by the auto proved, in fact, to be shackling. Most men and women today lead lives of physical inactivity, insulated from the outdoors by steel and glass, and dependent on others for power and services. The bicycle, as a self-generated form of trans-port, promises a second wave of liberation as we near the end of this century.

88

THE OLDER BIKE TOURIST

The 40-year-old biker who is in good shape can have the same cardiac ability as someone half his age who doesn't bicycle, says *Bicycling* magazine's Dr. David Smith. So, to ask a question similar to the one about women bikers: why aren't more older bikers on tours?

One answer is the same as that for women, having to do with social unacceptance. Another reason, probably, is a reluctance to take a chance on life. At a time when middle-aged women and men need a shot in the arm through fresh interests and experiences, they retreat into the pervasive modern life of ease (read indolence). Notwithstanding the recent emphasis on exercise and self-sufficiency for oldsters, bike touring has hardly caught on. The situation is much brighter in England, of course, where bike touring has always been popular and accepted by young and old alike.

And yet, bike travel offers just those features that are especially crucial for the older person. The exercise is substantial enough to promote good health and it reduces tension, without danger of overexertion or muscle injury. Bike touring brings older folk into the company of younger ones, and of people of new and varied interests, while a motorized group tour lumps together travelers of inbred and lethargic tastes. Most important, biking yields a real sense of accomplishment and of independence at a time of life when the fear of diminishing powers is potentially dangerous to the person's psyche.

For those in retirement, those advantages—as well as increased savings for a limited income—are especially beneficial. The usual idea of activity for a 65-year-old, the golf, shuffleboard or horseshoes, can hardly be called active at all. Those social events do nothing for the heart and lungs.

But a 70-year-old can lead a very active life. Clifford Graves, M.D., of IBTS is a prime example. And Wilfred Cresswell was 65 in 1976 when he began his around-the-world tour. The capability of the retiree diminishes in a very shallow curve with advanced age.

Some slight shifts of emphasis should probably be taken in account with age, of course. Slowing down, for one. That would seem contradictory to the advice for expanded activity. Still, many oldsters—mostly men, but some women, too—feel they must prove how young they really are, and they go all out to overextend themselves. Riding up a hill in stages, walking up, or even taking public transportation to the top doesn't diminish the enjoyment of a tour. Stopping sooner for the day and taking more breaks adds to relaxation, and increases the chances for meeting and talking to people.

The diet of the older person should be adjusted, too. In the last few years I've cut down substantially on meat, feeling intuitively that its fat content wasn't good for me. Philosophically, too, I believe that cows and sheep couldn't have been put on earth expressly to be eaten by man. The sheer inefficiency of a system that obtains protein through an additional link in a chain from grain to man doesn't appeal to me, either. Today we hear more about the deleterious effects of overindulgence of animal proteins, and the advice for the elderly to substitute vegetable proteins. At the same time, carbohydrates are recommended as the principal caloric source.

To camp in the open and brave wet nights may be too much to ask of an older person used to a lifetime of indoor comfort; inexpensive hotels or hostels can be substituted. The weight savings of not carrying a tent and sleeping bag while hosteling makes riding easier, too. A good choice is a country in which hostels have kitchens. The informality of a shared stove and easy conversation is a good setting to make friends.

Traveling by bike is particularly gratifying to an older couple, who are thrust into new experiences together. They pull their weight equally, and they share the other joys and responsibilities of that way of travel. No other mode asks as much of them in individual performance, in self-reliance, and in cooperation to meet a daily goal.

THE INNER GAME

Maintaining a healthy state of your internal environment—a positive attitude, self-control, perspective, and a buoyancy in the face of an occasional setback—could be as important to your tour as keeping the bike in shape.

Riding in a strange environment for any length of time, especially alone, plays havoc with your sense of community. "What am I doing here?" you ask yourself after a while. "Who are these people, and what can I mean to them?" Isolation from surroundings and transient contacts with people rob you of a social base; you are forced to draw on inner reserves.

90

A bike trip provides means to perform on one's own, independent of ties to family, job and society. There's no predetermined role on the road; you can redevelop at will your basic self—the elements of "privacy, liberty and a degree of sovereignty" that Charles Reich identifies in *Greening of America* (New York: Random House, 1970) as necessary to reach one's potential in life.

You have the perfect vehicle with which to exercise this new role, setting your own standards of dress, deportment, values and life-style. Any persona you adopt is fair game—athlete, vagabond, scientific observer—all are possible on a bike. Since you aren't dependent on services or support, other than sources of food, you can resist the tendency to conform to social expectations, as at home.

Bike travel forces inner reflection. You don't ride continually through scenic or interesting areas to be immersed in the sights. And you can't fill the hours on that vehicle with the trivia of other forms of transport, the small talk, card playing or movies of train or plane.

Some bikers try diversions to pass time. They sing, check their progress with a stopwatch, or engage in mental busy-work. But why fight it? Give in to your musing. Consider the state of your life, your work, the relationship to family and social group. Recall the events of the previous day or week and evaluate their significance. Test them against your values, or your prejudices. Compose a letter or an entry in a diary about the people you've met or things you've seen. Stop occasionally, right there beside the road, to jot down your thoughts in a notebook. Give your mind action, as well as your body. Consider, for example, that on a bicycle a person's legs can still take the intrepid traveler almost anywhere in the land-world.

PART II

COUNTRY-BY-COUNTRY DESCRIPTIONS

INTRODUCTION

This part deals primarily with information useful to a bike tourist. For further passport and visa requirements, the cheapest air fares, places to visit, exchange rate and such, check with your travel agent, the national tourist office of the country concerned, or a general travel guide.

You'd be in touch with those sources in any case, when planning your trip. *Let's Go, Europe, Fodor* (see Appendix I), and a dozen other excellent guides to countries provide many details useful to general tourists. This guide doesn't try to compete with them, except at the bicycling level.

There is some overlap, of course. But what is described as desirable for the motorized tourist is not necesarily good for the biker. A type of campground that is lauded in a Rand McNally camping guide may be all wrong for our kind of traveler; he would certainly find no use for electrical and water hookups or a children's playground, for example. And so, I include accommodations data and that for eating, but try to keep it relevant to needs of the cyclist.

The emphasis is on economy—campground use, both formal and free, cheap indoor accommodations, and cooking for yourself. People who can afford more luxuries aren't in great need of advice.

I include specific mentions of hostels and campgrounds, where bike tourists recommended them (or warned against them). Those shouldn't be taken as immutable ratings. The management of hostels changes often in some countries—notably France—and so may conditions, either for the better or worse. Campground conditions are more long lasting, the management usually being a private owner of the camp.

Information is sorely lacking in some countries. The guide depends to a large extent on contributions from other bike tourists. The number of those with experience in Europe is an infinitesimal fraction of the hordes of motorized travelers. Our two-wheel collective experience is bound to grow, nevertheless, and so will this guide. Write me what you've found out on your tours; I'd like to use it.

AUSTRIA
10

BIKING MATTERS
SUGGESTED TOUR

Across Austria, Lake Constance/Bodensee to Vienna. About 485 miles of cycling if direct, more if side roads are used. Two weeks' time, or three if riding more leisurely.

Start at Bregenz at the east end of the lake. Arrive there from either Switzerland or Germany by rail, or bike if you have the time. Take E17 south, then east, through Dornbirn, Feldkirch and Landeck to Innsbruck.

A difficult but more scenic alternative for this first leg is to go east on road 200, just north of Dornbirn, and then join 198 at Warth. Continue east on 198 to Reutte. If you wish to connect here with Germany, route 2, cycle a dozen miles north to Fussen.

At Reutte, take 314 to Lermoos. To reach Innsbruck, you can either swing north through Germany on 187 and 313, or cycle a tough route south along 314 and 189.

You'll deserve a rest at Innsbruck; the city is worth a stay. Ride parallel to the autobahn on 171; it'll take you to Worgl and a connection with 312, which takes you to Salzburg. You'll cut through a finger of Germany for some 25 miles. If you want to invest the extra climbing, take a swing south on 305 in this part of Germany through Berchtesgaden, Hitler's retreat.

You're out of the worst of the mountains on reaching Salzburg. The rest of the way to Vienna will have just some rolling hills and a lot of level road.

Take 156 north to Braunau, a beautiful town, then east on 309, 137a, 137 and 1 to Linz. The city isn't worth stopping at. Stick to 1 as far as Enns, about 15 miles east of Linz. Cross the Danube on 337 and turn east again on 3. It hugs the Danube all the way to Vienna. The views along the river are great, though some of the villages are self-consciously touristy.

You can leave this route for Germany at a few points between

Innsbruck and Braunau, to Czechoslovakia from Linz or Vienna, or to Hungary from Vienna.

MAPS, TERRAIN, TRAFFIC

Kummerly & Frey, 1:500,000 is excellent. What roads it doesn't show probably can't be cycled, at least in the mountains. The Austrian National Tourist Office will send you a 1:800,000 youth hostel map if you ask for it. Not bad, but it lacks road details and shows few symbols for places of interest. It has detailed information about hostels; unfortunately, it's all in German.

Mountains cover two-thirds of Austria. Cycling is difficult to moderate. It's hardly possible to make a circular tour west of Salzburg because the country is narrow, and there are few parallel roads east and west. But you can meander in the north in relatively flat country on scores of secondary roads, weaving along and across the Danube, for example.

The mountain roads are strenuous but negotiable for bikers in good shape. Tyler Folsom and Venita Plazewski went out of their way to climb a few high passes along 145 and 166 in the vicinity of Bad Ischl, east of Salzburg. The rest of their ride across Austria was moderate in comparison.

97

Traffic can get heavy on E17 and on other main highways during summer, but the smaller, secondary roads are nearly empty.

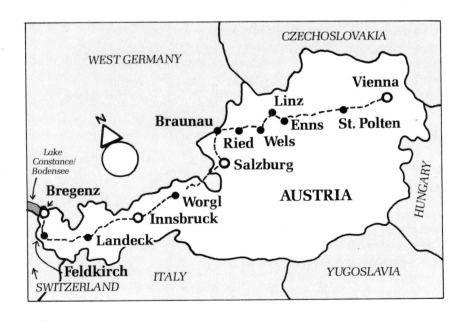

Roads parallel to autobahns can be pleasant, unless they cater to tourists.

Vienna and Linz environs are also heavy, and it's best to get out on a minor road as soon as possible. Watch where the autobahns are incomplete or under construction and empty into lesser roads. Traffic will be horrendous there.

Every road I cycled had an excellent surface, with no ruts or chuckholes. You'll get cobbles in towns, and often in villages, at the sides of narrow roads.

BEST CYCLING TIME

As on most of the Continent, avoid vacationers in cars during July and August. Vienna gets quite warm in May; the western and southern high mountain areas take much longer to heat up. But it's chilly in high country right into June during the night, so carry an extra sweater or long johns.

No part of the year is dominant for rainfall, but April and November are wettest on record. I found September very pleasant along the Danube. It may be a good idea to travel from east to west if crossing the country early in the season, to take advantage of the warming trend in that same direction. The opposite would be true if starting late in the season.

98

I noted no prevailing direction of wind, nor any days when it blew hard.

BIKE EQUIPMENT, RENTALS

The larger cities can supply parts like derailleurs and chains, but I saw no 27-inch tires. Bikes are rented at many railroad stations and in resort areas, but those are playthings meant for casual local riding. They're expensive, in any case. In Vienna, rates start at $7.50 a day, or $30 a week.

BIKE TRANSPORTATION

Trains will take bikes as a matter of course. You pay about a third of your ticket price for the bike. Place the bike on the train yourself.

GENERAL
ENTERING, LEAVING, HASSLES

You need a passport and nothing else. No hassles, and good bike and personal security.

AUSTRIA

LANGUAGE AND PEOPLE

English is the second leading language, being taught in schools and used widely by many people. When you're lost or looking for something in a city street, the second or third person you ask will answer, "Yes, of course, I speak English."

Austrians are reputed to be the amiable, comfort-loving southern cousins of the ambitious Germans. I found them not so much easygoing as at ease, but somewhat straitlaced. Friendly, but not effusive. People wear traditional native dress like a badge, with no self-consciousness—the men with knickers, suspenders, and long stockings, the women in peasant skirts and aprons—even as they shop in expensive boutiques.

Streets and buildings in small towns were scrupulously clean, service was prompt and correct. Hostels were always neat. Their wardens were efficient and friendly, but not outgoing.

The atmosphere in Vienna is cosmopolitan compared to the rest of the country. You hear a variety of languages in shops and coffee houses, and food reflects past influences.

OVERALL COSTS

Vienna was easily the most expensive city I've experienced. Away from it, I spent considerably less. I had to watch my schillings to stay under $8 a day in 1979, nevertheless. I camped out a third of the time and stayed in hostels the rest, and I cooked all meals.

Other bikers reported an average of $14 a day, but that was with hostels and some motel or hotel stops, and eating at least one meal daily in cafes. I estimate costs of $10 and $17 a day, for those two living styles, in 1981.

Would you believe $1.40 for a 4-ounce cup of coffee in a stand-up buffet at a gas station? I consider the cost of coffee a good barometer of a country's prices. When coffee is high, I tighten the grip on change in my pocket.

Even the mails were expensive: the aerogram that cost 22¢ in the United States was 52¢; an ordinary envelope and one sheet of paper took $1.05 in stamps to send to the States; a fee of 60¢ was charged to forward mail.

I was lucky to have been warned about the high prices by a German biker I met in Hungary. We stocked up there with cheaper food before crossing the border.

Banks are open mornings and half the afternoon (full afternoon Thursdays), and are closed weekends. Railroad stations in major cities stay open all week, 8:00 A.M. to 8:00 P.M. Cash your traveler's checks in large denominations, since there's a fixed fee for them. No fee is charged for exchanging U.S. currency into schillings.

ACCOMMODATIONS

You can find a single room in a small-town hotel or pension for $8.50. A double will cost almost twice as much. Major cities charge double those rates and more. The Austrian Tourist Office will send you a list of accommodations in cities, classified as category B, "moderate," at $13 to $18 a person, with two sharing a room. For the two lower categories, C, "budget" and D, "basic," they tell you to check with local information offices.

Those charges are increased by a $1.50 booking fee, when using information offices. You'd have to pay extra to find a room by yourself, in any case, through a number of phone calls.

Some 80 hostels are in Austria, but about a quarter of them bunch up in the lakes region around Salzburg. You can't depend on hostels for daily stops. Although preference is supposed to be given to visitors under 30, I've never had a problem that way.

Varying prices are charged, from $3.50 to $6.75. Special facilities are supposed to account for the higher prices. I found hostel offerings fairly uniform, though, with clean dorms, hot showers, and a comfortable meeting room. Some bikers in the country did tell me that some places they stayed in were in poor shape.

A small minority have kitchens. Of the five in Vienna, only the one on Pulverurmgasse is listed in the International Youth Hostels (IYH) Handbook as having a kitchen. When I stayed there in 1979, it had none, in fact. But people cooked with butane stoves on dining room tables, without reproval from the warden. In the matter of curfew, though, he was strict. Ten minutes late, and you paid a fine of five schillings before the door would be opened.

The tourist office will send "Camping-Caravaning," containing a list of the few hundred campgrounds in the country. They're distributed throughout, but most thickly in the Salzburg region, and in the western half.

Costs range from 60¢ to $4.50 a person, with a discount for an international *carnet* holder. Camps near cities average $2 a person. You'll be spared a parking fee, which is charged for motorized vehicles only.

Most camps have hot showers and a restaurant, and about half have food stores, with at least some provisions. About one-third have cooking facilities. For clothes washing, you either do it yourself, or use a laundromat in a large city.

Because Austria is so mountainous, and is full of forests—

almost half its area is in woods—camping in the open is easy. Water from streams is safe and plentiful in mountain areas.

FOOD

After a bed, food is the second culprit for an expensive stay. You can pay as little as $3 for a plate of food, but it'll be hardly a meal for a biker. A complete lunch will be more like $6, and dinner at least half again as much. The food is good, and in Vienna and the large cities, interesting because of Slav, Hungarian, Italian and German influences. You ought to splurge on a meal or two. If I had to choose between spending my money on lodging or food in Austria, it would be no contest; food would win hands down.

Pastries, cakes and tortes are imaginative and heavenly. Their prices are up in the clouds, too. I couldn't help indulging, but I had to ration myself, and I chose the less expensive strudel, with plebeian fillings.

To sit at a cafe and drink a leisurely espresso costs $1—more for an American-size cup—but you'll not be hurried as you read or write notes in a conducive atmosphere. A pint of beer in a bar costs $1.40.

Grocery food is reasonable, considering the alternative. It's 10 to 25 percent higher than in the United States for most packaged goods, and up to 50 percent more for meats and other necessities. It's all of good quality, the produce fresh and ripe, and the meat lean. Shops are open until 6:00 P.M., half-day Saturdays. Cooking is the only way to save on food. Butane cartridges are available, but kerosene for stoves is hard to find.

ADDRESSES AND FURTHER READING

Austrian National Tourist Office
545 Fifth Avenue
New York, NY 10017
and
3440 Wilshire Boulevard
Los Angeles, CA 90010

Michelin Green Guide, $7 in U.S.

BELGIUM
11

BIKING MATTERS
SUGGESTED TOUR

Castles and art; a circular loop from Brussels. About 380 miles without deviations. Two leisurely weeks. The tour includes a number of castles and monasteries, and famous cities with art and architecture. It ranges from easy cycling at the start to some hilly, but not forbidding, country in the southeast.

Start in Brussels. If you don't want to see the city—most of my correspondents advised to avoid it—ride northwest from the airport to Vilvoorde. Continue west to Grimbergen, Wolvertem and Aalst. Take 10 here west to Gent. The road parallels E5, which should take the brunt of through traffic. Lay over at Gent, an outstanding art city, with many other interests also.

Stay west on 10 to Brugge, a medieval city with great art and architecture. A secondary road that parallels 71 just to the east can be taken for most of the way to Kortrijk. Otherwise, use 71. Turn northeast on 9/14 for a couple of miles, then east on 9 to Ronse. There, take the secondary road through Ellezelles and Flobecq to Lessines. Continue to Ghislenghien, Attre, Cambron-Casteau, Lens, and Mons. Keep going in the same general southeast direction on 61 as far as Beaumont.

Turn directly east on 36 to Philippeville and Dinant. A tourist center here, and worth a stop. But it's expensive to sleep in, so try to arrive early in the morning and move on in the afternoon.

You are in the Ardennes by this time and will encounter some climbing. Avoid the work and save a few miles, if you want, by staying on 36 to Liege. Otherwise, cycle south on 47 to Beauraing, then east on 46 to the village of Wellin. On a minor road, go northeast a few miles to Ave-et-Auffe, then a bit farther to Han-sur-Lesse and Rochefort. Turn southeast to Saint-Hubert for an interesting pair of churches, then northeast on 28 to La-Roche-en-Ardenne. Scenic countryside and a Sound and Light exhibit of a castle in ruins here.

BELGIUM

Now swing northwest through a series of villages to Hotton and Grandhan and connect with 35. Stay on it a dozen miles to its junction with 36, where you turn left on a minor road to Villiers-le-Temple and Ombret-Rawsa. Cross the river to Amay and take a hard right, following the river road all the way to Liege. A number of churches and a museum in this art city.

Take 3 northwest out of Liege to Saint-Truiden and Leuven. See some churches and interesting architecture in the latter. If you have time, go northwest some 15 miles to Mechelen, where you can see some work by Rubens and a striking carillon in the Gothic Cathedral. Return to the airport south on a minor road that parallels and stays just east of E10.

Otherwise, continue west from Leuven until just before the outer ring motorway around Brussels, where you turn right for the airport.

If you come in from the region of Reims, France, you can connect with this route by taking 77 north out of Sedan (France) to Bouillon, then continue northeast on 28 to Saint-Hubert. To connect from Luxembourg, take a train toward Namur, but get off at

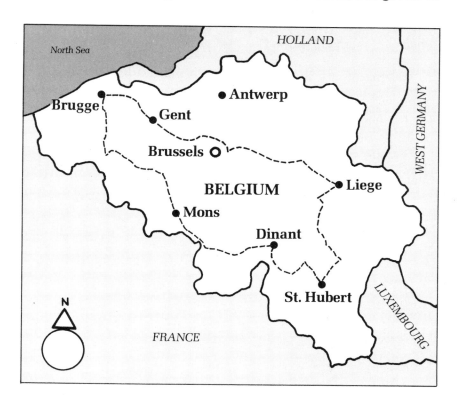

Libramont, 10 miles south of Saint-Hubert. Or cycle to the latter from Luxembourg on E9 and 48; it's only 55 miles.

MAPS, TERRAIN, TRAFFIC

A tourist map, 1:400,000, will probably suit your purposes. The Belgian National Tourist Office will send it free. It'll show all the secondary roads you'll need, and points of interest such as castles, churches and ruins. If you want more detail, buy the three Michelin 1:200,000 maps for Belgium (one of them, number 001, overlaps with Holland), at $2 each in the United States.

Belgium is one vast plain, except for the southeast Ardennes region. Hills there aren't high. The highest point is 2,000 feet; most of your climbing will be just a few hundred feet. A tour that mixes the two areas gives variety, as do alternating stays in cities and small towns. If you don't care for one part of the country, it's easy enough to shift to another. The distance across the entire country is under 200 miles at the most.

Roads are well surfaced, generally. You'll ride often on cobble-stones in cities and rural roads. Watch trolley tracks in Brussels, which can catch your wheel and spill you. Write to the Public Works Ministry (Ministere des Travaux Publics) for the road conditions along your intended route. Don't be surprised if your answer comes in French.

Bikepaths are fairly common, especially on main roads and entrances to cities. Most correspondents complained of their surfaces, citing the peculiar kind of large bricks or stones that make for a rough ride. You have to take the bikepath when you see the round blue sign with a white bike outline.

Signposts give directions to villages and towns; they seldom show road numbers, except on motorways. You ride from one town to the next on secondary roads.

Traffic is heavy in the west during summer, even on roads that parallel the limited access highways. This is true mostly going along that busy tourist trough that runs from Paris toward Gent, Brussels and Antwerp. Traffic on roads that run from the north-west to southeast is considerably lighter than in the Ardennes. In all parts of the country, however, the secondary roads provide some relief.

BEST CYCLING TIME

There's less than 10 degrees (F.) of average temperature vari-ation during the months between May and September. Any time during that period makes for good cycling weather. The coast is

104

more stable, while the southeast tends to a continental climate that has hotter summers. Winds on the coast are often stiff from the southwest. They moderate inland.

What with a good secondary road system, the influx of summer tourists is less acute than in some of the mountain-bound countries. If you plan to cycle in the southeast, June may be the best time, since you'll have longer light in the day and will avoid vacationers.

BIKE EQUIPMENT, RENTALS

The cities of the west and a couple of the larger ones in the east will have most of the usual spares. You won't find 27-inch tires though, except possibly in the capital. Nor do shops carry wide-range freewheels. Repair facilities are good, since 10-speed biking is common in this land of Merckx. Groups of jerseyed racers are common on the roads.

Still, you'll find 1-speeds the common bikes available for rentals. The railroad offers train and bike combinations at a dozen stations; the bike can be returned at another station. Write to the Belgian National Railroads in the United States. Shops offer rentals, too.

105

BIKE TRANSPORTATION

Bikes are carried on trains as a matter of course.

GENERAL
ENTERING, LEAVING, HASSLES

Passport, no visa.

No bikers complained about car drivers, even when in heavy traffic. George Cole wrote that no one laughed at their helmets when he and his family cycled there, in contrast to Holland where people were almost rude.

LANGUAGE AND PEOPLE

Flemish is spoken in the north and French in the south. Just about everybody is bilingual, and a good many speak English in addition. Road signs will have names of towns in the two official languages.

Questionnaire correspondents reported that people were friendly. I had no particular impression of Belgians, either positive or negative, but then I didn't ride slowly enough to meet any.

OVERALL COSTS

Average daily cost for hostel stays and a mixture of cooking and cafe use is about $12. Camping can cut costs only a couple of dollars, since formal grounds, with showers available, are expensive.

Banks are open midmorning to midafternoon. They charge a $3.50 fee for exchanging each traveler's check, nothing for U.S. currency. If you're not changing a check of a large denomination, go to the railroad station exchange window where there's no charge, but you'll get a lower rate.

Send for the leaflet, "Budget Holidays," from the national tourist office. It doesn't contain too many bargains, but the special fares on railways and the list of stations with bike hires may interest you.

The 50¢ stamp for a 5-gram airmail letter is more reasonable here than in most of Western Europe. Wait to write home until you get to Belgium.

ACCOMMODATIONS

Avoid the large cities if you want a cheap hotel. With some looking you may ferret out a double at $28. Sink in room, but no bath, of course. Nor a breakfast, at this price. Showers will probably cost you extra. You'll at least get more for your money in smaller towns.

106

The tourist office's leaflet "Budget Holidays" has a long list of "Social Holiday Homes," located in holiday centers. They average about $18 a day and must be booked well ahead of time. You may want to base yourself for a time in one of them, and explore the region. Inquire and book directly to the one that interests you.

The same leaflet has locations of youth hostels, national "stage" hostels, and houses run by Belgium's Friends of Nature (Amis de la Nature). That list of addresses doubles the number of hostels that is included in the IYH Handbook. It broadens the scope of your touring, since you could have as much as 40 to 50 miles between the international hostels. The leaflet also lists youth information centers, which will help you find a room.

The basic cost of international hostels is $2.75 in the north and $3.50 in the south. The four I stayed at all required a breakfast, hardly a bargain at $1.50 for bread, jam and some cheese. Other bikers also mentioned mandatory breakfasts, so that practice may be more widespread than just at the major cities mentioned in the handbook.

Of the 38 in the country, 10 hostels have kitchens. Almost all of those are in the north, and the kitchens are not always clean or roomy. Bathroom facilities and rooms vary greatly in quality, also.

BELGIUM

Those approved: Namur (incredible, can even wash clothes); Kortrijk (beautiful, modern); Tilff (pleasant, staff helpful); Oostende (friendly); Huizingen (beautiful setting, best alternative to Brussels); Gent (right in city, lock bike in basement, cold water); Antwerp (nice setting and building, comfortable); Brugge (always room, good showers); Saint Gerard (great setting in an abbey).

Not recommended: Brussels-"Centreurop" (dirty, awful facilities, no security—Morrie Paul had a sleeping bag stolen); Poperinge (simply hideous in all respects).

In spite of shortcomings—mandatory breakfasts, few kitchens, lack of hot water at some places—hostels are probably your best bet for reasonable accommodations.

Although Belgium has plenty of campgrounds—over 500 are licensed by the government—they offer little for your fee. George Cole, who used them with his family in 1979, reports that they were "just plain bad." They were very hard to find—no signs or good directions from the locals—and they were poorly run. The worst cases had a fee of $7 for the three Coles, plus $1.25 each for a shower.

In fact, of the 300 campgrounds listed in the camping leaflet distributed by the tourist office, only 5 are listed to have a hot shower. Those charge $3.30 to $3.85 for one person in a tent, more than a hostel.

Your only advantage at campgrounds is the ability to cook. But in that respect they also have shortcomings. One-third sell some kind of food supplies. Only a handful rent out gas cookers, whereas they're provided free in most of Western Europe's campgrounds. Belgian camps have much to learn about attracting tourists.

All in all, if you want to cook for yourself, you may as well camp in the open. You can do that easily in the southeast and some of the eastern part that sticks out into Germany. What with the built-up areas in the west, open camping is more difficult. A farmer may let you camp on fallow land. There's not much of that, except a bit in the north; the rest is usually in crops.

FOOD

A menu of the day in a city is $4.50 to $6, and a good modest meal at a restaurant can be had for $9. Food is similar to that in France. Prices are somewhat lower in small towns but not by much. Some hostels serve superb meals at $4.

If you devise a satisfactory strategy for making your own meals, you'll find food prices reasonable. They're hardly higher than in the United States, especially if you concentrate your shopping in supermarkets of towns and cities. Depending on what you buy, food can even be lower than at home, providing you keep your daily quota of pastries and croissants at a reasonable level.

A good-size loaf of bread is 70¢, a half-dozen eggs 85¢, a pound of pork chops $3. Most cuts of meat are under $3.50 a pound. A medium-size jar of jam costs 75¢; a half-pound of raisin cookies $1.10; a pound of delicious rice cake $2.50.

Belgians are third in beer drinking per capita in Europe, behind Germans and Czechs. Knowledgeable connoisseurs rank Belgian beer with the best. A can of popular Stella Artois beer in a grocery costs 50¢; a glass of it in a cafe is 65¢. A cup of coffee in the same cafe is $1 — more than the United States but less than Scandinavia, a good gauge of cost of living.

Shop hours are as in France: open in the morning, a break for a couple of hours, and open again to 6:00 P.M. or thereabouts. Supermarkets and some food stores in cities are open a couple of hours longer. On Fridays, many stores will stay open until 9:00 P.M.

ADDRESSES AND FURTHER READING

Belgian National Tourist Office
745 Fifth Avenue
New York, NY 10022

Belgian National Railroads
    Same as the tourist office

Ministere des Travaux Publics
Residence Palace
Rue de la Loi, 155
B-1040 Bruxelles

Ligue Velocipedique Belge
Ave du Globe 49
1190 Brussels
    They will answer your inquiries (in French), but their chief interest is in racing.

Nika Hazelton, *The Belgian Cookbook* (New York: Atheneum, 1970). It may seem strange that I recommend a cookbook, but 100 of its 236 pages touch on great descriptions of daily life, travel and culture. It's really the best of what's written about the country. Get it out of the library for a quick read.

BULGARIA
12

BIKING MATTERS
SUGGESTED TOUR

Sofia-southwestern loop; 300-plus miles, 10 days to 2 weeks.

No cycling through the heartland of Bulgaria is easy. This tour through the Rila Mountains is no exception. Many of the roads are in poor shape, but the tour largely takes you away from the main tourist routes. Cycling is difficult and low gears are definitely needed.

Start at Sofia. Ride E20 southwest. Leave it a dozen miles farther, taking the fork to Pernik. Continue to Kjustendil, short of the Yugoslav border. Turn east to Stanke Dimitrov. Mountains all around you.

Turn south on E20 to Blagoevgrad. On the way, a side trip can be taken to the stunning Rila Monastery. Turn east off the road at the village of Kocherinovo. It's a climb to 3,500 feet; when you get there, a 9,000-foot peak dominates the region. A couple of campgrounds are close by. Enough campgrounds are located along this route to stay at one each night, except for the first few days.

Continue south of Blagoevgrad a few miles to Simitli, where you turn east. Ride on minor roads through Razlog and Velingrad to Batak. Go north to Pazardzik. Turn west here for the return to Sofia.

Stay on E5 for some 35 miles to the village of Kostenec. Take the left fork at it to Samokov. Turn right on the road there, through Pancarevo to Sofia.

If planning to cross the country from Sofia to the Black Sea coast, you'll find few satisfactory routes. Cycles are forbidden on parts of main roads—E5, E27, and the last 70 miles of the main east-west road to Burgas through the "Valley of the Roses." Don Lemmon, H. Haalboom and Bert and Dinnie Nieuwenhis rode the main roads anyhow. They got away with it, though they were stopped by police. They told Lemmon that what he was doing was "sport" and they let him continue. But another time a cop made him walk the bike just before Burgas.

ADVENTURE CYCLING IN EUROPE

The best route I see to the Black Sea is a minor road northeast of Sofia to Mezdra, then to Lovec, partly on E27. Here, take a minor road to Levski to join E20, and ride to Bjala. More minor roads east to Targoviste, Preslav and Sumen. No other way to reach Varna from here except on E27.

Once on the coast, you face more bike restrictions. Lemmon rode the main road E95, but it was officially forbidden to bikers. There are only a few secondary roads running north and south to bypass the coast. You can combine those with E5 to get as far as Turkey. For example, some 35 miles west of Varna on E27, a road goes south through Vrovadia and Dalgopol to Aitos, then to Burgas.

A few miles south of Burgas, there are also ways to avoid the shore area. One minor road goes directly to Malko Tarnovo, through Drusevec. I found this road closed to traffic a few years ago because of extensive road work, but it should be in good shape now. Another possibility is to take a series of minor roads through Rose and Jasna Poljana to Gramatikovo. Both options bring you into E95 and Malko Tarnovo, a few miles from the Turkish border.

MAPS, TERRAIN, TRAFFIC

Usable maps for this country are made by Ravenstein and Geographia. Both maps are in combination with Romania. Complete Traveller sells them. Ravenstein has a 1:1,160,000 pocket version for $4, and a 1:1,000,000 conventional sheet for $5. Geographia's 1:1,000,000 is $6.

Kummerly & Frey sell a 1:1,000,000 also. Get it from CTC or try B. Dalton bookshops in the United States. It's a good idea to buy the map before arriving on the Continent, as neither the adjoining countries nor Bulgaria has any.

Much of the country is in mountains. The northern roads along the Danube and the strip on the Black Sea are relatively flat. The mountains become less severe in the southeast on the Turkish border. That part of the country is neglected, however, because of little desire to have dealings with the Turks, a traditional enemy.

Cycling is difficult. Secondary roads are poor—in engineering, maintenance and surface. Cobblestones are very common in villages and towns, and even on main roads. As an example, a 25-mile stretch of E20, between Sofia and Kulata, is cobbled. Gravel appears on main roads occasionally, also.

You at least take a chance on finding an adamant cop who'll give you real trouble if you take main roads that are forbidden. Sections adjoining those roads may have farm roads used by wagons, and you may be told to use them. Lemmon says the ones he saw were not fit for cycling.

111

Still, the scenery and the unspoiled land and villages may be worth the struggle. It's certainly one of the most offbeat places in Europe to tour.

Away from the main roads, traffic is almost nil. Even on many of them, it's light much of the time. Vehicles increase near cities, but drivers are careful and courteous. Most visitors to this country come from other parts of Eastern Europe, living it up at the Black Sea resorts and the health spas. They contribute little to the traffic.

There are trucks on the through, international roads, such as E5n from Sofia to Edirne, Turkey. That road is level, with a good surface (other than in villages), but the trucks make it unpleasant.

BEST CYCLING TIME

May through October has good weather. April can still be cold. The strong, warm sun and hard shadows I experienced in May reminded me of weather in Spain, especially so since I rode through vineyards.

There's no dominant rainy season. It's spread evenly in those months. When it did rain, I found it to be a light sprinkle during the night, stopping by morning.

Traffic is hardly a factor, and cycling at the height of summer can be pleasant if you stick to the mountains. If cycling close to the

Danube in the north, it would be better to avoid June and July, when it's hot in that plain.

BIKE EQUIPMENT, RENTALS

Alan Bubna wrote that he saw 10-speeds in all parts of Eastern Europe. I did, too, and one would think that parts would be available to service them. My experience proved, however, that the parts were scarce and when found were inferior. This was borne out in the frequent requests I had from those bike riders to sell them any spare parts I had.

I do know that I never saw 27-inch tires for sale in shops in Poland or Romania, though 700c sizes were sold in main cities in a few shops. I couldn't check the situation in Bulgaria, since I hadn't seen a shop there, but then I visited only Burgas and Varna among the large cities. My feeling is that there wouldn't be much useful in a bike shop other than incidentals like cables, ball bearings, brake pads, and probably 700c's in Sofia.

Lemmon saw 3-speeds for hire at the Black Sea resorts. They were meant as casual playthings for the visitors.

BIKE TRANSPORTATION

112

Lemmon flew his bike from Burgas to Sofia. The pedals and handlebars had to be turned, no box needed. The same procedure applied for a flight out of Sofia to Munich on Lufthansa.

Trains coming into Bulgaria from other countries will take bikes, of course. I don't know the policy within the country. The tourist office was unresponsive to transportation questions, and I cycled through the country and had no experience with trains.

Buses run throughout Bulgaria, but I couldn't find out if they take bikes. I saw group taxis (called *taksi*), on the Turkish *dolmus* model, running between communities. Many had roof luggage racks and conceivably could have taken bikes.

GENERAL
ENTERING, LEAVING, HASSLES

Only a passport is needed. No visa is required, but there is a Byzantine catch. It's conditional on having prepaid accommodations for 48 hours or more, or on being part of an organized group. That may cost you an arm and a leg; it's usually cheaper to pay the $14 for a visa before you arrive at the border. It'll also insure that you get through it without any complications.

One way you can beat the system is to purchase a few camping vouchers in advance from a travel agency specializing in travel to Eastern Europe. The Bulgarian Tourist Office will send you a list of agencies. Showing the vouchers at the border will satisfy the prepaid condition. The vouchers are nonrefundable in case you change your mind, though.

That's the theory, anyhow; what actually happens in Bulgaria, as well as in other Eastern European countries, often depends on the bureaucratic interpretation on the spot. An official can become very stubborn if he thinks you may not have enough days of camping vouchers, or if his view of the policy differs from the tourist agency's. And he's the man when it comes to getting into the country. To be absolutely safe, get the visa in the United States.

There were no reports of any kind of harassment in the country from either police or officials. I was stopped by the military on the road leading to the Turkish border for a passport check. It delayed me for a couple of hours when they weren't sure of what they read in it, but my detainment wasn't malicious.

Care should be taken to avoid loitering or taking photos in border areas or near anything that can be interpreted as important militarily, such as a bridge or a port area. Otherwise, no one bothers you.

113

LANGUAGE AND PEOPLE

If you know something of any Slav language, you can communicate with a Bulgarian. Given that you get past the Cyrillic alphabet when reading, of course. Menus and road signs may be printed in it.

English is almost unknown, spoken by just a few of the educated and some of the young. In the countryside, you'll seldom meet an English speaker, even in tourist offices or hotels.

The look of the country is clean and cheerful — roses and other flowers planted by the roadside, houses well maintained and surrounded by gardens and grapevines, well-preserved old homes in cities. Large Communist banners and heroic statues are seen everywhere, but they don't seem to inhibit laughter, music and an easygoing pace. Bulgaria is the only country that has a museum devoted to humor and satire.

All people I met were helpful and eager to communicate. A bicycle tourist of any kind, and especially one from the West, is still an oddity here. Everyone is curious. Children are polite and don't pester you for handouts. There's still a demand for jeans and other clothes and you'll be asked by young people to sell them.

You'll see a primitive society. Practices go back a hundred years. People work with their hands instead of with machines on farms, and oxen and horses pull plows. You'll be overwhelmed at the peace and quiet. Shepherds with their flocks may be the extent of your company on a day in the mountains.

Lemmon suggests you note the custom of nodding the head up and down for "no" and side to side for "yes."

OVERALL COSTS

Lemmon spent $15 a day in 1978 staying in hotels and eating in restaurants. In 1981 it should cost about $20. That figure can be cut in half or lower if you don't stay in hotels.

Bulgaria no longer requires a minimum exchange per day of visit. If you buy a currency voucher before you arrive, you'll get a 50 percent higher rate than the official one for your money. The government is, in effect, trying to compete with the black market with that tourist inducement.

Be careful of those black market exchanges. If you do indulge, change at least some money officially and keep the receipts. You may be asked for them, and you should have some plausible amount accounted for to justify your stay. Also illegal is paying for services with foreign currency. It amounts to a black market exchange, since your dollars will get you much more than Bulgarian levas at the official rate.

Bank exchange offices are open mornings and Balkantourist bureaus at borders and in hotels have a 24-hour money exchange service.

ACCOMMODATIONS

Hotel prices are fixed. The rates set by the state-run Balkantourist for 1980 ranged from $7 to $27 each, with breakfast, when sharing a double. At the Black Sea, they're 50 percent higher. Singles are about a fifth higher. Discounts of 40 percent are given off-season in the Black Sea hotels.

Hotels get full easily and usually have to be reserved. Private homes are cheaper and easier to book. A room for two can be as low as $10. Get the room through Balkantourist or deal with an individual. If the latter, the police must be notified. The host may ignore that requirement and you could pay less. All these prices are quoted at the official exchange rate, of course.

Orbita is an organization that caters to young people. It cooperates with other international youth organizations and offers doubles from about $10, singles for half that. The singles are dorm style.

Some 30 youth hostels or mountain huts, and 5 youth hotels are almost all located in the western half of the country. They're run by Orbita, and are allied with the International Youth Hostel Federation. Costs in 1980 were from $1.70 to $3. Two-thirds of them have kitchen facilities, for which there's no charge. Tent camping is not permitted.

In the western regions, you can almost build a tour around hostels, given that they're not full. If you start your tour in Sofia, it may be worthwhile to visit Orbita there and make reservations.

Over 100 campgrounds are well distributed, except in the inland parts of the east. There are dozens along the Black Sea. All have showers and kitchens. Most are open from June 1 to the beginning or mid-September. I stayed at a couple of camps in May without charge. A caretaker was at one of them, but he wouldn't take any money since the camp wasn't officially open. Cost is somewhat over $1 for a tent and another $1 for each person.

Camping in the open is officially forbidden, but no one will bother a biker. There are plenty of places in the mountains to pitch a tent. The Black Sea area is so developed that it's much harder to find a spot. You'd probably be happier at the campground and would find it more interesting. Most of the vacationers at them come from Eastern Europe, and it's the easiest way to meet them.

FOOD

Except that it's cheap, there's not much going for the Bulgarian cuisine. The best is of Turkish or Greek origin. Most meat that's served is grilled, and vegetables are separate dishes a la Turk.

A filling meal at a cafeteria should be under $2.25, and a combination of excellent Bulgarian yogurt or cheese and sandwiches even cheaper. The yogurt is plain, not the flavored kind found in the United States. Cheese is a white curd, like Turkish or Greek. You can live it up with a $4 meal.

The beer is pretty bad. Wine is no more expensive and is excellent. Coffee on the Turkish model.

The main meal is midday and restaurants stay open until 11:00 P.M. You may be surprised by a sour cream soup with lamb liver that's served for breakfast. It's about 60¢, with tea, at a cafeteria.

Country restaurants, those catering to passing tourists and relatively well-off Bulgarians, are a delight. Each is distinctive, terraced on a hill in many cases, sprawling, and usually half inside and half out, with a large overhang. Always a good view. It's easy to spend a couple of pleasant hours in one without realizing it.

If you see a large industrial plant near a city, try its employee cafeteria for a new experience. The food is plain and heavy, but unbelievably cheap, a big meal under $1.25. I stumbled into one in search of water and stayed to eat a meal. It was filled with earthy proletarians, all regarding me like a man from Mars. No objection from anyone, so I stopped at a couple of others when I saw them.

There's a basic problem in trying to cook for yourself. Except in large towns and cities, finding a food store is a major effort. Many villages are organized communes, with fenced-off barracks and stores. They're self-sufficient and closed to outsiders. The grocery stores you do find will be very poorly stocked. But if you can manage with what you find, basic staples in them are so cheap that you can eat on $1.25 a day. Most food will be canned, the majority imported. Hours are limited.

I never saw refrigeration in those stores nor vegetables or fruit, the latter sold in season mostly at markets. I wondered if any fresh meat was sold in the country at all, when I was dramatically presented with the answer at a small village.

As I wandered among the shelves of the rustic store, a man entered with a freshly killed lamb on his shoulder. He dropped it to the floor; the small crowd that had been waiting outside gathered around him in an attentive circle.

The man hacked the carcass into pieces, almost ritually, and the store clerk weighed them for waiting customers. Within ten minutes there was nothing on the sawdusted floor but a small pool of congealing blood. A primitive scene that quickened the pulse.

116

ADDRESSES AND FURTHER READING

Bulgarian Tourist Office
50 East Forty-second Street
New York, NY 10017

Orbita
45A Blvd Alexander Stamboliiski
Sofia

Arnold L. Haskell, *Heroes and Roses* (London: Darton, Langman, Todd, 1966). A long ride in a camper through Bulgaria. Accounts of encounters and experiences with people the author met.

CZECHOSLOVAKIA
13

BIKING MATTERS
SUGGESTED TOUR

Don Lemmon, Harvey Lyon, Alan Bubna, Tyler Folsom and Venita Plazewski cycled in Czechoslovakia within the last few years. Their trips and my two— 1971 and 1979—are the only bike tourists' sources I have for this seldom-visited country.

Rather than suggest a specific tour with limited data, I simply repeat all their findings for the roads traveled. From the West German border to Prague, E12 is excellent in surface and light in traffic. Most of the route is level or rolling hills.

From Prague to Hradec Kralove and to the Polish border at Nachod, E12 is somewhat hillier and the traffic even lighter. The surface is still excellent.

In the south, the road from Bratislava to Komarno has a good surface and light traffic. The route is level, following the Danube. From Vienna to Brno on E7 the highway varies from two to four lanes but often has a brick surface in villages. It's fairly level along a river.

A minor road from southeastern Poland (south from Krosno) to Svidnik and Presov has a good to excellent surface and is very lightly traveled. It has a few hills. Presov to Kosice on E85 is level, with somewhat more traffic. Surface is excellent. Still south to Hungary, the minor road that branches off from E85 has a few hills but is still excellent in surface. Traffic is thin.

From these experiences and information I received from a Polish cyclist who tours Czechoslovakia, this seems an excellent country, not yet invaded by hordes of tourists.

MAPS, TERRAIN, TRAFFIC

The largest scale map for Czechoslovakia is a 1:600,000 Freytag-Berndt, available from CTC for about $5. Geographia offers the same scale map at $6, and Ravenstein has a 1:800,000 pocket map for $4, both at Complete Traveller. American Map Company sells a guide to Czechoslovakia, which includes a folding map.

The country is mountainous, with plateaus and river valleys veining the land in all parts. Main roads run through those, accounting for the cited roads being fairly level. If you get onto secondary roads, there are plenty of chances for mountain cycling, though.

The landscape is lovely, reminiscent of the southern Pennsylvania hill area or Vermont, but also with dramatic high mountains in the northern regions. A variety of terrain, mountain villages, castles and medieval towns provide touring interest.

Traffic is heavier than in Poland, lighter than the States. It depends on where you cycle. The eastern parts are generally less visited, while the area between Prague and Austria is more popular.

BEST CYCLING TIME

April is still cold and May is a better time to start. Fall weather is unpredictable. Occasionally even August can get very cold, as Folsom and Lyon found on their trips. But September is usually pleasant. My last trip was in that month and the weather was great.

Rain is distributed evenly during the season. It tends to be somewhat wetter in midsummer than in fall. Winds are variable and not strong.

BIKE EQUIPMENT, RENTALS

The Favorit, the best bicycle that Eastern Europe has to offer, is made here, and racing is popular. Lightweight bike parts, including 27 X 1¼-inch tires, are sold in major cities. I've not seen

rentals. I think the concept is foreign here; bicycles are either utilitarian or you use them for serious sport. In either case, one would own the bicycle and not hire it.

BIKE TRANSPORTATION

No problems on trains. Put bikes on yourself, if you wish. I don't have information on buses, but those I've seen didn't seem to have room for bikes.

GENERAL
ENTERING, LEAVING, HASSLES

Passport and visa needed. Check with your travel agent or Cedok, the Czech travel agency, for the current requirement of mandatory daily exchange for each day of visa. In 1980 it changed from $10 to $15. Time will be saved by applying for the visa and prepaying the exchange at home.

I've never been searched coming either in or out, and no other bike tourists reported it. Numerous newspaper articles have cautioned about police surveillance, and of rooms being bugged routinely. I've not had anyone follow me, certainly neither by bicycle nor slow-moving car, though I suppose it was possible to watch me pass at checkpoints along the road. The idea of that is a bit preposterous, considering the logistics involved in keeping track of a meandering biker across the country.

119

The warnings are also there about any contacts with Czechs (see *New York Times* Travel Section, December 17, 1978, for example), and especially in changing money on the black market. Both Lyon and Lemmon talked with people without any encounters with watchful police, and I routinely had a conversation with a patron at each cafe I stopped at.

As for the black market, I had what seems to me a revealing incident. I tried to change money at a bank in a town near the border and was told I was in the wrong bank. The one doing the changing was in the next town, 30 miles farther, and it was closed for the weekend besides. I pleaded with the manager to find some way for me to change a few dollars to get past the weekend.

"Why don't you just ask a private citizen to change money?" she asked. "You can get a much better rate that way." She didn't whisper this advice to me, but said it in a conversational tone in front of the bank's employees.

I told her I knew no one and hesitated to ask people in the street. "If you wish," she replied, "I'll change some for you personally."

I assumed she meant that she would give me the official rate and work it into the bank funds somehow, but she offered double the rate. I was amazed at what was happening, right in a state bank and initiated by a bureaucrat, but no one else there seemed surprised.

LANGUAGE AND PEOPLE

Czech and Slovak are related but distinct languages, the latter closer to Polish and the southern Slavs than to Russian.

There's some English known by the young in cities, but none in small towns and villages. German is more likely to be understood in the western parts. Russian is spoken more here than in other Eastern European countries.

Czechoslovakia has always been the most Westernized of the Slav countries. Its economy is in good shape compared to most of the other eastern countries, though the evidence of Communism is more obvious. The red flag is displayed everywhere, even on apartment houses and over shop entrances. A billboard every few kilometers and a handbill every fourth pole prescribe socialist messages along the highway.

120

When I was mistaken for a Pole in Prague, I was sent to the Solidarita Hotel, filled with Eastern Europeans, for half the cost of comparable Western-style hotels. The Czechs there were more candid in their opinions about living conditions in the country, and were at ease with me. The same was true with peasants, who thought I was a visiting Pole.

But when they knew I was American, I heard no complaints and their attitude was somewhat defensive. I was also offered the more expensive items when I shopped, and I detected some envy. Still, I never felt enmity.

OVERALL COSTS

The mandatory daily exchange of $15 will more than pay for camping costs, occasional stays at private homes, and very good eating. When using hotels you can double your costs. Lyon spent over $30, and I just $5 in 1979 when I camped in the open, to give an idea of the range possible.

I had a 48-hour transit visa the last time I rode there. It didn't require a minimum daily exchange; no bank receipts or any accounting for money were asked with it. If you happen to be passing through the country, as between Poland and Hungary, this is one way to beat the exchange. You can even repeat the crossing, say by cycling through Hungary, reentering Czechoslovakia and leaving at the German border. You'd need a multiple entry visa for that.

CZECHOSLOVAKIA

Banks are open 9:00 A.M. to 6:00 P.M. Monday to Friday and to noon on Saturday. There's no need of one ordinarily, since you'll make the money exchange at the border, unless you must change more money later. If so, note that all banks don't exchange money for tourists, as mentioned in the incident above. Don't get caught in a small town like that, and carry a bit of extra money all the time.

ACCOMMODATIONS

The better hotels in large cities need reservations, though not usually in towns. Book through the local Cedok tourist office. That office will not send you to a cheap hotel knowing you're a "rich American," except by mistake. Go to the hotel yourself and take a chance on a vacancy.

Second-class hotels, the cheapest you'll ordinarily be offered, cost about $15 a double, $10 single (all prices cited for 1980). The room will be small and the bed narrow. Rooms in private homes can be booked through the tourist office, or you can often arrange a stay by asking around.

Hostels charge $2 to $4. Only a minority of them have kitchens, and many of those in schools have no hot showers.

About 60 hostels are spread evenly in the western two-thirds of the country. It's possible to plan an entire trip around them in this small country. In the eastern part, Slovakia, you have to rely on hotels and campgrounds.

There are hundreds of campgrounds in all regions. Prague alone has ten. Make your own arrangements, without prior booking by a state agency. They open generally in May and close the end of August or September.

All campgrounds have stores in camp or very close by. Most have showers, communal kitchens and restaurants, either on the premises or within a few kilometers. Many of them offer bungalows and chalets for rent. A few have washing machines and even saunas. A bus stop is usually close to a camp's entrance. Fares are dirt cheap.

A person in his or her own tent pays less than a couple of dollars. Per person, chalets are $4 and bungalows $10.

As in other Communist countries, camping in the open is officially forbidden. I've camped in woods, along rivers and lakes, and in people's backyards at their invitation. Open camping is easier away from suburban areas, and in eastern Czechoslovakia.

It's probably best to have a stamp or two in your visa showing you stayed some nights in camps or hostels. Otherwise, you might run into a bureaucrat who's a stickler for regulations when you leave. When you have a few nights accounted for, it's easier to maintain that you were often stuck in the middle of nowhere at nightfall, than when there are no entries at all. In any case, the worst that will happen is that the official will wag a finger at you.

FOOD

With Hungary, Czechoslovakia has the best food in Eastern Europe. Great cooking, relatively cheap, many eating places, and a pleasant atmosphere are found everywhere. To my taste, food is better in Slovakia, with its Hungarian influences, than in the western parts. In the latter, meals are heavier, leaning to Germanic dishes with dumplings and potatoes.

Other Eastern Europeans come to both Czechoslovakia and Hungary to gorge themselves on meat, which is of good quality and plentiful. A substantial meal can be had for under $2 in a *hostinec* cafe, and you can live it up for twice that in more expensive restaurants.

Beer is excellent and cost is about 30¢ a pint. Pilsener came from here (Plzen), and the story has it that the Germans confiscated many of the famed beer barrels and the beer recipe during past occupations. Wines are also good, though expensive and not as popular as beer. Don't spend your time reading or writing notes in beer halls. It's a place for talk. Go to the quieter wine bars or coffee shops instead.

Groceries are well stocked with hams, cold cuts and other cooked meats. Bread is excellent. So are tarts and pastries. Fruit out of season is hard to find. You may go long between stores. There are no villages in the Polish or Romanian sense. Farm workers live in towns and are driven to large collectives for the day's work.

Cooking for yourself is no problem, but it seems hardly worthwhile when you have to spend $15 daily. Save on accommodations, and eat well instead in this country.

122

ADDRESSES AND FURTHER READING

Cedok-Czechoslovak Travel Bureau
10 East Fortieth Street
New York, NY 10016

A Guide to Czechoslovakia, American Map Company. Historic, cultural and recreational coverage. Includes maps; 413 pages softcover, $8.

DENMARK 14

BIKING MATTERS
SUGGESTED TOUR

Denmark is such an easy country to cycle in—there are always minor roads to choose among, and bikepaths are numerous on main ones—that you can hardly go wrong with just striking out in any direction and following your nose. You have a further advantage in that the country is so small—less than 100 miles across at its middle, and 240 miles north and south on the mainland—it's almost impossible to get lost. You soon bump into either water or the German border to tell you where you are.

Rather than outline a tight course with specific roads, I indicate only the towns of a circular route that touches on representative parts of the country. You'll pass from the sophisticated capital through fishing villages, historic towns, farmland and the sand dunes of beach areas. Cycle the secondary roads between the indicated towns directly, or digress as you will. The tour is largely modeled after one taken by the Allen Manthei family in 1976. Rosemary Smith and I touched parts of it in 1979 on our way to Norway.

Round-Denmark, about 575 miles, two weeks. Make your way out of Copenhagen with the aid of a street map (a free one from the tourist office will do). Head south to Koge. If you take E4, instead of secondary roads, you'll be mostly on bikepaths.

You can now circle the bump of the Stevns peninsula on minor roads or take the more direct way through Harlev to Fakse Ladeplads, on the Baltic Sea. Continue south through Allerslev and Kalvehave to the island of Mon, then turn west to Bogo. Catch a ferry there to Stubbekobing, and cycle south to Nykobing.

Head west to Nakskov, at the other end of Lolland Island, using minor roads (as through Nysted, Rodby, Sollested), although the main highway is not too busy.

North of Nakskov, past Sandby, take a ferry to Spodsbjerg. Ride to Rudkobing, then over the bridge to Svendborg, using

123

bikepaths. Make your way northwest to Kolding across Funen Island, either going through Odense or along the southern shore through Faborg and Assens. The second alternative is the more scenic.

Take country roads to Vejle, a beautiful town. Lay over here and enjoy. Now to Silkeborg, directly north, through the lake region east of A13. Take minor roads through Uldum, Nim and Ry, for example.

Ride north-northwest to Nykobing, through Kjellerup, Frederiks, Gronhoj, Monsted, Stoholm and Skive. At the latter, swing north of A26 the rest of the way to Nykobing—a ferry the last seven minutes. Cycle west some more into Thy, and meander along the sandy shores facing the North Sea.

Head northeast and recross the sound into Logstor, halfway between Nykobing and Aalborg, to the east. Now south to Gedsted, and east to Alestrup, Hobro and Mariager. South to Randers.

Reach Ebeltoft, southeast of Randers, by any back roads. Take

a ferry across the Kattegat to Sjaellands Odde, on the spit that juts out of the northwest tip of North Sealand. Ride east, take another ferry to Frederiksvaerk. Return to Copenhagen, avoiding the main highways.

MAPS, TERRAIN, TRAFFIC

Local tourist offices issue four 1:325,000 regional maps that are detailed enough for touring on minor roads. They are free, and contain other useful information, such as campground locations and points of interest.

If you want more detail, it'll cost you. Buy any or all of four regional maps, Geodetic Institute 1:200,000, at bookshops in Copenhagen for about $6 each. On those, use the black roads instead of those marked red or yellow for least traffic.

Denmark is almost uniformly flat, with an exception in the lake region southeast of Silkeborg. The hills there are minor, but the contrast with the rest of your cycling days will be somewhat startling. Natives refer tongue-in-cheek to that region as Denmark's little Switzerland.

Road surfaces are almost uniformly excellent—even the smallest roads are usually asphalted. In the northwest, some drifting sand may be found on some roads along the shore. Avoid the smallest roads there. Gravel may be found occasionally on minor roads, those shown on the 1:200,000 maps with the thinnest black lines.

Signs are clearly marked, and it's easy to find your way around. Bikepaths in and at entrances to cities are plentiful. Their asphalted surfaces are much better than the rougher ones in Belgium and the Netherlands. Some cobblestones in towns.

Traffic on minor roads is sparse, more so as you go farther north. Avoid main highways, especially at the height of the season.

The scenery offers little drama, and you'll have no unpleasant surprises. It's one of the most comfortable and least difficult countries to cycle—a perfect one for an introduction to foreign touring.

BEST CYCLING TIME

May is transitional. We had wonderful weather in the middle of that month—sunny, and just cool enough for good pedaling—but it can get wet and cold. June is more certain for warmth, and days are long. Schools go on vacations about June 20.

There's some tendency for more rain in August. The prevailing wind is from the west and southwest, and it's more pronounced along the western half of the mainland, sometimes very stiff in the northwest.

125

BIKE EQUIPMENT, RENTALS

Denmark is a strong biking country, with much of the populace on two wheels and 20,000 members in the militant Danish Cycling Federation. Consequently, many shops and repair facilities exist throughout the country. Bike parts are available for 10-speeds, but not specialized ones like replacement sprockets, or even spokes to fit your bike. But you can buy chains and major components. Bring a spare 27-inch tire, at least.

Of the European countries that have bike rental facilities, this would be the one in which it would make most sense to rent. That is, if your vacation is local and you won't be passing through to Sweden or Norway. The 3-speeds that are available for hire ($20 a week, and up) are perfectly adequate for Danish terrain. If you haven't a suitable bike at home, or don't want the hassle of transporting it, rent in Copenhagen (Koebenhavns Cykelboers, Gothersgade 157) or ask in towns at the tourist office. A hundred renting locations are dispersed evenly through the country and train stations have bikes, too.

Or take one of the two dozen organized tours, sponsored by the Danish Tourist Board. Write for their "Bicycle Holiday" and "Active Holidays" leaflets, which give tour prices and show the routes, and the towns with bike rentals. Maximum daily mileage is 40, but you can digress from the route on your own if you want to do more.

A typical circular tour of eight days, using hostels with half board (one main meal provided) and including use of a bike, costs $145 (1980 prices). Children pay a third less. If you opt for hotels and inns instead, you'll pay $140 more, children one-half. When you bring your own bike, the hire cost will be deducted.

126

BIKE TRANSPORTATION

Trains take the bike as baggage. Check it into the station the day before if you want it to arrive at the same time as you. Cost is up to about $2.75, depending on distance. That's for delivery to major stations; to smaller ones it'll cost $7 and more.

Bikes aren't taken on buses. On ferries, just roll the bikes on, baggage and all. Pedestrians and bikers are let on first, before motor traffic.

GENERAL
ENTERING, LEAVING, HASSLES

Just passports, no visas.

Denmark is one of the most tolerant countries in Europe. As

long as you don't panhandle blatantly on the streets, foment a riot, or fornicate in public, you can do as you wish.

We met Heinrich, the self-styled "King of the Road," and his consort Bertha along the road. They had all their belongings packed on a bicycle, and they wheeled a baby carriage containing their bitch Molly and her new brood of puppies. They've roamed the country for years in that manner, living off the land and the largess of people they befriended. The fact that they've been able to do so reflects on the acceptance and support of Danes for their eccentrics.

There's sexual freedom, too; you can bathe at a nudist beach, and the tourist bureau writes "exposure at many other beaches accepted as long as not offensive."

Rock festivals and Copenhagen's Tivoli amusement park appeal to the young, as do various outdoor sports and holiday opportunities. A walking tour, drawing a hand-cart that contains your camping gear, is one example of the emphasis placed on healthful fun.

LANGUAGE AND PEOPLE

English is widely spoken, especially in Copenhagen and other cities. All cyclists that wrote me remarked on the friendliness of the natives and of their cheerfulness. But in spite of the apparent hedonism of the capital, with its sex shows and music, the Danes are not frivolous. People work diligently. The country is clean— windows seemed to be washed continually as we rode through small towns—and you won't find glass or garbage on the highways.

127

OVERALL COSTS

Expensive if you eat in restaurants, and if you insist on hotels. Cooking for yourself and staying in hostels will cost about $11 to $13 daily. That's calculated from our experience and that of other bikers. Camping will cut that cost somewhat.

The Danish National Tourist Office will send you leaflets on inexpensive lodging and eating places, and the booklet "Low Cost Vacationing in Scandinavia." Or you can get those from an SAS office in Denmark or from your travel agent. The booklet includes suggestions for transportation, recreation and shopping, as well as rooms and meals. Tourists 65 and over get discounts on domestic air and railway fares.

Banking hours are variable and you should inquire about those. You'll also get different rates if you cash traveler's checks at hotels, exchange bureaus or tourist offices. Shop around a bit.

ACCOMMODATIONS

Hotels are high if you seek the ordinary comforts. Modest doubles in the capital start at about $30. Country inns and rooms in private homes could be half that. Check with the local tourist office for the latter, or at Copenhagen's "Use it" center.

With its emphasis on and appeal to youth, Denmark offers various lodgings that emphasize minimum comforts and maximum savings. A Sleep-In at Copenhagen exemplifies this spirit. For $5.75, including breakfast, you find a bed and crash down in your own sleeping bag. No kitchen, no family rooms, and no separation of sexes; people keep very much to themselves.

Hostels are the other large system with reasonable rates for indoor stays. Over 80 of them are distributed evenly in the country. You'd not have to ride more than about 30 miles between two of them. Average price in 1979 was $4.50 each, without breakfast.

We found the standards of cleanliness and the facilities probably the best anywhere. Almost all hostels had kitchens and family rooms. Technically, the private rooms are meant for married couples with children, but the tolerant Danes allow any couple to use them. Often, these rooms are as lavish as a hotel, with individual showers and decorative touches.

Hostels are full from about mid-June to the beginning of August, when schools are not in session. In mid-May we were frequently the only customers.

Among the best hostels: Rudbel (comfortable, good facilities); Ennderudskow (delightful country area, worth effort to find it); Vejle (attractive, an unforgettable pleasure); Ry (great area on lake); Hirtshals (beautiful building on water's edge, view of lighthouse, wind-swept beach); Korsor (motellike, new); Arhus (good setting in forest area); Somarke (nice spot, less crowded since hard to get to by nonbikers); Nykobing (one of best); Tisvilde (modern, clean, relaxing); Randers (individual cabins, beautiful); Helsingor (manor house, clean baths, food store); Skanderberg (beautiful lake, laundry, sinks in rooms, with two to four bunks); Frederikstad (friendly, small rooms, good kitchens); Hobro (good kitchen).

Not recommended: Alborg (barrackslike, regimented atmosphere); Bellahoj, Copenhagen (crowded and grim); Gjerrild (not clean).

Campgrounds are also distributed evenly throughout Denmark. Everyone reported them excellent, with good facilities, clean and well maintained. Charge is about $2.50 a person. You'll need a camping *carnet,* or buy a temporary pass at any campground for $1.80.

Send for "Camping and Youth Hostels" from the tourist office or the Danish Camping Union. Local offices in the country also have information and pamphlets on camp offerings.

Camping in the open is somewhat more difficult than in other countries. It's permitted on beaches and public land, but Denmark lacks woods, and the countryside is well developed or inhabited. You'll be given permission to camp on private land if you ask.

FOOD

Danish food is excellent, but the cheapest lunch will be $6, with a beverage. A dinner is half again as much, more if you have an alcoholic beverage. The amount of food is generous.

Grocery food is among the best in the world. Deservedly renowned are cheeses and other dairy products, meat and fish, both fresh and delicatessen types, sausage, and bread.

Rolls and pastries are heavenly. We ate a couple dozen varieties of "Danish." Each local bakery we visited—and there were many—seemed to have yet another new offering. Various beers are superior to any in America. You'll enjoy the food you prepare for yourself, even if you're not much of a cook.

Shop hours differ, but most are open 9:00 A.M. to 5:30 P.M. (later on Friday), half-day Saturday. Though food stores are closed on Sunday, you can buy some provisions at a bakery, mostly dairy products and packaged goods. All bakeries open at 7:00 A.M. daily; it's wise to shop for fresh rolls in the morning.

The sight and smell of bakery goods drive you wild. Even the design element in their tasteful arrangements is provocative—oversized bagels tied by ribbons overhead, the creams and fruit fillings of strudel, and the breads and rolls set in patterns in display windows.

ADDRESSES AND FURTHER READING

Danish Camping Union
Gammel Kongevej 74D
Dk-1850 Copenhagen V

Danish National Tourist Office
75 Rockefeller Plaza
New York, NY 100'9
        and
3600 Wilshire Boulevard
Los Angeles, CA 90010

Dansk Cyklist Forbund (Danish Cycling Federation)
Kjeld Langes Gade 14
DK-1367 Copenhagen
        The Federation will send you a copy of "Bicycle Holidays in Denmark," and will answer your questions.

FINLAND
15

BIKING MATTERS
SUGGESTED TOURS

TOUR 1. Round trip, Helsinki to Rovaniemi, at the Arctic Circle. About 600 miles each way, the tour takes four to five weeks in its entirety, or public transportation can be taken from Rovaniemi back to Helsinki or Turku.

Leave Helsinki on National 2 through Forssa to Pori, on the coast. Join N8, which goes north all the way to Oulu. A number of side roads closer to the Gulf of Bothnia may be taken, for example, north of Pori through Merikarvia and continue through Pietarsaari. Check locally on the current condition of the roads. These side trips take you through interesting fishing villages and waterfront camping grounds.

At Oulu join E4, then leave it just beyond Kemi. There, take the road on the east side of the Kemijoki River, through Tervola to Rovaniemi. The road has few accommodations, but you can cross the river occasionally to buy food on the other side, where the main road has more villages. Traffic is very light.

At Rovaniemi you can take either N4 or N79 north to Norway and North Cape.

Returning south from Rovaniemi, take N78 to Ranua and Pudasjarvi. N78 joins N20 east for a few miles, then continues south to Puolanka. Take the secondary road to Vaala there, and circle the lake to join N5 at the village of Mainua. South on N5 through Iisalmi, Kuopio, Mikkeli and Lahti to Helsinki. As an alternative, take E80 about 9 miles south of Kuopio to Tampere and Turku, where steamers connect with Sweden.

The first half of this tour takes you mostly along the gulf, although you'd have to ride on side roads to actually see it. The second half is completely in forests and lakes. Only a tenth of the land is cultivated, and most of that in the south.

The entire route is flat, except for some gentle hills on the return leg. Campgrounds are all along it, with no less than 30

FINLAND

youth hostels on or within a few miles of the road. The farthest distance between any accommodations is 50 miles.

TOUR 2. Southeast lakes circle, 370 miles, 10 to 14 days. A relaxing tour among a score of the 60,000 lakes in Finland, in an area with many water sports. Ferries cross the lakes and you can meander

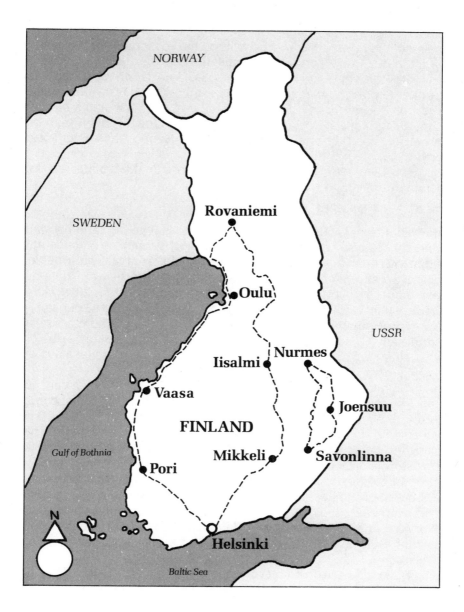

among them in side trips. There are plenty of accommodations—10 hostels and 13 campgrounds on or near the route.

Start at Savonlinna, about 220 miles northeast of Helsinki. An interesting town, with a castle, an opera festival in July, and a hostel. You can make it your headquarters for side tours in the area, too.

Take N71 to Puhos, joining N6. North to Joensuu, then N73 and a side road to Ahveninen. Continue on same road; when you come to the railway, follow the tracks on the coast road to Vuonislahti and Lieksa. There's an outdoor museum there.

Stay on the lake road to Nurmes. Join N18, turn south to Juuka. About 15 miles farther, turn right at Ahmovaara on a side road to Polvijarvi and Viinijarvi, joining N17. A few miles east of that village take N70 south through Juojarvi (or through Liperi on a parallel road) to the villages of Vihtari, Sappu, then Enonkoski and back to Savonlinna.

For bike tours in other regions, write to Matkailuasiamies, Kunnantoimisto, 43100 Saarijarvi.

MAPS, TERRAIN, TRAFFIC

132 The German Ravenstein 1:1,500,000 is a good planning map and could be sufficient if you ride only in the north; any roads not shown on it for that part of the country would be virtually unridable. The map shows campgrounds and places of interest, but lists no road numbers other than the "Es" for European highways. A Ravenstein 1:750,000 is better in the south. Buy in the country.

The Finnish Suomen Kiekartta 1:200,000, in 12 sheets, is best for detail. It would be expensive to buy a number of them, but 1 or 2 sheets could do for a circular tour of a thousand miles. Buy in the country.

Finland is fairly flat south of the Arctic Circle, either a coastal plain or a slightly elevated plateau inland. The only hills of any note are in Lapland in the north, and those are modest. Traffic is light on all secondary roads, and even on main roads in the north. The southern part of the coast road has a lot of truck traffic up to about Kokkola.

Most roads in the south have good surfaces and an adequate shoulder, but in Lapland even main ones may be dirt and gravel. In the northeast, avoid the rough roads from Kaamanen to Neiden, Norway, and from Sodankyla east to Kotala, near the Russian border. But the hard-pressed gravel road from Kaamanen north to Utsjoki is OK.

Bikepaths are common on main roads and in big cities. They're of good quality and lead directly between cities, instead of meandering, as they do often in Holland or the United States.

Settlements are sparse in the north. You'll see an occasional Lapp house or tent, resembling the teepee of an American Indian. ("How many laps to go?" called back Rosemary, as we passed one of them during a long stretch of empty road.) Otherwise, there'll be lonely miles with only pine forests for companions. The country is stark, primitive and beautiful. One correspondent wrote that the northwest finger of land that points to Norway is exceptionally remote and scenic.

BEST CYCLING TIME

It's a toss-up: freeze in May or get eaten by mosquitoes a month later. At least in the north. Mosquitoes are very thick and awful in Lapland. In the beginning of July we found them intolerable, even wearing layers of clothes, net hats and gloves. They dived into the pot of food when the lid was opened, attracted by the heat, and their sound on the tent walls was like a heavy rain. No abating during the night either (midnight sun and it doesn't get dark), and there's no escaping them. After a few days we gave up and took a bus south, out of the region.

Mosquitoes thin out and fall colors are brilliant by September; cycling can be excellent for a couple of weeks during days that are still warm. But nights are longer and colder in fall, while in late May you have more daylight hours. One night in June we rode until about 3:00 A.M. in the weird light.

133

It rains somewhat more frequently in fall. In Helsinki during early summer it averages eight days a month.

BIKE EQUIPMENT, RENTALS

There are 10-speeds sold in the country and you should be able to find 27 X 1¼-inch tires and basic components in the larger cities of the south, with some searching. The more common size is 28 inches. Repair facilities are scarce, though, so bring a freewheel remover, chain-link tool and any other specialized tools needed for your bike.

Cycles may be rented at the Stadion hostel in Helsinki and some holiday towns, such as Joensuu in the southeast lakes region. A few organized tours also exist. Check with the national tourist office for current ones.

BIKE TRANSPORTATION

Cycles are taken on trains and on buses for a nominal price, except not on buses in cities. The railroad stops at about the Arctic Circle. Beyond there, bus service is good. Bikes are carried either in the back of a bus on racks or on top, or in a back luggage compartment if there's room.

GENERAL
ENTERING, LEAVING, HASSLES

As in the other Scandinavian countries, you need no visa or inoculations. No problem whatsoever at borders.

LANGUAGE AND PEOPLE

Very little English spoken away from the big cities. The second language is Swedish; the country was occupied by Sweden in the past. A phrase book or dictionary is useful to point out words. Since Finnish belongs to a non-European language group, originating in Asia and related only to Hungarian and Estonian in Europe, you'll find it difficult.

It's hard to believe that Finns are thought to stem from Mongolia in ancient times; most are light colored and have blond, or at least very light brown, hair. They're friendly but shy, but not so standoffish as Norwegians or Swedes. Lapps ignore you, mostly. We tended to stare at their colorful costumes—worn as everyday clothes on visits to town; I had thought they may have been only for special times—but they paid no attention to us and our bikes.

The air is pure everywhere and Finns take pride in honoring ecological principles. The country is clean and neat.

Cleanliness is almost a religion. No other explanation could account for the sauna, a devilish introduction to what I imagine would be the wrong part of an afterlife. Heated rocks raise the temperature to a point where breathing is difficult. Occasionally you throw a ladleful of water on the rocks to raise the humidity and feel the heat even more. As if that were not punishment enough, you flail yourself masochistically (or each other) lightly with birch twigs, leaves intact. At intervals you run out to take a cold shower. I was able to stand about three ten-minute intervals. The sauna opens your pores and guarantees absolute cleanliness.

OVERALL COSTS

We spent about $8 a day for food and lodging; André Everett about $5.50. André camped in the open more than we, and was a house guest a few times. Rock-bottom costs in 1981 should be about $7 a day.

"Low Cost Vacationing in Scandinavia," available from the tourist office, suggests ways of saving money. Retirees get a 25

FINLAND

percent discount on domestic air flights and 50 percent on state railways. The differential between the Finnish markka and the dollar, as well as living costs in Finland, has not risen very much in the past few years. The cited costs should not rise greatly in the near future.

ACCOMMODATIONS

In small towns a cheap single room will start a little below $11. Doubles are only slightly higher. The cheapest single in Helsinki will be almost twice as much.

Over 110 hostels are sprinkled throughout the country. They're thickest in the southeast lake region. Those in the north open June 1 or later, earlier in the south. Most close by the end of August.

Prices vary depending on region and offerings. A dorm bed in a hostel with cold water and no showers costs $3.25. With a shower and in a double room, two people pay $5.25 each. The latter cost jumps to $10 in the best category of hostel, which has TV and a meeting room, and which includes sheets in the price.

Many hostels, but not all, have kitchens. Most have family rooms, meant for a man and wife, with young children, but any couple is accommodated if the rooms aren't full. Only the higher category hostels are certain to have showers. Lower graded ones may have only hot or cold running water in sinks. Some hostels even have washing machines.

Saunas are common. About $2.75 lets a couple inside for a liberal amount of time—longer than you can stand, in any case.

If you plan to attend a festival or a night entertainment, a hostel is a poor choice. The hostel will likely be full because of the event, unless you make reservations, and the usual 11:00 P.M. curfew will force you to return early. Better to camp instead, or try to get a cheap room.

Many hostels allow camping, alleviating curfew conflicts but still getting the advantage of kitchen and washing facilities. Write to the Finnish Youth Hostels for a free booklet that shows map locations of hostels and what they feature. It's much better than the information in the IYH Handbook.

We didn't use many hostels in the country, but we liked the one at Inari in the north. It had a pleasant atmosphere, private rooms, and use of the family kitchen, all in a private home. A dorm was being built in back at the time we were there, so the private rooms and kitchen may not be available in the future. Jorma Kaukonen liked Lieksa (great facilities, private bath).

Poor hostels, reported by other bikers, are at Savonlinna (closely packed, dirty); Helsinki's Stadion hostel (stark, charges if late return, after curfew); Kemi (dilapidated, one toilet, one sink, no mirror, no shower).

Open camping is possible anywhere outside of cities. Sources, both national and in the United States, differ on how or whether "everyman's right" applies, as in Sweden and Norway. Cyclists should try to get permission, or let close-by residents know they intend to camp. In most of the country it doesn't matter, though; forests are widespread and open to camping, with few signs of civilization nearby.

Remoteness from people is one of the problems with camping in the wild, in fact. Standing water may be all that's available (don't drink it), and you won't find someone from whom to get a fresh supply. Mosquitoes and distances between stores are other problems.

An organized campground with an equipped, screened kitchen and a camp store or kiosk offers more comforts and conveniences. A camp may even have an adjacent cafeteria and a sauna. Well over 300 camps are strewn all over the country. Some farm houses offer "yard-camping" and use of facilities, also.

Some campgrounds are very crude, with outside, unscreened kitchens, and are hardly worth stopping at, but most have the amenities. Many camps are situated in drained areas, and the number of mosquitoes is minimal.

136

Cost for a tent and two people is usually $2.75. You may get a cheaper rate if you take it up with the owner. Argue that you'll take a spot which a motor camper couldn't get into, and that you'll use less of the camp's facilities. Camping season starts late May and lasts to early September. It's shorter in the north.

Few camps were mentioned by my correspondents; most camped in the open. Reported as agreeable were: Rovaniemi (good facilities), and Peura (pleasant spot, lots of room) in the north; Punhahayir (nice setting), and Rauma (beautiful) in the south. We found an especially bad camp south of Antila in the far north (no screens in outdoor kitchen, poor facilities).

FOOD

Cafe and restaurant prices are lower than in the rest of Scandinavia, although still high compared to the rest of Europe. A small meal-of-the-day can cost as little as $3 in a cafe, but you'll spend twice that by the time you add beverage and side dishes to satisfy hunger. People bring in their own food and order just coffee in cafes, without objection from waitresses. A cup of coffee, at 60¢, costs less than in any other northern country. If you can find a smorgasbord for $3.50 to $4.50, it would be a bargain way to fill up.

Groceries cost up to twice the prices in the States, and could be higher in remote places. In the north meat and other basics are hard to find in stores. Some typical prices (in 1979): 1 quart milk, 45¢; a smoked fish, 40¢; two big sausages, $1.50; hamburger meat, under $3 a pound; eggs, $1.50 a dozen; cheese, $4 a pound; jam, $2 a pound. Fresh fish and produce in season are a good buy, relatively. Snacks and cooked food are reasonable: a pound of smoked, unboned fish is $1, large cooked sausage 75¢. Crayfish are a big delicacy, abundant in late summer. Weak beer costs about 60¢ a bottle, but liquor is expensive. Vodka has a good international reputation.

Store hours are generally 9:00 A.M. to 5:00 P.M., weekdays, half-day Saturday and closed Sunday. In big cities, supermarkets may stay open longer, sometimes until 10:00 P.M. On weekends, you can buy limited varieties of food in kiosks and in gas stations.

Mushrooms and berries fill forests and sides of the road, starting in midsummer. But get a mushroom book to know which to pick, or ask the locals.

ADDRESSES AND FURTHER READING

Finnish National Tourist Office
Scandinavia House
505 Fifth Avenue
New York, NY 10017

137

and

Scandinavian Tourist Office
3600 Wilshire Boulevard
Los Angeles, CA 90010

Finnish Youth Hostels (SRM)
Yrjon Katu 38B
00100 Helsinki 10

David Bradley, *Lion Among Roses* (New York: Holt, Rinehart & Winston, 1965). Adjustment of a family to a work stay in the country, and through it a report on the people's temperament. Well written.

Sylvie Nickels, ed., *Finland; an Introduction* (New York: Praeger, 1973). A number of authors, mostly Finnish, write on various aspects of the country. A good basic guide.

FRANCE

16

BIKING MATTERS
SUGGESTED TOURS

TOUR 1. Loire Valley, about 600 miles if all by bicycle, less if some by train. It can take from two to three weeks, depending on how many churches and castles you inspect.

From Paris make your way to Versailles, then on N306 to Rambouillet and D906 to Chartres. Or take a train to avoid Paris traffic. Chartres is a picturesque town, with the famous Notre Dame Cathedral.

Now, ride on D921 and D955 to Chateaudun, with its castle and old town. Then on D924 and D917 to Vendome, and D917, D305 and D304 to Le Mans. Next, D309 to Sable; D21, D28, D20 and D923 to Cande; D19, D33 and D178 to Nantes. Those many small roads will avoid traffic along the more direct N23. Lots of churches and castles along this route.

A return to Paris, east along the Loire River, takes you through the heart of the castle country. Any number of routes are possible. D17, D751, next to the river through Saumur and Chinon to Tours, is good and takes in historic spots. The region around Tours is the heart of the chateau country.

Continue on D751 to Blois, or take a side trip on D40 to Chenonceaux, then D764 to Blois. Next, D33 to Chambord, and the most magnificent castle of all. Continue D103 and D15 to Orleans.

You can now take a train directly to Paris or cycle on D97 and D49 to Etampes, then N191 and D83 to Melun. From here, the 30 miles or so to Paris are all busy, so take it easy. Or take a train.

This tour is virtually all flat, with some rolling hills in the Le Mans region, and some short climbs when leaving the river valley.

TOUR 2. Alsace, and wine region; about 640 miles for the complete circle from Reims and return. Easy to moderate mostly, some hard hills through the Vosges Mountains. About three weeks. Wine festivals are mid-August. "Degustation gratuite," they'll say, announcing free sampling.

FRANCE

Take a train from Paris to Reims, or cycle the approximately 100 miles on departmental roads. The Reims cathedral is worth seeing, and the city is pleasant.

Cycle D9 south through the champagne-grape-growing region to Eparnay, if you wish to hostel there, or turn east on D1 to Chalons. A short ride east on National 3, and then a right turn onto RD394. Make your way to D902 and D901, which take you to St. Mihiel. Now, D907 will lead to N57 and Nancy, in the Moselle wine region.

Go east on N74 and D38 into Saverne. There, take D41 into Strasbourg. You are now in the Alsace, where both wine and beer are renowned. Follow the Rhine south along D468 to a point east of Colmar, at N59. Or take some of the hilly roads west of N83 in the Vosges for some good scenery. At N59, take D2b and D20 south through Mulhouse, onto D432 to Altkirch. There, turn west on D419 to Belfort.

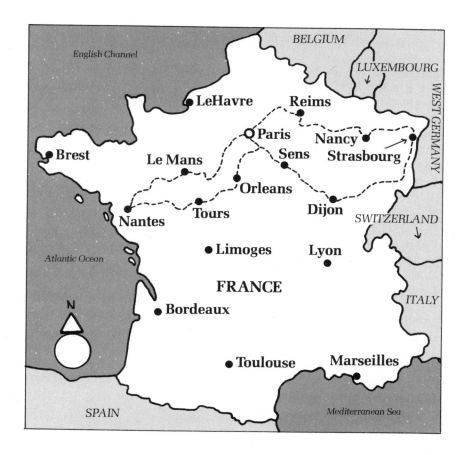

A short distance on N83 brings you to an intersection with D9, which goes to Vesoul. Then, D474 and D70 bring you to Dijon. About 30 miles northwest on N71, you'll see D6 forking off to the left. It leads to D19 and to D905. That goes northwest almost to Sens. There you can take a train, or cycle back to Paris. Or return to Reims on D939, D439, D951, RD51 and N51. The tour can be interrupted also at Strasbourg, Mulhouse, or Dijon, all of which have trains going to Paris.

Many more good tours are possible: in Brittany in the extreme west, in Provence in the southeast, and in the Pyrenees. If going to Spain, avoid the Biarritz area, taking the harder but less crowded inland roads instead. Along the Mediterranean, try not to cycle weekends or at the height of the vacation season. Your options of roads there are limited.

MAPS, TERRAIN, TRAFFIC

The Michelin series of maps, of course. Even Michelin 989, the 1:1,000,000, overall France, is adequate for distance rides, and when you're not interested in detailed exploration (about $3 in the United States, or get it and other maps from the CTC or in France). The 989 shows one- and two-lane, departmental roads (D numbers), which are certainly sufficient for pleasant bicycling. Michelin shows no contours, but steep hills are indicated on roads, with ominous darts. The tourist office issues no maps useful for bicyclists.

Roads in the north and east are well marked, those in the central and Pyrenees region not so well. In the latter, you're better off with one or more of the 45 maps in the 1:200,000 series. That also shows local roads (VO and VV), which take you completely off the beaten track.

"Scary, smelly, intimidating, dangerous," were the complaints of most riders about traffic on N roads, shown in red on maps. Harsh comments about cities, also. But city cycling is all right if you avoid the largest avenues, those through streets that abound with cars. Smaller roads in the country have no shoulders, but those have so few drivers that it makes no difference.

There seem to be no dirt roads in France. There must surely be some, but I've never seen any except for those that connect the most remote villages with a larger road. None of my questionnaire correspondents complained of any road conditions. The pavements are excellent and well-marked roads are the rule.

Cobblestones are found in cities. In the northern ones you may encounter a sort peculiar to northwestern Europe. These are *setts,* big, round, granite cobbles that are rough on backsides. The surface is often polished and slippery when wet or contaminated with oil. Back streets of some towns have cobbles, too.

Bikepaths are infrequent, except in approaches to cities and towns. Where they exist they're compulsory.

The great river valleys are flat and so is a vast plain in the north, with Paris about its center. The south and east are mountainous, and you should be geared down to below 30 if carrying a load. A conventional 10-speed, or even a 3-speed, will do for the rest of the country.

Prevailing winds in the northwest blow west to east. If traveling in one direction only, take advantage of those. In the south, along the Rhone valley especially, the mistral blows from north to south, sometimes fiercely. Winds in the eastern parts are more variable.

BEST CYCLING TIME

In the north, May is rainy. I found fall delightful in the north, and April and late fall best along the Mediterranean. July and August are hot in the south.

August is the worst time for traffic, also, as most of France takes its vacation then. In addition, it poses problems in small towns, where many of the shops are closed for vacation.

Le weekend is a busy time on the highways everywhere. The city motorist heads wildly then for the country and seashore. Avoid especially the July 14 and August 15 holidays, and weekends nearest the first of July, August and September. Best not to cycle from midday Friday to midday Saturday.

141

I noted that traffic was worse in 1979 than in 1974; the higher yearly ownership of cars makes it certain that it'll get worse yet. Gas prices won't be a deterrent. While the Americans were complaining of shortages and prices, the French, with a cost per gallon considerably higher than ours, were driving with abandon.

BIKE EQUIPMENT, RENTALS

If your bike has English threads and 27 X 1¼-inch tires, bring any spares you think you might need. But 700c tires are available everywhere. Repair shops are not common away from large towns and cities. Mechanics are competent and helpful, and will take care of you on the spot. In August, vacationing bike shop owners will close down and you may not be able to buy anything anyhow.

Rentals are hard to find, except in Paris and railroad stations. Where found, most rental bikes are clunkers and unsuitable for touring. They'll have limited gearing and will lack proper racks and accessories. Best to bring your own.

BIKE TRANSPORTATION

Few long-distance buses exist in France. Local ones take bikes where there are no train services. Bikes ride flat on the roof.

Trains are good, but you may have to plan for delays if you go through any large cities with car changes. Ask if there will be transfers. If so, get a ticket to the transfer terminal, pick up your bike, and buy another ticket to your final destination. You'll be more certain to have the bike arrive with you.

If the train arrives after the baggage room is locked, you may have to wait until the next day anyhow, especially when you cross a border into France and have to wait for a customs official to pass you through. Some bike tourists count on a bike arriving late, sending it ahead to a destination and visiting a couple of days in a large city in the meantime.

Many trains, classified as outer suburban services, take neither cycles nor luggage. The timetable indicates which. Cost for bike transport is $3, no matter the distance.

Allow an hour or two ahead of time to check it in. You can often load and unload it yourself, either securing it with a strap or hanging it up. That may be the best idea; Brian MacDonald's bike was handled poorly on trains, getting scratched and gouged. He even saw bikes stacked on top of each other. Take all luggage off and either carry it or send as baggage at extra cost.

142

GENERAL
ENTERING, LEAVING, HASSLES

Passport only. No problems in or out of the country. Some surliness by Parisian salesmen and ticket vendors was a complaint of a few bike tourists.

Occasionally, police ask for your documents along the road, a customs evasion control. They may search baggage for drugs if you look scruffy.

LANGUAGE AND PEOPLE

The French believe their language to be the most beautiful in the world. Cyclists who speak none of it may be disdained or ignored. But in tourist areas they react with arrogant contempt when you try to communicate in French. Waiters persist in speaking English, though it may be no better than your French. If they insist on English, baffle them by talking fast and idiomatically. They'll soon allow you to practice your French.

Small cafes have no need of posting menus in English, in

contrast to those that cater to tourists. In fact, you're better off in those neighborhood eating places. If a restaurant has an English menu, it'll surely be more expensive. You'll need some familiarity with food names, at least, to eat in native cafes.

You'll need some French also for deciphering the names of staples, if you shop anywhere but in supermarkets, with their familiar packaged goods. Take a short course in French, or at least bring a Berlitz or similar phrase book.

A few American correspondents complained that city people acted antagonistic. I've not found them so, but except for young French cyclists I met on the road not many were friendly either. I've never been invited into a French home, although I've had pleasant, casual conversations with people in cafes. That's not surprising; Hugh McLachlan has lived at the same address in Paris for 20 years and has only been offered something in someone else's apartment twice, and one of those times by a foreigner.

You'll find people more easygoing and friendly in the south, more businesslike in the north. But overall, bike tourists should not count on the openness which seems so natural elsewhere.

A French person won't be impressed by the fact that you're a bike tourist, for the above reason and because bikes are used in a utilitarian way. However, people tend to accept you more as a special kind of foreigner, who's willing to see the country in a nonconspicuous manner, and they'll respect you for that. There's more brusqueness off than on the bike.

143

France is a place to see things, rather than to meet people, in any case. Make the most of the sights and the cycling.

OVERALL COSTS

If you share a camp and make your own meals, you should be spending about $9 a day. Costs will rise somewhat if you indulge yourself in extra good food and wine. I spent over $9 in 1979, eating lavishly and drinking wine with meals, and staying at a lot of hostels. Ann Conklin, with a group of a dozen, spent $12.50 a person in 1978. She hosteled, and ate hostel dinners and in restaurants.

Costs will obviously be higher with hotels and restaurant meals. The country is about on a par with England, less expensive than Scandinavia, more than Spain.

Banking hours are 9:00 A.M. to noon and 2:00 to 4:00 P.M., what they used to be in the United States a generation ago, but a few are adopting American hours. A bank may sometimes be closed Monday instead of Saturday. Jim and Jean Scheu found train depots a dependable place for money exchange. Someone always spoke English, and they got advantageous rates. The depot had a list of hotels, with rates, too. Credit cards are only accepted in the more expensive shops; they're not economical for a budget in France.

Allow about eight days for mail to arrive. There's a small, nuisance charge for picking up mail at *poste restante.* You should use hotels, hostels and campgrounds as addresses instead, but make sure they're open. Ask the proprietor to forward or return mail; the post office can seldom be relied on.

ACCOMMODATIONS

You won't be able to find a hotel, with private bath, in a large city, for less than $28. In tourist towns and a large community, a tourist bureau *(syndicat d'initiative)* can help you find a room.

Hotels are considerably cheaper if you stick to small ones and don't ask for a room with bath. The cheapest are in rural areas, and when you avoid the high season of July-August for touring; the cost out of that season will be $9 or so. The price is the same single or double. A full-board hotel will cost $17 a day.

A hotel may be cramped for room and have no indoor storage for a bike, especially in a large town. Conversely, country inns often have very good bike security, in a shed or barn.

144 Many hotels and inns expect you to eat supper in their dining room. Check into that before you book, but you can hardly go wrong in choosing their menu of the day. "It's worth waiting for," is the kind of remark cyclists made to describe meals in those small hotels. Still, look at the menu before asking to have a look at the room.

If your budget can stand the few extra dollars, the small French hotel offers the best value in Western Europe. When you share a room with someone, it may cost hardly more than a hostel. But as insurance against not finding a suitable one, it's still wise to carry a tent.

Besides being relatively inexpensive and offering good food, hotels offer another advantage, according to Jim and Jean Scheu. They had a flat at the end of a cycling day and decided to fix the tube in their room. To their delight, they found that the bidet in the bathroom proved to be the perfect receptacle in which to find the source of the tube's puncture.

Another possible accommodation is a Relais Routier, a series of hotels and inns that cater to truck drivers. They are found on truck routes, and usually at entrances to towns. Meals are supplied at all hours at reasonable cost.

Hostels in France are somewhat distant from each other, 30 to 60 miles apart. It's possible to cycle between two of them each day, but your route may be severely restricted if they don't happen to be along it. For Tour 1, Loire, for example, only 7 hostels are on it. Tour 2, Alsace, has 16 hostels, but a few are bunched together.

If you arrive at a hostel to find it full you'll be stuck, unless prepared for tent camping. Happily, many small-town hostels and those in the country are either combined with campgrounds or have space around them for tents. Hostels like these are a real bargain. You pay a third of the price of a dorm bed but enjoy the same bathroom and kitchen privileges. And you don't have to abide by the hostel curfew, coming and going to your tent at any time.

I always found space in hostels, even in midsummer, but a few cyclists said they saw people turned away. I believe, though, that most French hostels are informal enough in applying rules so that a cyclist arriving after dark could always find some space to sleep on, even if only on the floor. That's unpredictable: you may run into prudishness, as in Chartres. Its room for marrieds is not available to unmarried couples, according to a pair of my correspondents. In case of that restriction, you might use subterfuge by wearing a ring and claiming a recent marriage. A show of propriety is what's required.

Only a few hostels have private or family rooms. Most are dorms with double-decker bunks. Hot showers are not common, and conditions can be pretty bad, with dirty kitchens and rooms, and little supervision of unruly youngsters. A woman at the St. Mihiel hostel said that was because wardens are volunteers, not paid except in keep, and there's little monetary support. The ratings and prices of French hostels have little relationship to their quality. The most expensive often offer the least.

145

Recommended hostels: Tours (tremendous dinners); Phalsbourg (in charming old chateau, nice view from a hill); Reims (wonderful kitchen, lots of hot water, clean); St. Quentin (posh looks but cheap, good facilities); Vezelay (superb).

Not recommended: Beaugency (dirty, boys and girls shared dorms, smoking in dorms); Chateau-Salins (miles off highway on dirt road, very dirty, no shower, dog wet all mattresses on bottom bunks); St. Mihiel (no hot water, carry bike up three flights); Lille (no kitchen, no hot water, dirty, top price); Aubigny (dirty, smells, bad vibes).

Free camping in parks, woods or fields is easy to find. As elsewhere in the world, water is a problem; you'll have to cart it in. Permission to camp on someone's farmland may not always be granted by suspicious owners—offer to pay something—but there's always another spot farther on.

Official campgrounds are abundant and cheap. A camping *carnet* seems to get you nothing in the way of discount or consideration, as it does in Scandinavia. Most camps have some kind of shower, although it's often cold. You must pay for showers with warm water.

The *Michelin Red Guide 610,* "Camping in France," costs $7 and is worth the price if you'll stay long in the country. But you don't really need it. Grounds can be found in almost every town, and routes to them are very well marked. "Camping Caravaning" is free from the French Tourist Office.

A washing machine in a campground wasn't reported by any questionnaire correspondents. I've never seen any. Laundromats in France, except in Paris and the large cities, are very hard to find.

Camps in the Riviera area are always crowded in summer, with vehicles bumper to bumper. I found that beach camping was easy and more pleasant, as long as I stayed away from developed sections. If you travel early or late in the year, camps may be closed, but no one will bother you if you use them anyway.

France is reasonably free of thievery, but there's no point in taking chances. Secure your bike indoors when you can. I'd not leave it on a street ever, no matter how many chains and locks were on it. When in a camp, take your things inside the tent and lock the bike to a fence or tree. Jim and Gerri Thorsteinson had some money stolen in a campground.

146

FOOD

Restaurant food ranges from excellent to uninteresting. The French cuisine is deservedly famous. Food is one thing the French are quite serious about.

A fixed price meal will cost $5 to $6, probably with some wine. Frequent only those restaurants with menus posted outside. Food quality and value can be found at hotels where you stay; they're apt to have family atmosphere, and meals will be served with pride and prepared with care.

Lunch is best eaten in the open air. If France had only its cheese, bread and wine, it would still deserve fame for tasteful eating. Add some fruit, have a picnic on a grassy spot away from the road, and your day will be complete. Try a different cheese each day that you're in the country, and you'll hardly dent the varieties. Table wine is cheap, and it's not strong enough to hamper the rest of the afternoon's biking—if you don't overindulge. If you do, so what? Find a camp nearby and stay the rest of the afternoon. Life should be easy in France.

Buy a crusty roll with butter and a coffee for breakfast in a cafe. That is, if they serve fresh rolls. If not, pick up a melt-in-the-mouth croissant or a roll from a nearby bakery, bring it into the cafe and order just coffee. That's what the locals do.

FRANCE

Watch yourself in cafe toilets. Many of them are still the hole-in-the-ground type, with two metal or ceramic footsteps to stand on when you squat. Flushing is primitive and may be incomplete. A brush is usually provided, with which to clean down and reflush. Take care when entering and leaving the cramped space, since the light is controlled by the door lock and toilet doors may swing in. You can easily take a misstep.

Cooking for yourself is a delight in France. It has probably the best meat in Europe. For a treat try a *charcuterie,* where all sorts of delicatessen items are sold. Produce is cheap and always of good quality. It's tree or vine ripened and succulent.

Some sample prices (in 1979): the typical, long French bread, 40¢; a half-pound of dark bread, 40¢; pastry, 40¢ to 55¢; an assortment containing two onions, a cucumber, a tomato, and a pepper, all medium size, 60¢; six eggs, 85¢. Per pound: peaches, 65¢; grapes, 75¢; pork chops, $2.35; most other cuts of meat, $2.90 to $3.50. In a cafe, coffee costs 40¢ a cup, and beer 60¢ for a quarter-liter.

A Reisling wine in Alsace costs $3 a liter. Table wine is as cheap as $1. Hugh McLachlan cautions against cheap wine, though. Much of it is full of chemicals and is questionable. He believes no wine should be bought without an *appellation controlle* statement on the bottle. That and the wine's cost—it should be no cheaper than about $3 a bottle—are the best indications of quality.

147

He further suggests not to buy an aged red wine. With aging, a wine "deposits out," and shaking it on a bike will reintroduce those bitter deposits into the body. Better to buy younger wine. If you lay over somewhere and don't shake the bottle too much after buying, you can let aged wine settle out again, and leave the dregs in the bottle.

Tapwater from a municipal supply is drinkable but may have a chlorinated taste. Restaurant water is always safe. Not all bottled water should be drunk liberally. Most comes from spas and is for medicinal use. Try to find mineral-free water, labeled on the bottle as such. Fruit-flavored drinks are available and can safely slake your thirst, too.

Marcia Horner, who cycled from the Loire Valley to the Pyrenees in 1979 with her husband, Michael, said she loved to shop in French food stores. The *boulangerie* (bakery), *boucherie* (butcher), *laiterie* (dairy products), and *epicerie* (groceries) offer the best in their specialties. My favorite French word was *patisserie,* the pastry shop, where much of my daily budget was left. French pastries almost match those in Denmark, and I snacked on them continually.

Supermarkets vie with the specialty shops, forced by competition to try for the same high standard of food quality. If you don't feel up to conversing with a shopkeeper, the *supermarche* lets you pick at your ease among the offerings, just as at home.

When you don't feel like cooking a meal from scratch some evening, look for a deep-frozen *cassoulet* (stew with mutton, goose sausage, vegetables, in port wine), a bouillabaise, coq-au-vin, frog's legs, quail, or some other fancy, precooked meal in the supermarket. It'll put a dent in your budget, but you'll get a taste of French cooking at its best without paying a bundle in a restaurant. An occasional treat like that heightens a tour's memory.

Food stores are open from 9:00 A.M. to 6:00 or 7:00 P.M., and even later. Most of France closes its shops at noon for two or three hours. The practice is being changed somewhat by the supermarkets (and that French creation, the larger *hypermarche*), which stay open all day and into late evening. But tradition still prevails in common Monday closings. Food stores are open, however, on Sunday mornings, though in some towns they may be closed. Bread is available each day. Watch your hours, which may change from region to region and by season, and stock up for weekends.

Butane (*Butagaz,* commonly) is available in S-200 cartridges. Kerosene (*petrole*) is sold by the liter in a paint store (*marchand de couleurs*).

148

ADDRESSES AND FURTHER READING

French Tourist Office
610 Fifth Avenue
New York, NY 10020
and
9401 Wilshire Boulevard
Beverly Hills, CA 90212

French Cycle-touring Federation
8, rue Jean-Marie Jego
75013 Paris

Touring Club of France
65, av. de la Grande-Armee
Service Camping
75116 Paris

Francois Nourissier, *The French* (New York: Knopf, 1968). The good, bad and indifferent of 50 million Frenchmen, comparable in analysis and wit to Barzini's *The Italians.*

Michelin Green Guides to Paris and six regions of France.

NOTES ON CYCLING IN CORSICA
(FROM NORMAN FORD)

An offbeat cycling spot, Corsica has probably 1,500 miles of roads around it, and in the interior. Surfaces are acceptable, and traffic is light during the off-seasons: May to June 15, and September 12 to November 1. "*Never* go in summer," warns Norman Ford.

Most roads are hilly and mountainous. You'll need low climbing gears, and a lot of stamina. Use the Michelin map 090, Corsica, 1:200,000. It costs $2 in the United States. You'll be rewarded with fantastic scenery and a lot of beaches, cliffs, piney woods and scrubby hillsides.

You should learn some basic French to communicate and to shop, English being rarely spoken. People are friendly toward Americans, but regard bikers as eccentric. No Corsican would be seen on a 10-speed, considering that a bike is degrading—proper travel is by car.

Shops close in the afternoons and Sundays, otherwise there's no problem buying food. Wine is cheap. Ford estimates 1980 cost per day at $20 a person, buying food at markets and staying at second-class hotels. Many hotels close after mid-October. There are no hostels. Camping could cut costs in half. There are many campgrounds, but you can find a free site easily in the sparsely peopled countryside. Ask permission when you can, of course.

A number of ferries reach Corsica from France and Italy. From Nice the fare is about $20 one way. Don't rely on public transport on the island. It has just two short railroad lines, and bus service is unreliable. Bike shops are few; they carry some bike parts but no 27-inch tires. You'll have to be self-sufficient.

GERMANY (WEST)
17

BIKING MATTERS
SUGGESTED TOURS

TOUR 1. Mosel River and castles; 310 or 370 miles, depending on alternatives, up to two weeks. Most of this tour was supplied by William Stagg, who lives and works in the Frankfurt area.

Start at Frankfurt. There's a train station under the airport, and you can take a train to Wiesbaden, about 38 miles west. Make sure the train has a baggage car. When you get there, ride south about 4 miles to the intersection with 43 and turn west (may be signed B42).

Or you can cycle there. Follow the signs from the airport toward the Wiesbaden autobahn. Don't take the autobahn. At the second traffic circle out of the airport, pass the access sign to the autobahn and continue toward "Unterschweinstiege" and the Airport Hotel. At the third traffic circle, take the second exit out of the circle. The hotel will be at your right. Take the small asphalt road on your left, just before the hotel, to Schwanheim/Kelsterbach.

Go straight on this road about 4 miles until you join 43. You'll have gone over a small bridge and railroad tracks. Go west on 43 toward Raunheim a bit over a mile, and look for a small road to the right, just before a large refinery. It follows a fence, on your left, and takes you over the Main River. Walk the bike across the bridge to the village of Eddersheim. Take the first main road left, toward Florsheim.

You are now on 40. Continue past Kastel, which runs parallel to the Rhine. Cycle all the way to Koblenz either on 42, on minor adjoining roads, or by crossing the river to 9, with its adjoining minor roads. Loads of castles and churches on both sides of the Rhine.

The Mosel flows southwest out of Koblenz. Follow it on 49 as far as Cochem. Cross the river there, and continue on the secondary road that stays with the river. Recross the river into Nehren, on its other side. Ride on 49 to Alf, where you'll join 53. Stay on it until you can cross over the river to Reil. Take the secondary road out of Reil along the river as far as Traben. Rejoin 53 and cycle to Neumagen-Dhron. Take the secondary, river road out of there to Thornich. Cross the bridge and rejoin 53. It will take you into Trier.

All this crossing and recrossing will keep you along the river and will minimize traffic. Campgrounds and other accommodations are all along this route. Watch also for "Weinprobe Stands," which ask you to sample the local wines. Those are made from grapes grown on the almost vertical vineyards along the road.

From Trier onward, the cycling becomes harder. Take 52, east of the city, eastward to Freisen. Cross under 62 and ride into Kusel

and Altenglan. More castles and churches all through this area. You can now cycle either down the river Glan, northeast to the Mainz area, and back to the starting point, or east to the Worms/Heidelberg area.

For the latter, ride out of Altenglan to Rothselberg. A few miles farther, join 270 and go southeast as far as Otterbach. Turn left to Otterberg, Enkenbach, and Eisenberg, and continue on the same road to Worms. Explore that historic area.

Out of Worms, the land is level. Take 47 east to Gerspenz, and 38 north. Don't stay on 38 into Darmstadt but continue north to Dieburg. Now, go a short way north on 45, then turn left to Langen, between Darmstadt and Frankfurt. Make your way to either Wiesbaden or Frankfurt on minor roads, referring to a detailed map of the area.

TOUR 2. Romantische Strasse, the Romantic Road, Frankfurt area to the Austrian border. About 280 miles for its entire length, it can be an easy 10 to 14 days. It's a hackneyed route, but still has much of interest. It can link with an Austrian tour, or you can return by train from Augsburg.

In the latter part of Tour 1, turn east at Gerspenz onto 47, the Nibelungenstrasse. Stay on it until you run into 27 at Walldurn. Ride about 15 miles east on 27 to Tauberbischofsheim. The Romantic Road runs south from here. It changes numbers, but you won't get lost; it's a recognized tourist route. Cyclists say that it's not crowded, however, if you avoid the height of the summer season.

You'll pass through the medieval cities of Rothenberg, Nordlingen, Augsburg, Landsberg, and end at Fussen. It's the easiest way to Austria and Italy, and you'll see the expected "picture postcard" version of Germany. For an appreciation of it, refer to a *Michelin Green Guide* for Germany.

The roads will often be minor and two lane, and sometimes major, as along 17 south of Augsburg. But a bikepath adjoins the highway in that latter part. The road has only a few stretches of hills; most of it follows river valleys. Hostels and campgrounds are frequent along this route.

MAPS, TERRAIN, TRAFFIC

The German National Tourist Office will send you a 1:800,000 map, which is sufficient for overall planning purposes. It can even serve for one-route tours, such as the second one described above. The map shows symbols for places of interest and campgrounds.

To find minor roads, and to negotiate difficult turns on secondary roads and bypass cities, you need more detail. The Shell Gen-

GERMANY (WEST)

eral Karte 1:200,000 maps got praise from cyclists, as did Michelin of the same scale. Buy them in a large town before you get out into the country. There are five in the Michelin series, only for the western part of the country. They cost $2 each in the United States. The Shells cover all of West Germany.

Another map series in the same scale is Mair's Generalkarte. The maps show even cart paths. The whole country is covered in 26 sheets, costing $3.25 each from the American Map Company. For the smallest roads for given areas, such as along the Mosel, or near large cities, Stagg suggests a few 1:50,000 maps. A line of those is printed by the German government, and another by Ravenstein. Write to Rudolf Rother (see section on Addresses and Further Reading) for the latter, asking about a specific area.

Except for the northern third, Germany has a varied topography: hills, winding rivers, and many heavily forested areas. The most known of the latter is the Black Forest, a broad region in the southwest. It's a satisfying touring area, if you're up to a lot of hill climbing on minor roads. The few main ones through it are filled with tourists and are too overdeveloped for pleasant cycling.

All cyclists commented on the excellent condition of roads. Surfaces are sound and gradients gradual. The secondary road system is well developed in all but the most mountainous areas, and you can always find some relief from a sudden influx of traffic. Road signs won't necessarily carry numbers, but towns will be clearly indicated. You'll find cobbles in some old parts of cities and in smaller towns and villages.

Bikepaths are not as common as in Holland, though they follow many main routes as along the Rhine. I usually found their surfaces better than in the Low Countries. Most were paved and there were few of the brick types found in Belgium, and often in Holland. Where they exist, you must ride on them. Look for a sign with a white bike on a blue circle, which indicates mandatory paths.

Even though a main highway may have no alternate bikepath, you may find that cycles are not allowed on it. I was stopped by a policeman on 12, a main road from Munich to Austria. He told me to get off the road, although that warning wasn't posted and there was no parallel road for me to take. Nor was there much traffic that time of year, September. After we looked at the map together and he realized that there were no real alternatives, he agreed that I should continue.

Besides the usual roads, a cyclist can ride *Wege*, access roads for farmers and forest workers. They're usually concrete, and autos are prohibited. A 1:50,000 map will show them.

153

BEST CYCLING TIME

Weather is pleasant and fairly stable throughout the cycling season. Evenings are cool in summer— Munich has an average low of about 53 for July and August, for example. It makes for good sleeping in a tent. Rain is evenly distributed from spring to fall. There's no appreciable prevailing direction of wind except on the northern coast, where it comes from the west.

As elsewhere, the vacation months have the most traffic. It's somewhat lighter, though, than in France or Italy, not because Germans travel less, but because they travel far—into France and Spain, as well as Scandinavia. Though there are crowds in resort places, in the Black Forest and Lake Constance, for example, you won't find the mass exodus from cities during weekends that you do in France.

BIKE EQUIPMENT, RENTALS

Both 27-inch and 700c tires are widely available, though not necessarily in the smallest towns. Wide-range freewheels are not, those above 28 teeth. But you can find Shimano, Sun Tour and European components easily enough. Good to excellent bike shops are common in cities. One of the best, according to Stagg, is Brugelmann's in Frankfurt. It's Germany's "Bike Warehouse."

Bikes can be hired at some 250 railroad stations. Fees are $4.50 a day, but a ticket allows a 50 percent reduction. You won't find them to your liking, the bikes being heavy recreation types. Bike rentals at good cycle shops may satisfy for a short, local tour, but might be inadequate for any hill climbing. Ten-speeds are scarce and their gearing will be on the high side.

Write to the tourist office or the German Cyclists' Association for any questions on rentals or biking matters.

BIKE TRANSPORTATION

Buses don't take bikes. A train with a baggage car will carry a bike, if you have a paid passenger ticket, to any destination in Germany for about $1.55. Ask for a bike ticket at the window, remove panniers (usually), and take the bike to the baggage car. The handlers load it. When leaving the country, you're advised to bring it a day early in order to have it arrive with you.

On two separate occasions that I shipped a bike—once from Munich to Strasbourg, France, and the other from Frankfurt to Czechoslovakia—it arrived with me, although at night the second time. The customs office wasn't open and I had to wait until morning. I watch the time of my arrival now. It's best to take a night

154

train. Saves on accommodations, too, as there's no problem stretching out on the seats.

GENERAL
ENTERING, LEAVING, HASSLES

No visa, just a passport.

A few questionnaire correspondents commented on the mirth with which people greeted them when they wore bike helmets. Otherwise, there were no comments about harassment, from either the public or officials.

On our swing through northern Germany in 1979 we noted some rude behavior on the part of young teenagers, who guffawed at us and our laden bikes. When Rosemary Smith talked to them friendlily, their laughter soon turned to curiosity, and then to respect for our touring effort. People often came to us and offered to help when we stopped and looked lost. In one town we asked a woman for the way to a hostel. She started to explain, then went into her house for a bike and led us to the hostel.

Stagg points out that motorists must take driving courses, which include the rights of bicyclists, before they can get a license. And so German drivers are courteous, or at least respect your right to the road. You get no hassles on the road. By the same token, you're expected to act responsibly on the road; stop for red lights, signal, and generally follow the rules.

Germany is one of the safest countries in regard to dogs. They don't run loose, and are either on leash or under voice control of owners. I've never been chased by one in the country.

LANGUAGE AND PEOPLE

English is widely spoken, more so by the young and by city people.

Germans are an energetic people. What they sometimes lack in charm and patience, they make up by an almost compulsive sense of order (trains always on time), neatness and efficiency. Americans will probably find these qualities a pleasant change if they come from a Mediterranean country, where chaos often reigns.

But German manners may disconcert. On the northern trip that we took, they punched out their answers to us 10 decibels louder than necessary, accenting them with jabs of fingers in our direction. On the other hand, during two trips farther south I rode with young Germans who were among the gentlest of people. Still, my lasting impression of the people is that quality of brusqueness.

155

You'll be called Mister or Miss, rather than by a Christian name, at least by older people. The young have taken to first names, though, once they become friendly. When they're fellow bikers, certainly.

A small German town is dead by 10:00 P.M. Not dead like an American town where most places are closed down, but the boisterous young still hang out at the gas station or pizza joint. In Altotting or Husum, no one is about. I was told that local ordinances prohibit noise near bedtime, and police enforce it. It's peaceful but unnatural.

OVERALL COSTS

The half-dozen tourists who cycled 1978 to 1979 spent about $10 a day when mixing hosteling and camping, and cooking for themselves. With all hostels and cafe eating, the cost approached $20. The one person who rode with his bike club in a group tour spent $35, using hotels and restaurants. Smith and I spent $15 each. We used hostels, with meals, and we made a lot of pit stops for coffee and pastries. Costs in 1981 should range from $12 to $24, if not using hotels.

156
Money exchanges can be made from 6:00 A.M. to 10:00 P.M. at border railroad stations. They stay open for arrivals of international trains, also. Banks are open in the morning and a couple of hours in midafternoon, closed on weekends. No fee is charged when exchanging currency for marks.

Ration your letter writing. A 5-gram airmail letter (1/6 ounce) costs 75¢. You get a bargain if you make it longer. Up to 20 grams (7/10 ounce) it takes a $1.15 stamp. I didn't dare ask what it would take to mail a package, or even a roll of undeveloped film.

ACCOMMODATIONS

Doubles in small-town hotels, including a continental breakfast, start at $22 to $28. It's nearly impossible to do as well in a large city, where some searching will get you a double for $33 to $39. Singles will cost 25 percent less.

A tourist office, often near the railroad station, will help you find a room. It won't necessarily be a cheap one if you look late in the day or are in a popular area. Don't expect to take a bike into your room, though most places will have a safe place to store it.

Rooms in private homes are cheaper. A double can be as low as $11. Check with the local tourist office.

Germany is where the hostel movement started. Some 600 are scattered throughout, least thickly in the area above Munich. Even there, the farthest distance between two hostels is 50 miles. You can sleep in them for your whole stay, unless a hostel is full; school groups are ubiquitous and fill up the room fast. They're also loud and uncontrollable. Ian Davis advises you watch your baggage; the kids pilfer a lot. If you're older than 27 you may be bumped by a younger person, who has priority in German hostels until 6:00 P.M. In Bavaria, hostels can't be used at all by those over 27. No camping on grounds.

Hostels vary in price from $3.75 to $4.75, depending on the standard of comfort. The ones we stayed at all had hot showers and were very clean. Family rooms were rare, but dorms usually had only four bunks to a unit.

Many hostels have a mandatory breakfast, which adds $2.50 to the price. The breakfast is a skimpy one, and you can buy the ingredients cheaper yourself. Dinner's aren't a bad idea, though, at $2.50 to $4. Check first, as they're often just cold cuts. Lack of cooking facilities is the greatest drawback to German hostels. You're thrown into restaurants or forced to eat hostel meals.

Bikers recommended these hostels: Husum (delicious food, quaint and historic building); St. Goar (excellent meals); Bernhastel-Kues (excellent meals); Munich/Miesingstrasse (comfortable); Rothenburg-Spitalhof (good facilities); Pullach (easy atmosphere, late curfew); Nordlingen (clean, modern); Bonn-Bad Godesberg (great setting); Bonn (modern, comfortable, nice setting); Celle (good facilities); Cochem (not crowded since inconvenient to hitchers, good meals); Hannover (clean, modern, friendly staff); Reinhardswald (pleasant setting, friendly staff); Berleburg (remote and not crowded, friendly); Freudenstadt (pleasant, comfortable, friendly warden); Titisee/Veltishof (beautiful, atmosphere, highly recommended); Freiburg (beautiful, fabulous, and not crowded).

157

Not recommended: Bremerhaven (large and regimented); Dinkelsbul (no showers); Munich/Wendl-Dietrichstrasse (regimented); Rothenburg-Rossmuhle (no hot showers); Trier (noisy); Kassel (large rooms, uncozy); Koln (run by a Valkyrie—beware! crowded).

Send for a camping map and leaflet from the national tourist office. For more detail, buy the camping guides printed by the Deutscher Camping Club. Camps cited in the leaflet are recommended by the German government and are more expensive, from $4.50 to $7.50 for two in a tent. Showers are commonly extra. A car or caravan is charged the same as a pup tent, but you might get a break from a sympathetic manager. Less well-equipped camps, run by cities or individuals, can be cheaper.

Hot showers at all camps, apparently. Some arrangement is there for food, a provision store, restaurant, or both. Kitchens at many places.

The choice between stays at hostels or campgrounds depends on your eating preference. Since you can't cook meals in hostels, you'd spend more in restaurants, unless you eat out of cans. Camps can be as expensive as hostels, but you'd save money in the long run by cooking.

Open camping is forbidden officially, but some of the bike tourists camped occasionally. I did a few times without being challenged. It's certainly acceptable when permission is asked of the owner of a field or wood.

FOOD

Restaurants open around 11:00 A.M. and serve what is considered the main meal of the day until 2:00 P.M. They begin dinner at 5:00 P.M. In between, most are open but the fare is limited. Fast-food stands *(snell imbiss)* sell wurst, french fries, potato salad, and occasionally hamburgers.

Budget meals in restaurants start at about $7. Fish is fairly cheap in the north, and a wurst, sauerkraut and potatoes are reasonable anywhere. You can buy snacks at street stands for $1.70. McDonald's will serve as an antidote if you have a "Big Mac" attack. The hamburger outlets are proliferating in the country. A small beer is 60¢, a glass of wine about 80¢ and a cup of coffee $1 to $1.70.

Supermarkets are everywhere and have the best prices. You'll find it easier to shop in them instead of small stores, if you don't speak German. Quality of food is high. Try the many excellent sausages and good cheeses. Prices are reasonable considering the alternative of restaurants. German bread is excellent and pastries are good, so you can stuff yourself with those carbohydrates, at least.

Stores open 8:00 to 8:30 A.M. and close some time after 6:00 P.M. during weekdays. In small towns they close after lunch for a couple of hours. Saturday closings are at 2:00 P.M. except the first Saturday in the month when they stay open until 6:00 P.M. or so. In tourist areas store hours may be longer, and shops may be open Sundays.

Camping Gaz C-200 cartridges are very common. Kerosene is extremely difficult to find.

ADDRESSES AND FURTHER READING

German National Tourist Office
630 Fifth Avenue
New York, NY 10020
and

GERMANY (WEST)

Broadway Plaza, Suite 1714
700 South Flower Street
Los Angeles, CA 90017

German Cyclists' Association (Bund Deutscher
    Radfahrer)
Otto-Fleck-Schneise 4
6000 Frankfurt/Main 71

Deutscher Camping Club
Mandlstrasse 28
D 8000 Munich

Rudolf Rother
Postfach 57
8 Munich 19

George Bailey, *Germans* (New York: Avon, 1974). A probing examination of what makes the German go—the pluses and minuses, the contradictions, energy and tragedy of their drives. Very able, a fair treatment, and interesting.

Michelin Green Guide, $7 in U.S.

GREECE
18

BIKING MATTERS
SUGGESTED TOUR

Peloponnesus loop; 595 miles, two to three weeks depending on sightseeing. Almost all on main roads, the tour is still difficult in parts. It follows, for the most part, the route taken in 1978 by Tyler Folsom and Venita Plazewski.

Leave Athens on the street Petrou Rali to Perama, some 10 miles west. A ferry takes you to the island of Salamis. If you get into the airport too late to do any cycling that day, stay over at the Voula campground. It's well equipped and can be found easily by referring to the tourist office pamphlet "Pireus—Apollo Coast."

Cross the island of Salamis and take another ferry to the mainland, then Megara. Ride west to Corinth. You've entered the large peninsula of Peloponnesus, full of archaeology, picturesque villages and mountains. Weeks can be spent exploring it.

Take the road south to Navplion and Argos, through Loutro Elenis and Ligourio (names will be spelled differently on maps, whether Greek or anglicized). Now south along the coast to Leonidio. This is not the usual tourist route to Sparta, and it will have less traffic.

Take a minor road southeast through Kosmas (at close to 4,000 feet, the high point of the mountains). It becomes rougher as you go along. The last part, before Geraki, is dirt. Swing west to Sparta.

From here, cross the rest of the peninsula, through Kalamata, to Pilos. The main road, more or less along the coast, will take you through Kipaissia and Pirgos to Patra. Side roads can be taken, either inland or to the shore, but most are likely to be rough, though ridable.

Take a ferry across to the mainland a few miles northeast at Rion. Cycle the main road along the shore east to Itea. Swing north and east on a secondary road to Delphi and then Livadia. Another main road leads through Thiva to Athens.

160

GREECE

For easy cycling, you can ride the northern shore of Peloponnesus from Rion to Corinth, and retrace your route to Athens. This road

parallels a toll road that takes much of the traffic. It has few places of interest, other than the villages themselves.

This tour can connect with Italy or Yugoslavia either at Patra or by cycling to Corfu, where ferries arrive from those countries. The main road along the coast from Corfu to Athens is fairly easy.

Another tour possibility, easy cycling but with much interest, is from Athens to Thessaloniki (Salonica) in the northeast. A national highway goes there, but a number of more interesting secondary roads are better: along the large island of Evia, north of the peninsula on which Athens rests, and parallel roads to about 20 miles north of Larissa. Above there, you'll have to take the highway most of the way.

That main highway had occasional bikepaths when I rode it. Otherwise, I saw no signs forbidding bikes, and police passed me without saying anything. But the highway was uninteresting and bypassed villages. I soon left it.

Except for Crete, none of the islands offers enough roads for an extended tour. They're pleasant for stays, of course, and a bike is handy for local transportation.

MAPS, TERRAIN, TRAFFIC

162

The Greek National Tourist Organization's 1:1,000,000 map is useful for planning purposes. The tourist office will also send a very good map of Athens.

The Geographia 1:1,000,000 doesn't show much more. A Freytag and Berndt 1:600,000 can be bought in-country. So can Esso maps.

The country is mountainous, the ranges running northwest to southeast. The only flat areas (relatively, since they still have local hills) are south of Larissa and in the immediate area of Thessaloniki. The country is abundantly indented with coves and small spits of beach that make for a great variety of scenery.

The main road surfaces are good. So are secondary roads in the plains. But mountain roads will be rough stone or dirt and you won't get far on them. Most secondary roads there go only for limited distances. The best bet to avoid traffic on main roads is to limit your touring to early spring or late fall, when fewer tourists come.

BEST CYCLING TIME

Mid to late April is about the start of good touring in most of the country, a bit earlier around Athens and south. The weather is good through October. Rains come in November and last until March.

Summer is hot everywhere, and it's full of tourists. Greece has two-thirds as many foreign visitors each year as its population. A third of it is in the Greater Athens area, and many of the tourist crowds come there, too.

BIKE EQUIPMENT, RENTALS

Athens has a few good bike shops near the National Museum, on Stadiou Street, for example. They have a full line of 10-speed parts, except wide-range freewheels and small chainrings. I was able to buy 27-inch tires there, and I saw those in other cities and towns.

Bike rentals are supposed to cost about $2 a day, according to the tourist office. I never saw any so I don't know what kind of bikes they have, but I doubt they'd be satisfactory for Greek mountains.

BIKE TRANSPORTATION

Trains and ferries take bikes without an argument. I had to talk a bus driver into taking my bike a short way to Kavala when I had trouble with a rack and needed some hardware. Robert Woods was refused bike transportation on a bus, also. There seems to be no clear policy on this; other bikers wrote me that their bikes were taken on buses without question.

163

GENERAL
ENTERING, LEAVING, HASSLES

Passport, no visa.

The machismo of the rest of the Mediterranean is not as strong here, probably because of the number of tourists. Traditions are still strong, however, and single women may be considered fair game by Greeks on the make. In some of the smaller remote villages, Western women may be stared at, but seldom are bothered.

LANGUAGE AND PEOPLE

English is common in tourist areas and in large towns, not in peasant villages. The Greek alphabet may be used on some signs and you should become familiar with it. It's similar to the Cyrillic; if you learn one, pay attention to the other, also. Signs along roads are poor and they may be in the Greek alphabet. You may have to ask directions, so learn a few phrases.

My impression of Greeks was that they were neutral to tourists, sometimes disdainful. The fact that I was on a bicycle seemed to make little difference in their attitudes. They were most interested in me when they learned I planned to go to Turkey. They were then concerned, warning me with a knife-to-throat gesture. Later, the Turks gave me the same warnings about Greeks.

There's more warmth in places off the tourist path. Those places will be hard to find if you stick close to the national highways, from which cars take a lot of side trips. Make local inquiries about the condition of minor roads, but even if the surfaces are bad they may be better choices than main ones.

A promising touring area is in the mountains of the north, across from Corfu to Thessaloniki. It's tough cycling, but few tourists go there.

OVERALL COSTS

It's one of the cheapest countries in Europe, if you're willing to forgo constant stays in hotels and if you camp. With a combination of those and some cafe eating, you can get along for as little as $7.50 a day, sharing costs with another. That's away from Athens and tourist-oriented places, of course.

Cheap prices may be on their way out. It was reported in a *New York Times* article in May 1980 that tourist officials will try to discourage visitors with lower incomes by raising prices significantly.

164 Hotel prices for 1980 had already risen almost 20 percent by the time of that pronouncement. Still, if the bike tourist doesn't stay at that many hotels, his costs shouldn't be too much higher. The dollar cost of the Greek drachma didn't rise between 1978 and 1980.

Tyler Folsom warns of buying traveler's checks in Greece. You pay two ways: a 1 percent commission on the checks themselves, and a further loss when dollars get exchanged to drachmas and the drachmas to traveler's checks. Banks are open 8:00 A.M. to 1:30 P.M. weekdays.

ACCOMMODATIONS

A double in an Athens hotel, often with bath and air conditioning and including breakfast, could be had for $30 in 1979. Rooms without the amenities are always cheaper, and so a double in a hotel can be as little as $7, and a room in a pension half that.

Prices are supposed to be fixed—they're posted in the room—but they can be discussed when tourists aren't plentiful. If you're traveling with a group, ten or more get a discount of 15 percent. The tourist office gives help in finding a room, and the Tourist Police are helpful at most large towns.

Hostels cost $1.70 in 1979. There are close to 30 of them in the country, but less than 20 on the mainland and not all convenient for bike tourists. For example, 7 of the 20 are on mountains from 3,000 to 8,000 feet high.

About a third of hostels have kitchens. Some allow camping at a nominal charge. Altogether, hostels can't be counted on for routine stays except in large cities, where they offer an advantage of a cheap price.

YMCAs in the largest cities can often be better than hostels. I stayed at the one in Thessaloniki for just a slightly higher cost, and I had a room to myself and no curfew. The place was nearly empty at the beginning of June.

Campgrounds are distributed a bit better than hostels, but most are along the shores. If your tour is shore bound, you can depend on them. They're run by either the National Tourist Organization of Greece (NOTG) or the Hellenic Touring Club.

The NOTG camps have showers, most have cooking facilities and restaurants, and some have shelters in case of rain. All these features are advantages for the bike tourist. They also offer power outlets, sports and amusements, of dubious value for bikers but for which they pay.

The Hellenic camps are more modest, though they usually have showers and food stores. NOTG charges about $3.75 for two in a tent, while Hellenic's are about half that. The NOTG camps also have huts for hire, for about $7.50 a couple. They're cheaper for each person when in a larger hut. Camping *carnets* get you a 10 percent discount.

165

Woods used many camps and liked them. He cited especially Nea Makri (friendly manager); Delphi (well equipped, view of valley); Itea (well maintained, excellent restaurant). He gave a "thumbs down" to only Olympia (scruffy looking).

Camping in the open is officially forbidden. Police pay no attention to this, unless provoked by flagrant disregard, near a highway or on a tourist beach. No biker reported any harassment.

FOOD

The cost of restaurant meals is also controlled, according to class. A third-class restaurant ranges in price from $3.60 to $4.80 (all prices 1980). In a village or small-town tavern, you can get a satisfying meal for $2.50. Restaurants serve late, past 8:00 P.M., and they're closed between 4:00 P.M. and then.

In mid-June, fruit trees ripen and fruit is abundant and cheap. Fill up on peaches, apricots and grapes. Watermelon costs only 8¢ or 9¢ a pound.

Beer is about 50¢ a bottle, but wine is a better buy at about $2 a bottle. Coffee is about 25¢ a demitasse.

There are plenty of cheap vegetables with which to cook, but meat is only somewhat lower, or the same price, as at home.

Selection away from large towns is limited, and you may have to do without or depend on canned meats or sausage for your base. Living out of cans is not the cheap way to go: a medium-size can of cooked beans costs 65¢, for example.

The staple cheese is *feta,* distinctive but easy to like. You can live off it, bread, tomatoes, onion and fruit. It's your best recourse in the absence of a good grocery store. Snacks of *souflaki* on pita bread, at about 30¢, are good fillers, too. You can buy them anywhere.

Grocery stores have odd hours, usually 8:00 A.M. to 2:00 or 3:00 P.M., and again in the evening on certain days of the week. Ask locally.

ADDRESSES AND FURTHER READING

Greek National Tourist Organization
Olympia Tower
645 Fifth Avenue
New York, NY 10022
and
627 West Sixth Street
Los Angeles, CA 90017

Automobile and Touring Club of Greece
2-4 Messogion Street
Athens, 610

Herbert Kubly, *Gods and Heroes* (New York: Doubleday, 1969). Anecdotal and very readable, but still a reflective account.

HOLLAND
19

BIKING MATTERS
SUGGESTED TOURS

With the greatest bicycle density in the world—two bikes for every three inhabitants—Holland would seem to be the best touring choice in Europe. It is for those sold on the safety of bikepaths, and for cyclists who enjoy riding in a country which is almost literally flat as a pancake.

Other bike tourists, who seek wildness or natural variety in terrain features, will be disappointed. After a couple of days, the novelty of riding along paths wears off. They yearn for some vantage point from which to look down at scenery, and are happy for the relative height of a dike.

Still, most of my questionnaire respondees were enthusiastic about Holland, with such remarks as: "Bikers are respected here; people are most hospitable; great for beginners." It's significant that the only serious complaint among those who liked the country was a remark about the lack of a bikepath for a few miles in the vicinity of one of the cities in the eastern part.

I'll not outline or suggest a route. Any route yields the same sort of riding, as such. Instead, I suggest that you read the standard tourist literature, or some other reference, and decide which cities or points of interest you'd like to see. Then just cycle between them.

The bikepath network is so extensive that you can't help but ride on it, even if you don't seek out a path. And the country is so full of history, museums, architecture, ancient towns, and, of course, windmills and people in traditional dress, that you should have no problem in finding something to your tastes.

MAPS, TERRAIN, TRAFFIC

A Michelin 1:400,000 shows all of Holland and costs $3 in the United States, and three sections of 1:200,000 are $2 each—all less from the CTC.

167

ADVENTURE CYCLING IN EUROPE

It seems hardly worthwhile to spend money on a map when the location and identification of Dutch roads are hardly the criteria in your cycling. The general, 1 inch = 10 miles map (about 1:635,000) that the Netherlands National Tourist Office provides

should be good enough; it shows the location of cities and towns and the main roads between them. You cycle on bike paths, guided by signposts.

The tourist office will send you also a cycling route map, about 1:850,000. That contains some of the principle routes in the country, the few of the thousands that are possible for cyclists. It also shows the main roads that are suitable for bikers. If you want more detailed cycling routes, you'll have to send for them from the Royal Dutch Touring Club (ANWB). They print a series with a scale of 1:100,000 and sell them directly or through in-country tourist offices (designated by the initials, VVV).

The Stichting: Fiets! is another source of information about cycling routes. This cycling organization sells a 72-page pocket atlas of maps and bike routes for about $8.

But you can always get information on local routes from the nearest VVV office, located all over the country. Or you can simply follow your nose and the ubiquitous signs for cycle paths.

There are three basic signs. A white bike outline on a round, blue background means a mandatory bikepath. A black horizontal rectangle with "Fietspad" printed on it indicates an optional bikepath, and you can use the roadbed if you wish. The ordinary signpost **169** showing distances between towns includes directions and mileages for cycling routes as well as for cars. Those for bikes are a white background with red lettering and a red bike outline.

Bikers even have separate traffic lights, as do pedestrians. They're always provided for in the transportation system. If not allowed over a bridge, for example, a ferry will take them. The road tunnel under the Maas River, at Ondor, even has a separate tunnel for bike users. Escalators at both ends take them up and down to the tunnel.

Holland's highest elevation is 1,050 feet, in the extreme southeast. The average elevation is a little over 30 feet. In fact, a lot of the time you might be riding below sea level, where one-fourth of the country lies.

You could cross Holland in any direction in about two days, if you were able to cycle in a straight line. But you can't, not if you travel bikepaths. They meander, crisscross roads repeatedly, are often filled with mopeds and pedestrians, and frequently are constructed of large stone blocks or uneven bricks—all detrimental to a brisk pace.

Traffic is no problem, unless you include the periodic congestion of cyclists themselves. That happens mostly in urban areas and during school commuting hours. It's refreshing, in a way: better by far to rub elbows with bikers than with trucks.

BEST CYCLING TIME

Temperature variation is not profound in Holland, but most months have some rain or mist for half the days. And so, even a few degrees of warmth make a difference in comfort. We found the moist cold penetrating at the start of May, although it could not have been much below 50°F. We would have been better off to wait a few weeks before starting. The amount of rain increases during July and on to October.

Winds are reputed to be strong from the west, but we didn't note that. It may have been because we were traveling northeast and we were inland, away from the open land next to the sea.

BIKE EQUIPMENT, RENTALS

This land of bikes is a haven of 1-speeds—high black monsters that haven't been seen in the United States since before World War II. A small percentage of 3-speeds are seen here, and even fewer geared machines, the last manned by serious racer types. Except for foreigners, I never saw a woman on a 10-speed.

The country is riddled with bike shops—5,500 reported by Stichting: Fiets! Most 10-speed components are available, though not everywhere. You'll have to settle for a Presta valve tube if buying a replacement, so have an adapter if you own a Schrader type of pump.

Rentals are offered by bike shops, railway stations and by regional bike tour organizations. Costs start at about $10.50 a week, and depend on the quality of bike. If you want an exhaustive list of bike hiring firms, the Stichting: Fiets! will sell you almost 800 addresses for about $2.50. It almost goes without saying that most of the rentals will be heavy 1-speeds, but in this kind of country you don't need a Masi.

For information about organized tours write to the Netherlands National Tourist Office. They'll send "Holiday on Two Wheels" and further details for tours, with or without rentals.

BIKE TRANSPORTATION

Trains with baggage cars will take bikes. You handle the bike. No bicycles on buses.

GENERAL
ENTERING, LEAVING, HASSLES

No border problems; just bring a passport.

Like Denmark, Holland is a permissive country. Youths find it a fun place; there are six nudist beaches, and hedonism is almost institutionalized. But the Dutch are cracking down on the influx of drug use, so be warned.

You'll not be considered an oddity on a bike, of course, though you will stand out from the utility bikes with your 10-speed and touring baggage. A lot of my respondees commented on the mirth with which Hollanders greeted them when they wore bike helmets.

LANGUAGE AND PEOPLE

Much English spoken, especially by the young, and you'll not want for communication. With a past heritage of sea trade and colonization, the Dutch have always been internationally minded. They don't hesitate to enter into conversation and to offer to help you. The outstanding instance I remember is when I was lost in a suburb of Dordrecht and asked an elderly man the way to Amsterdam. He said he didn't know the streets in the area, but that he'd find out for me. He hobbled into the middle of the street and waved down the first car that came along. The couple in it started to explain the way, but decided to show me. They took a U-turn—they were actually headed the other way themselves—and told me to draft the car. I did, for about 3 miles, while they made all kinds of turns and finally deposited me on the main bikepath that would lead to the capital. Other bike travelers can tell of similar experiences in Holland, I'm sure.

171

OVERALL COSTS

A half-dozen bike tourists reported daily costs of $8 to $10 in 1979. They split their stays at hostels and official campgrounds. Eating was also divided, between restaurants and self-cooked meals.

Costs in 1981 should be only about $1 a day higher. The Dutch guilder rose a few percent more, relative to the dollar.

ACCOMMODATIONS

Cheap hotels in the cities can be found for $11 a person. Better ones will be considerably more. The tourist office will book you a room for a $1.50 fee.

Eight of the largest cities have sleep-ins. A list of them is printed in the tourist office's "Holland Likes You." They're just what they're named; nothing but a bunk to lie down on for $3. Co-ed. Watch your belongings.

Fifty hostels are distributed fairly evenly about the country. They are probably the best choice for indoor sleeping, but their practice of a mandatory breakfast is irritating and a poor value. Cost per person averages $5, and a bed goes up to $8 in some places.

Dorms are the rule, some of them in rustic lofts. We found them always clean. Just before schools let out, in June, classes of kids may be there for group holidays; they may keep you up half the night. I heard of no hostels with family rooms for couples.

Only a half-dozen have kitchens. Bathrooms may be primitive, but there's usually a cozy meeting room where you'll find international travelers with whom to talk. Bike security is adequate; lock your bike and remove all valuables, anyhow, whether the bike is placed inside or in an outside open shed.

Best-liked hostels: Valkenswaard (modern, good facilities); Bunnik (beautiful setting, convenient to Utrecht); Schoorl (pleasantly situated in the dunes); den Oever (little but fabulous, at sea dike); Arnhem (good facilities); Sneek (good breakfast); Kortenhoef (on piles over water, pleasant, but primitive shower); Putten (big dining area, relaxed); Meppel (very good, can use kitchen).

Bad marks were given to Scheemda (regimented, noise), and den Haag (good setting, but the food was plastic and no seconds given).

Campgrounds are numerous. The ANWB's "Camping Holland" lists addresses, and the local tourist offices will steer you to the nearest one. Usually no camping *carnet* is asked for, but some do require it.

Campgrounds are sophisticated, with stores and even a restaurant here and there. They're very clean. Cost is as low as $1.50 a night for each person, more often $3. Showers are extra. A few have only cold water.

Holland is not a country for free camping. It's not allowed, to start with, and difficult in any case. Land is valuable and is developed highly, either in homes, cultivated fields, or business establishments. Someone might let you camp on their postage-stamp-size lawn—most homes and lots are doll-like—but it's doubtful. You're more likely to be able to camp in the open along some of the beaches, or the somewhat less populated eastern border with Germany.

FOOD

Eating out can raise costs dramatically. A three-course, fixed-price menu is $6.50; that's the best you can do for a regular meal. Sandwich shops will allow cheaper eating, but they're no bargain; you can buy the ingredients yourself at less cost. The best values for hot meals are either Chinese or Indonesian restaurants, those at train stations or the sidewalk stands.

But don't discount stopping at a cafe, even if you don't eat there. You can stretch a cup of coffee in a pleasant atmosphere an hour or longer, while you read, write, or just watch the goings-on.

172

The hostel breakfast that you get as part of the lodging price is bread and butter, chocolate sprinkles or a spread (surprisingly good), jam, a couple of slices of cheese and pressed ham, and tea. It doesn't vary from hostel to hostel; you never get an egg or cereal.

Supermarkets are only somewhat higher than in the United States—Spar markets are good—and you can buy food reasonably in an expensive country. Even if you don't have a stove, delicatessen dishes and meats, smoked fish, bread, cheese and fruit let you eat well. Stores are open six days, 8:00 A.M. to 6:00 P.M., mostly closed Monday mornings. Watch the holidays, too, which might catch you without food.

ADDRESSES AND FURTHER READING

Netherlands National Tourist Office
576 Fifth Avenue
New York, NY 10036
and
681 Market Street, Room 941
San Francisco, CA 94105

Stichting: Fiets!
Europaplein 2
Amsterdam

173

Royal Dutch Touring Club (ANWB)
Wassenaarseweg 220
The Hague

Anthony Bailey, *The Light in Holland* (New York: Knopf, 1970). What makes Hollanders tick, by an unusually perceptive observer. Readable and intelligent.

HUNGARY
20

BIKING MATTERS
SUGGESTED TOUR

Western Hungary; 440 miles, two weeks (or three, with layovers at the Danube bend and Lake Balaton). Tibor Pollerman took this tour in 1979. He, Donald Lemmon, and Zbigniew Zur provided most of the material for this chapter.

Leave Budapest on highway 11, and cycle around the Danube loop and into Esztergom. It's simply beautiful in this part of the Danube Valley. You can ferry across at Visegrad and stay at a campground or at hotels in the area to relax a day or two.

Continue on 11 along the Danube. It'll join with 10. At Almasneszmely go south to Tata. Keep south on an unnumbered road, first to Oroszlany, then a few miles west and south to Mor. Still on an unnumbered road, west through Szapar to Zirc. Turn south on 82 to Veszprem. Another unnumbered road goes southwest to Tapolca.

Now directly south to Lake Balaton, where you reach highway 71. Campgrounds are here and you can rest a while in a resort area. Ride west to Keszthely, and south on 71 and 68 through Marcali to the intersection with 61 at the village of Bohonye. Turn left to Kaposvar. Change to 66 there and ride southeast to Pecs.

No bikes are allowed on 58 at rush hours (7:00 to 9:30 A.M. and 4:00 to 6:30 P.M.). Avoid those hours or take alternate roads to Harkany, just a few miles away from the Yugoslav border. Turn east through the town of Siklos to the village of Villany. Just beyond it, swing north and east to Mohacs. All but the last bit on 57 are unnumbered. Two famous battles were fought at Mohacs against the Turks, the first disastrous and the second victorious.

Cross the Danube, staying on 57, and then turn north on 51 to Baja. If time is short, you can take a train here for the 100 miles to Budapest. Or cycle it on 51, continually along the Danube.

HUNGARY

MAPS, TERRAIN, TRAFFIC

Budapest's Cartographia Company prints a Hungary 1:500,000, as well as the "Road Atlas of Hungary," 1:360,000. The first costs $1.25 in Hungary and is more than adequate. However, the second has 100 pages of much more useful information: 40 pages of Hungary, town maps, lists and locations of hotels and campgrounds, shops, and points of interest. Texts are in English, Hungarian,

German, French and Russian. It costs $5 in-country but may be available by mail from Kartografiai Vallalat.

A Geographia 1:525,000 can also be bought in the United States for $6 from the Complete Traveller. But maps are much cheaper in Hungary.

Hungary is one vast plain, except for a line of low mountains running northeast to southwest of Budapest, and some hills in the south, above Pecs. Avoid the plains, which of themselves have about as much interest as the miles of cornfields in Kansas. (There's an amazing amount of corn grown in Hungary.) The villages and towns are worth seeing, but the terrain soon palls.

The highest peak has an elevation of just over 3,000 feet, but a few of the roads have sharp grades. The worst climbs, in some of the most lovely terrain, are north of Eger, northeast of Budapest. According to Zur, who has cycled there for years, it's the best touring region in Hungary. It has caves, vineyards, local folklore and castles, besides great scenery.

Roads are excellent, all those marked on the maps as "surfaced, dust-free." Pollerman says that the secondary roads he cycled were much smoother than those in England, and they had very little traffic. Lemmon called the roads he traveled excellent, those from Budapest through Szolnok to the Romanian border at Gyula. Gerard van der Veer cycled much the same roads and agreed. So did I, using northern roads between Czechoslovakia and Austria.

Traffic is very light on minor roads, sometimes nonexistent. Main roads are also light, except in the vicinity of large cities on Sunday afternoons, when cars pile up for miles with weekend returnees. You'll meet cows and farm wagons, even on main roads, during the week.

Bicycles are not allowed on main roads, those of single-digit numbers. My correspondents found, as did I, that although police sometimes stopped them they'd not press the issue, not being able to explain what other roads could be taken. There are plenty of good secondary roads to take with no need to travel the main highways, anyhow. The minor roads are where you see how people live.

Budapest has a lot of cobblestone streets and traffic, and it's best not to use your bike within the city. Stretches of cobblestones are in some towns and villages, too.

BEST CYCLING TIME

Hungary has a long autumn, and cycling is good well into October. April is just warm enough, too. May and June are the wettest months, though October has some heavy rains, also, in the southwest. There's hardly any rain in summer. The driest part is the east, which is also the hottest in summer. Winds are light, with no dominant direction.

Traffic is hardly a factor. Hungary gets as many tourists a year as her population—a surprising fact in this seemingly unknown vacation country—but the bulk of those come to the Lake Balaton region or to the capital. And a large proportion of them are from Eastern Europe. I saw almost no foreign car plates in the north in September.

That tourists come to Budapest is not surprising: all who were there were taken by it, and van der Veer, a Hollander, called it the most beautiful capital in Europe. If you stay away from the capital or from the lake, where accommodations are harder to find, a summer trip can be pleasant. Visit the mountains where it's cooler.

BIKE EQUIPMENT, RENTALS

I saw no bike shops at all. Parts were available in auto parts, hardware and department stores, but they were for utility bikes. Those, and small-wheeled, heavy folding bikes, are what you see natives using.

177

Some 10-speed parts may be available in Budapest—there are bike racers in the country—but none of my informants knew that from personal experience. Alan Bubna said shopkeepers wouldn't believe his 27 X 1⅛-inch tires had tubes. They tried to sell him tubulars. Bring all spares with you.

Mechanics and blacksmiths are talented in improvising repairs and they're helpful. It's doubtful that you can rent anything resembling a touring bike anywhere in the country.

BIKE TRANSPORTATION

A bike doesn't necessarily travel on the same train as a passenger, but it usually arrives the same day. Pollerman was charged $2.40 to take his bike on a regular train for 120 miles. For an optional express, it costs an extra $1.50. Unlike in Poland, a bike can be checked at a baggage room in a railroad station for a few days while you visit a city.

Buses don't have luggage space for bikes. Ferries cross the Danube frequently. A crossing cost me 8¢. Pollerman used a bike carrier bag to send his bicycle home from the airport. It avoided any problems with ticket clerks in handling it.

GENERAL
ENTERING, LEAVING, HASSLES

A passport and a visa are required. For latest requirements— fee, photos, application—check with your travel agent or write directly to the Hungarian embassy or consulate.

Although a visa can theoretically be gotten at the border, in practice that's a poor idea. You'll have to wait, at the least, and may run into bureaucratic wrangles. There are no provisions to get a border visa when coming in by train. Get one in advance and be sure of easy entrance.

I wasn't searched at the border, either entering or leaving. Harvey Lyon was just waved in when he came by plane, but was subjected to a lot of red tape with customs officials when taking his bike out by train. When at borders, ignore the long lines and ride right up to the guards. They'll take care of you without a wait.

Once in the country, you're likely to be stopped for a passport check, especially near borders. I was stopped on the road twice almost immediately after entering and twice again on my last day near the Austrian border. On both days my examiners were auxiliary police in plain clothes. They were polite, though they spoke no English except "passport," and they didn't hold me long. It was very mysterious and I couldn't find out why.

Since then, Pollerman wrote me that he was stopped, also, near Yugoslavia, where they were looking for smugglers and black marketeers who work across border areas. He speaks Hungarian, and that's what the officials told him.

In the middle of the country, there's no problem with police in any way. No one watches or follows you.

You're supposed to register with the police within 24 hours of entering, but not abiding by that doesn't seem to be crucial. At least, it wasn't for me. My visa wasn't stamped until the third day when it was done by the manager of a campground where I stayed. There were no consequences. I didn't ignore the regulation purposely, in any case; no one told me and I didn't read the application or travel folder carefully. But stay on the safe side and register.

LANGUAGE AND PEOPLE

Part of the same language family as Finnish, Hungarian is hard to learn. Without a formal course, you're not likely to get past a few phrases.

German is by far the most useful second language, but van der Veer suggests that if you speak it, make it clear that you're not German. English is known by only an educated few, mostly the young and in the largest cities. Even in tourist offices, you'll seldom find someone who knows it.

Still, people are friendly to Westerners, even if there's no verbal communication. This is evident in stores and cafes where you're helped, and on the road when people approach you as you look at a map. Van der Veer says, probably a bit cynically, that much of this friendliness is tied to a business interest, that is, black market money exchanges or buying of Western goods. That may be somewhat true, since I saw a few transactions going on between tourists and waiters in cafes.

OVERALL COSTS

I spent $5 a day in 1979, sleeping in campgrounds and in the open, and eating suppers in cafes. Pollerman spent the same amount under the same conditions, sharing expenses with a companion. So did Bubna in 1977, with a mix of various accommodations and cafe meals. Lemmon spent $15 a day, eating all meals in cafes and sleeping in private apartments that he booked through the tourist offices, and in motels that he found himself. Prices in 1981 shouldn't be more than about $1 a day higher. With Turkey, this has to be **179** one of the cheapest countries in Europe to tour.

Hungary doesn't require a minimum daily exchange of currency as it once did, and as other Eastern Bloc nations still do. Its money is at a pretty stable rate, though there is some black market demand for Western money. The fact that you get only a small advantage on that market—on the order of 25 forints for a dollar, compared to 20 officially—shows the greater strength of the Hungarian economy over that in Poland or Czechoslovakia. More favorable black market exchanges can be found, but many of those offers are from the police, who will entrap the unwary. Bubna says a 3:1 or higher ratio can be found, but that there's no need to trade on the street—a bank in Vienna gives almost that much.

ACCOMMODATIONS

Stay away from the state-run Ibusz hotels. Their cheapest doubles in regional hotels cost about $20, and more in Budapest (all accommodations prices 1980). A double in a moderately priced hotel, away from Budapest or a resort, can be had for $12.50. For $5 or less, two can get a room in a private home. That can be arranged through a tourist agency, or you can deal directly with the owner when you see his "to-let" *(szoba kiado)* sign. A train station or bus terminal in a resort or a small town may have the name and address of a person who arranges locally for tourist rooms.

Budapest has 8 hostels and there are 14 more in the rest of the country, all in large cities or resorts. They're not cheap—$3 to $6—they don't have kitchens, and no camping is allowed at any. They're also liable to be booked by groups (individuals can't reserve), and travelers under 30 have priority.

Distances between hostels are not great, but their locations may mean you'd have to go out of your way during your tour. Hostels should be considered only an additional accommodation, not the mainstay. As a couple, you're actually much better off to stay at hotels or private rooms.

Scores of campgrounds are located selectively around the country. A third of them line Lake Balaton. Most of the rest are near border crossings and in the western mountains. The only ones in the eastern plains are at towns and cities.

Prices vary depending on category and services, such as swimming pools. Most have hot water. About $5 for two in one tent is the average cost, assuming the official exchange. Holders of camping *carnets* get a 20 percent discount. The same discount holds at the beginning or end of the season. Camps open in early May and close in mid or late September.

180

Holiday chalets, with two to four beds in a room and no special amenities, and fully equipped bungalows can also be rented. Inquire at the tourist office.

Camping in the open is illegal. I camped on river banks and in woods, and once with a German companion in a cemetery. No one interfered. Pollerman also camped in the open and he saw others doing it, so the authorities must ignore it. I believe they're more apt to enforce the regulation with motor campers, who are likely to damage the terrain and who are more obvious.

You'll get permission to camp on someone's property easily enough, if you can make your wishes known, of course. Zur, a Polish bike tourist I met and befriended in Czechoslovakia, told me he never takes either a tent or sleeping bag when he cycles in Hungary. He depends on being allowed to sleep in barns or in spare rooms of farms and village hosts. Although he speaks no Hungarian, he makes his requests in sign language. "Where there is intelligence, there is communication," he told me. Invariably, he is not only invited into the home to sleep, but is also fed supper and breakfast, too. He always offers to pay, but has never been accepted. His is a daring logistics strategy, but it tells something of the hospitality given by Hungarian peasants.

FOOD

A full meal for two, with wine, at a well-known restaurant in Baja cost Pollerman $5. It would be more in Budapest. I usually

HUNGARY

spent $1.50 to $2 for a complete meal in a small restaurant or big city cafeteria, including a veal cutlet or chicken paprikash or some such meat. There was always more than enough to satisfy my hunger, which can get voracious after a day's cycling.

Hostels serve a package of three meals for $3 to $5. Bistros sell baked sausages for 50¢ a quarter-pound, including a large slice of bread and a spoonful of mustard. A pint of beer is 30¢. Hungary is a wine-producing country, and excellent types can be bought inexpensively. Food prices should be no more than about a fifth higher in 1981.

Visitors from other Eastern European countries, especially Poland, are common. They fill up on meat, which is both scarce and of poor quality in their own countries. As soon as they cross the border, they flock to shops to buy salamis and hams, and they gorge themselves in restaurants. Not only meat, but the other wonderful Hungarian foods appeal to them. Portions of the fanciest cream cakes (real cream), pastries, or strudel are seldom more than 25¢. Their quality is superb; the famous Austrian pastries were introduced from Hungary.

Foodstuff is very cheap, and you can cook for yourself for $1 a day. Fruit is vine or tree ripened. Cherries and strawberries sell at 32¢ a pound. Ice cream is sold at 5¢ a scoop. A bar of chocolate is 15¢. If you're crossing the border to Austria, stock up. Food there is four to five times as much as in Hungary.

Shop hours are as early as 6:00 A.M. and up to 6:00 or 7:00 P.M. Only the Lake Balaton region has stores open on Sunday.

ADDRESSES AND FURTHER READING

Tourist information is sent by the consulate:
Consulate General of the Hungarian People's Republic
8 East Seventy-fifth Street
New York, NY 10021

Hungarian Camping and Caravaning Club
VIII Ulloi ut 6
Budapest, 1085

Kartografiai Vallalat
Bosnyak Ter 5
Budapest XIV

Paul Ignotus, *Hungary* (New York: Praeger, 1972). A history of the nation by an authority. The writing style is somewhat turgid, and you certainly won't read it cover to cover, but it'll answer any questions of fact.

ICELAND
21

BIKING MATTERS
SUGGESTED TOUR

Although there are over 6,800 miles of roads in Iceland, only the 900 miles of the Ring Way (Hringveg) goes continuously around the island. On the others, you'd largely loop from the Ring Way, or go into dead-ends and have to retrace your way. Western Iceland has a wealth of alternative roads, if you'd rather not circle the island or ride across it. "Tracks" will take you through the interior, if you want to rough it. They're open to traffic at the end of June.

In 1979, André Everett rode counterclockwise from Reykjavik to Akureyri for over 700 miles, before his rack broke and he had to finish the tour. Most of the data in this chapter is from his notes.

About 100 miles of roads, radiating from Reykjavik, are paved. The paving may be only in the center and the sides of the road will be dirt. The rest of the island's roads are gravel, crushed lava, sand, mud, loose rocks, or snow. You'll pass glaciers so close to the road that you can throw stones at them. The conditions, road surfaces and weather range from good to bad. Some portions of road are terrible, according to Everett. Dick Phillips, a British authority on Iceland, says they're worst when grading is in progress, but it's unusual to encounter more than a couple of kilometers that are unridable.

Roads are not especially steep, but you may need a somewhat lower gear to overcome the greater resistance of the road surface. Says Everett: "It's a country for adventure, rough-stuff, nature, geology, birds, and cyclists. Definitely not for the hotel and restaurant crowd."

MAPS, TERRAIN, TRAFFIC

A 1:1,000,000 map of the whole island ($6), or a 1:750,000 sheet (about $13.50), would seem to suffice since there's only one road. But, points out Everett, that leads to problems. Iceland neglected putting numbers along it, and a side road may join the main one. You won't be able to tell one track from the other. Everett got lost once because of that; his map set him straight.

A compass does no good to tell direction. The needle goes berserk there, and you can't be sure of any reading. It's best to use landmarks shown on a detailed map.

The maps he used were the Island Ferdakort 1:250,000, four sheets, double sided. They're available at about $7.50 each in Iceland or from Dick Phillips (see the section on Addresses and Further Reading). Phillips is the best, charging about the same as in Iceland, and he's a source of various publications that are very hard to find elsewhere. Although he runs no bike tours now, concentrating on walking tours, his information is valuable to bike tourists.

Everett recommends you buy and study those maps before setting out. They're engraved, with fine detail, are well contoured, and show nearly every building in the country. If you buy them from Phillips, he'll mark positions of shops and accommodations on them, if you tell him the areas you'll visit.

Much of the southern coast is basically black gravel. Called the "wet desert" because the gravel is soaking in water, it has few people and little vegetation. Most of the country is treeless.

183

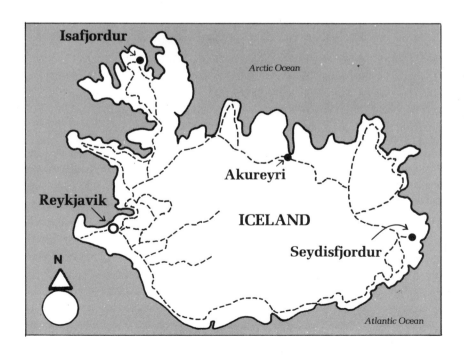

Traffic can be nearly nonexistent. Everett said he saw from ten vehicles an hour to five per day. The first Monday in August is a holiday and traffic may pick up somewhat.

BEST CYCLING TIME

June to August is satisfactory, but even in mid-July you may get winter weather. The average *maximum* daily temperature in July and August is 57°F. The longer days of June give you most daylight and the scenery is still "snowy" in appearance then, but some hostels don't open until the early part of that month, so check it out.

Most rainfall is in the extreme southeast and in the Reykjavik area. June is least rainy but the windiest. Winds can be fierce anytime, though, in the barren and open country. And you can have snow in June.

BIKE EQUIPMENT, RENTALS

184

You'll need wider tires than what's available for 27-inch wheels, according to Everett, both for comfort on the rough roads (two screws were shaken out of André's eyeglasses), and to avoid breakdowns. The practical choice is a 26 X 1¾-inch tire; better yet, 26 X 2¼ inches, at least for the rear wheel. An additional advantage of this size is that the tires are available there—only certainly in Reykjavik and Akureyri, though. Phillips believes you can get along on 27-inch wheels well enough.

But even Reykjavik has complete service just for 1- and 3- speeds. You'll not find cables, derailleurs, brake shoes, or any other spares you take for granted in shops at home. Other than tires, take spares with you. You're not likely to find rentals, either, except for 1-speed clunkers.

A solid carrier is needed to withstand the road battering. If you have a steel one, there are shops that can weld a break. Flats won't be as common as you'd expect, since there's very little glass, and no thorns.

Choose rugged components, not lightweight ones or those likely to be jammed by mud or grit.

BIKE TRANSPORTATION

Buses carry bikes, unboxed, for $1.50. They'll stop anywhere on their route. They don't run often, though. Iceland has no trains, and sea travel is impractical, being irregular and costly.

ICELAND

GENERAL
ENTERING, LEAVING, HASSLES

No visas or inoculations. If you're thinking of bringing in any food to beat the prices, leave out fresh meat; it's prohibited by customs. But dehydrated meat is allowed.

No problems of any kind otherwise, in a country that has no dangerous animals, no snakes, no mosquitoes, and no poisonous or itch-producing plants.

LANGUAGE AND PEOPLE

Except in farm country and remote places, English is common, and Danish and German are understood widely. Icelandic is specialized, a forerunner of other Scandinavian languages; it hardly pays to attempt learning it.

You'll find intelligent and civilized conversation with a literate people. The urban area of Reykjavik, with half of the island's population of 200,000, has more bookshops per capita than any other city in the world. The capital has 20 publishing houses and six newspapers.

People are completely trustworthy and open. Everett says the attitude of the natives was "friendly, mildly curious, and quite impressed by a bike tourist. Security is 100 percent."

Cities are smokeless, being heated almost exclusively by hot springs. Swimming in heated outdoor pools is a favorite sport in the capital.

185

OVERALL COSTS

Everett's living costs in 1979 were $6.30 a day, and he said he could have cut them somewhat by camping more. He used hostels about half the time. André took the trouble to learn Icelandic, and he was able to ask permission to camp on private property.

Ongoing inflation is high—an astounding 50 percent rate when Everett visited—so expect costs to mount yearly. However, Iceland's krona has been falling relative to the dollar, so the effect is tempered for American bicyclists.

Married couples and families get reductions on in-country air travel. A group of over a dozen can hire a private bus reasonably.

ACCOMMODATIONS

As elsewhere, camping will save you money. The law allows you to camp anywhere in the open, and farmers will usually allow you to camp on their land. You won't find a lot of grass though, says

Everett; rocks are the rule. Formal campgrounds, with basic facilities, exist only near sizable settlements. They cost about $3 for two people in a tent.

Some camping is almost necessary, in any case. Eighty percent of the land is uninhabited. Lack of facilities throughout the country would restrict your touring scope. Six youth hostels are on the mainland, two of them in the largest cities. They cost less than $4, have kitchens with electric hot plates and utensils, and provide hot showers (water smells like sulfur).

Unofficial hostels, called *svefnpokaplass,* are run informally in the summer. They charge varying prices. The ones controlled by the government have a standard rate of $11 a night (1980). Only a few have kitchens, and they may have hot showers. You might sleep on the floor in some of them, in your own bag. Write to the Icelandic Youth Hostel Association for a leaflet of their locations, or ask at the information office in the country or local people.

Dick Phillips runs one of the hostels at an old farm at Fljotsdalur, in the south-central farm area, about 85 miles east of Reykjavik. Says Everett: "It's in rustic shape, leaks in the rain, you may sleep in your own bag on the attic floor if the 15 beds are full, and its water is ice-cold, from a nearby stream. But it redeems itself in friendliness. Kitchen, too." Costs $2.25 in 1980.

Some government huts at passes are meant for snowbound drivers in winter. You can sleep there, but clean up afterward and use none of the fuel in them.

Icelanders feel a strong concern for their environment. Nature conservation signs, urging the visitor to respect nature, are posted in all national parks, reserves and protected areas.

Temporary, summer hotels in schools, all called "Hotel Edda," are run by the Government Tourist Office. In 1980 they were charging from $23 for a single to $38 a double, with shower. They serve no food. Private accommodations in Reykjavik cost $18 a single, $25 double, with breakfast, in 1979. Hotels started at over $20 single, without breakfast.

FOOD

Restaurant meals are expensive. Lunches start at $7 and dinners at $10 (all food prices, 1979). Cafeterias are cheaper, but a sandwich starts at over $2. Even if you can afford to eat that way, you'd have a problem in finding an eating place out in the country. And so, as with accommodations, you'll have to do for yourself.

Food shops can be found in any settlement of a dozen families. Knowing where they are ahead of time may save you from eating emergency cereal rations at supper. Ask. Shops may be part of a general store, but they'll contain the basics. Normal hours are 9:00 A.M. to 6:00 P.M. weekdays. They're closed weekends, so stock up. In Reykjavik and Akureyri, food chain stores stay open longer.

Kiosks are often attached to gas stations; they vary in what they sell, from junk food to many food items. They're open when food stores are closed, but don't count on them to supply complete supper food.

Prices are two to three times those of the United States, but such staples as rice, pasta and margarine are comparatively cheap. Lamb is the most common meat and is expensive. Even fish are costly. It may pay to bring some freeze-dried meats with you.

Farmers may sell you potatoes (if in season), eggs and milk. Stove fuel is available: "Esso Blue" kerosene, Bluet gas cylinders; and low-octane gasoline for multifuel stoves.

Water is safe everywhere, but streams with hot-spring sources and glacier rivers shouldn't be used. Beer is weak (1.8 percent) and expensive. Liquor is outrageously priced. Bring a bottle with you, make some tea and spike it. Only a few bars can be found anyway.

ADDRESSES AND FURTHER READING

187

Iceland National Tourist Office
75 Rockefeller Plaza
New York, NY 10019
        and
3600 Wilshire Boulevard
Los Angeles, CA 90010

Iceland Tourist Bureau
Ferdaskrifstofa Rikisins
Reykjanesbraut 6
Reykjavik

Icelandic Youth Hostel Association
Post Box 1045
Reykjavik

The English Bookshop
Snaebjorn Jonsson & Co., PO box 1131
Hafnarstraeti 4 og 9,
Reykjavik

ADVENTURE CYCLING IN EUROPE

Dick Phillips, Whitehall House
Nenthead, Alston
Cumbria, CA9 3PS
England (October to April, otherwise in Iceland)

André Everett
1919 "D" Street
Lincoln, NE 68502

Katherine Scherman, *Iceland — Daughter of Fire* (Boston: Little, Brown, 1976). The geography, history and culture of this unusual island. The best work on Iceland, by a skilled writer.
Iceland in a Nutshell, 4th ed., 1974. A soft-cover guidebook published in Reykjavik and available from Dick Phillips, about $3.25.

188

IRELAND
22

BIKING MATTERS
SUGGESTED TOUR

This tour is the one taken by Rich and Kathi Stafford in 1979. It loops around the western part of the country, up to 1,000 miles with side trips, and takes four weeks at an easy pace.

A small part of the route goes through a bit of western Northern Ireland. The Staffords said they were nervous in the region, with the sight of bombed-out buildings, armaments, and British military, but they didn't run into any problems themselves. That part of the tour can be bypassed, however, if you'd be concerned.

Start at Shannon Airport. You can store your bike box in the claim area until your return. It's standard practice at the airport.

Ride north to Ennis, where you can pick up tourist literature at the tourist office. Now northwest to Lisdoorvarna and the fishing village of Doolin. Have a Guinness and listen to some traditional Irish music at Gus O'Connor's pub. You can visit the Aran Islands from here, too. Five miles farther on, at Moher, are the cliffs—over 700 feet high, and you'll see the waves crashing below, against the rock face.

Head north and east across the Burren to Kinvara, a desolate area of barren limestone that has eroded over the centuries into fantastic shapes. Many Stone Age dolmens and mysteriously constructed cairns here, too. Continue through Oranmore and Headford on a level road to Cong, the setting 28 years ago of the movie, *The Quiet Man.*

Next cycle to Leenane, at the head of a 10-mile fjord, and then north to Westport, and on to Achill Island. Go over the bridge and around the island, a hauntingly misty place of sandy beaches and high, ragged cliffs. Retrace your route through Newport to the city of Ballina, or you can continue north from Achill and turn east at Bangor.

Now north to Ballyshannon and Donegal. Circle the peninsula, through Kilcar, to Ardara. Return to Donegal. Cross the border at **189**

Pettigo and circle Northern Ireland's Erne Lakes, returning to Ireland at Cavan. The Staffords went farther north, visiting relatives. You can skip Northern Ireland and just skirt the border on minor roads until you meet the national highway.

You can now ride that main road directly southeast to Shannon Airport, or take minor ones that parallel the main road. The attractive

town of Athlone is worth a stop. Deviate from the main road at Ballinasloe, at least, to cycle the western shore of Lough Derg through the picturesque village of Mountshannon. Return to Shannon.

MAPS, TERRAIN, TRAFFIC

Gary Conrad liked Geographia's Touring Map of Ireland, about 1:220,000, which he said was colorful and easy to read. You can buy it for about $6 from The Complete Traveller.

Bartholomew's series of five maps, 1:250,000, is also practical. Each map costs about $1.50. They're available from CTC. The Ordnance Survey 1:125,000 maps are too detailed and costly, while Geographia's International Series, Ireland 1:570,000 shows too little.

James Donlon, who has cycled in Ireland each of the last five years, has the best suggestion: buy the Shell road map that is sold there for 30¢. He finds it excellent.

Ireland is basin shaped and has mountains along the coast. Those are more formidable in appearance than in fact. Most ranges are below 2,500 feet and the highest peak is at 3,400 feet. But what it lacks in height, the terrain makes up in ruggedness. The western coast has steep cliffs and hundreds of small islands, which combine with the mists formed by the Gulf Stream to give a wild look to the land. The interior is mostly flat.

Almost all roads are narrow. Some are quite steep, but most hills are undulating. In the west the surfaces can be rougher. Jean and Hartley Alley thought roads in the southeast too rough for skinny tires. But roads overall are generally excellent in surface and condition.

Traffic can be heavy around Cork and Dublin and in places like the Dingle peninsula and the Ring of Kerry, where summer tourists throng. In the off-season you can meet sheep on a main road, as did the Staffords and Gary Conrad, the latter even encountering them on the road between Dublin and Cork.

The Alleys rode the southeast coast late August to mid-September. It had little traffic, not being promoted to tourists, and they found it pretty just the same. They said the B&Bs treated tourists better because they had little business.

Irish drivers are courteous and careful. That could stem from their being accustomed to a great number of utility bikes on the road, or from the natural gentleness of the natives.

BEST CYCLING TIME

The western coasts are considerably wetter than the eastern regions. But the Staffords said rain usually fell only during the early morning hours. It's drier early in the season, before midsummer.

191

May is warm enough for cycling. Buy some warm clothes for insurance. It can get wet and cold anytime. The Alleys had perfect weather in fall. They had only 2 days of rain in 23 cycling days.

Prevailing winds are from the west and southwest. They're not usually strong, but occasionally you'll get stiff headwinds if cycling westward.

BIKE EQUIPMENT, RENTALS

Conrad couldn't buy a replacement for a front derailleur or other 10-speed parts he needed outside of Cork and Dublin. Nor did he find a shop that could fix a rear derailleur. But the Staffords found a replacement 27 X 1¼-inch tire with no difficulty. A half-dozen recommended repairers are listed in the CTC Handbook, almost all in or near Dublin and Cork. Many other bike shops exist, but they cater mostly to the local 1-speed customers.

Cycling is becoming quite popular in Ireland, and it can be expected that more multi-speed bike parts will be available as bike tourists visit.

Rentals are becoming common; a large center at Killarney is one example. Information about the over 100 rent-a-bike dealers can be had from Raleigh Industries. Most bikes rented are 3-speed, with 10-speed types rare. The bikes will be equipped with carriers and accessories, but gearing and frame sizes are limited. You'd still have to bring extra tools, panniers and other necessities.

192

Prices are $5 a day and $28 a week, hardly worth it for a long tour. For limited riding, or day rides in the area, the bikes are adequate.

BIKE TRANSPORTATION

Conrad complained that the train he used was dirty and was slower and more expensive than in England. He couldn't load his own bike. A bike will cost one-third of your fare. In some parts— County Mayo's coast, for example—you may be 40 miles from a railway line.

The Staffords used a bus for a short distance, with a small charge for the bike. It's carried on the roof or in the baggage compartment, subject to room. The bike can be damaged, so watch the loading.

GENERAL
ENTERING, LEAVING, HASSLES

No problems, no hassles. The Alleys said dogs are sometimes a problem.

IRELAND

LANGUAGE AND PEOPLE

You'll hear Erse, the Irish version of Gaelic, throughout the country but mostly in remote regions and in the extreme north. Your English will be understood, of course. Signs will be in both English and Gaelic.

Almost all bike tourists who visited commented on the people's outgoing and friendly natures. People greet you on the road with "It's a lovely day." Most everyone asked Conrad if he was having a good time.

Even if you're not Irish, you'll be welcomed as an American. Besides the ties of immigration, there's been a traditional affinity with the United States.

OVERALL COSTS

With bed and breakfast stays and most food eaten in public places, you'll spend $15 to $20 a day. If you camp out and cook for yourself, you can cut costs in half. Dale Petrick spent $6 a day in 1978, staying in campgrounds half the time and hostels and B&Bs the rest. He cooked most of his meals.

Write to the Irish Tourist Board for "Travellers Guide" and "Land of Youth," booklets that will provide general information on costs.

193

ACCOMMODATIONS

Hotels, with breakfast, start in the vicinity of $27 in cities, a third less in the countryside. The local tourist office will find you a room for a 75¢ fee.

Your best bets for indoor stays are the hundreds of Irish home accommodations. These B&Bs cost from $8 to $11 a person. The breakfasts they serve are not your skimpy continental type. They'll feed you sausages, bacon, occasionally liver, eggs, superb brown bread and butter, cereal, and tea or coffee. The meal is especially pleasurable as it's eaten in the amiable company of host owners and their guests. You can order a dinner, also, if prior notice is given.

The CTC Handbook includes a couple hundred B&Bs that were recommended by member users, and the Irish Tourist Board will send you a 60-page booklet full of them, including detailed descriptions of their offerings and prices. Some listings announce bikes for hire. You don't have to depend on listings, though; rooms are plentiful.

Curiously, the proprietors' names indicate that all are women, the mass of them listed as "Mrs.," the rest "Miss." I'm not sure what that means, whether men don't want to be associated with the trade, or if the booklet wants to impress the reader with the homey atmosphere of B&Bs.

The 48 Irish hostels are scattered all along the coast, except for a few around Tipperary and a handful south of Dublin in the Wicklow Mountains. If you were to take a coastal tour of Ireland your greatest distance between 2 hostels would be 70 miles. But along the border with Northern Ireland, you'd not run across a hostel right across the whole island.

Hostels in the quiet countryside are more pleasant than those in cities. Only those rated "superior" have showers or a bath. All but one (Ben Lettery, County Galway) are shown in the YH Handbook to have kitchens. Only a third or so provide inside bike security; in the rest, bikes must be left outside. A night's stay is about $2.75.

Hostels that were remarked on favorably by bikers were: Arthurstown (nice view); Foulksrath Castle (atmosphere, modern interior); Killarney (comfortable, spacious); Loo Bridge (interesting former railroad station); Ballydavid Wood and Mountain Lodge (scenic); Limerick (clean, well laid out); Ballinclea (clean, pleasant).

Negative marks were given for: Cork (excellent bike security, but houseparent a military type who barked orders and demeaned); Mountjoy Square, Dublin (highly insecure, with many off-street transients and in a run-down neighborhood). In Dublin, stay at the Donnybrook hostel.

"Caravan and Camping Parks" is available from the Irish Tourist Board. Approximately 70 campgrounds are listed, all offering features in excess of the minimum standards required by the tourist board for camping. All but a few include showers. Their features include many not relevant for bicyclists, such as solid surfaces for cars, tennis courts, electrical connections, and children's pools. Scores of simpler campgrounds exist, which will do as well for bikers.

Camps are more open, and not as organized as British ones. They resemble those in the United States. Prices vary according to what they offer, but a typical site that's listed in the booklet is $3.

As with hostels, most camps are along the coast. In the interior, you must depend on either B&Bs or open camping. Farmers will readily give you permission; you might offer to pay. Camping along or near the road is not officially allowed.

FOOD

A good-size lunch costs from $6.50 up; a pub lunch of a sandwich or a hot specialty like a kidney pie and beer will be half that. Meat is good and commonly available, as is fish of various kinds. Guinness stout ranks with the best beers in the world, and is served in pubs for about $1 a pint.

Pubs open midmorning and close at 11:30 P.M. Sundays from 12:30 to 2:00 P.M. and 4:00 to 10:00 P.M. The pubs play an important role in daily life, being social and family centers for neighborhoods or villages. Drinking is secondary to talk and visiting. Not that there isn't hard drinking in the country. Marcia and Michael Horner said they saw more serious drinking in Ireland than anywhere else in Europe.

Food stores are open approximately 9:00 A.M. to 6:00 P.M., with a half-day off midweek. Small general stores open after Sunday mass. Some food stores sell at night, looking somewhat like America's 7–11s. You can often buy a few foodstuffs in pubs, too.

Most food staples are higher than in England, up by about a fifth, except for meat. Dairy products are somewhat cheaper. You'll have no problem buying anything you need to make your own meals. All villages have stores, and fresh-baked bread is common.

ADDRESSES AND FURTHER READING

Irish Tourist Board
590 Fifth Avenue
New York, NY 10036
and
510 West Sixth Street, Suite 317
Los Angeles, CA 90014

195

Irish Raleigh Industries Ltd
8 Hanover Quay
Dublin 2

Eric Newby and Diana Petry, *Wonders of Ireland* (Briarcliff Manor, N.Y.: Stein & Day, 1970). Their personal choice of 484 natural and man-made wonders, with maps. Through these sketches, you get a feel for the past and present of the Irish. Hard-cover and too heavy for panniers, but read it for inspiration before you go.

ITALY
23

BIKING MATTERS
SUGGESTED TOURS

Italy's attractions are well known: art, history, culture, resorts, scenery, joy of life—it's all there. Add to that the constant stimuli of sights, sounds, smells and the vigor of the people, and you're always stimulated. Choosing a tour depends on your interests, whether art cities, peasant villages, beaches or mountain cycling.

With all the obvious possibilities, I offer instead two offbeat tours to suggest the contrasting choices: a visit to the less frequented south, and a rugged tour of the northern mountains. You can pile on the miles with easy cycling in the southern tour, with some moderate climbing inland. Or you can do some hard work in the compact Dolomites, with their unusual formations and grand scenery.

TOUR 1. Southern boot loop, from 550 to upwards of 1,000 miles; two to four weeks.

Start at Foggia, coming by train from either Naples or Rome. Or connect at Bari or Brindisi, from Yugoslavia or Greece. Cycle from Foggia to Barletta, on the Adriatic, through Trinitapoli. The coast road can be taken to Bari, if off-season. But a more interesting route is south to Andria, then a dozen miles farther to visit Castel del Monte. Return to the coast through Ruvo, Terlizzi and Bitonto, and into Bari.

Again, avoid the coast road; cycle parallel to it, via Capurso, Conversano and Ostuni, and return to the coast at Brindisi. About 7 miles south, take a left on a road back to the Adriatic. You'll now hug the sea all the way around the heel of Italy to Taranto, passing through such interesting towns as Otranto and Gallipoli.

Stay on the shore road all around the toe of Italy also. Or take a shortcut across the boot 40 miles beyond Taranto, just past Scanzano Ionico. Turn west on the main road to Salerno. You need not stick to that road, except for a few unavoidable stretches. There are alternates or parallel roads almost all the way, though they'll all be harder cycling and will increase mileage.

ITALY

If taking the long way, you reach Reggio de Calabria, the southernmost large city. There are virtually no parallel, secondary roads from Taranto to here, most roads dropping from the mountains to the sea. Calabria is primitive and the beaches are uncrowded—empty in the off-season—and people are very friendly. Development will inevitably come; some has already started.

A motorway goes north from Reggio and will drain off much of the fast, through traffic. You'll stick to the shore road as far as Sapri. There, you have a number of choices to get to Salerno. All are about equally difficult, except the inland road that parallels the motorway. It follows the river and is more level, though not more

interesting. You're really as well off to stay on the shore road as any other.

Once in Salerno, the roads are all tourist filled. There are resorts all the way to Naples. If you wish to skip Naples and return to Foggia, cut across the mountains north of Salerno to Avellino and Benevento, turning east on the road to Buonalbergo, then Foggia.

TOUR 2. Heart of the Dolomites. Some 205 miles; as outlined here, this tour has much more potential. You can weave in and out of this area on a number of peripheral, scenic roads and probably add another hundred miles for a two-week trip. Some of those side trips are suggested below.

The tour is only for the stout hearted and strong legged. It was contributed by Lucy Grey, who cycled the region in 1976 and 1978. She says it's for those who enjoy mountain cycling and are traveling light. Grades are steep, up to 16 percent.

Start at Balzano. Trains come here from the south, and also from Innsbruck, Austria. Cycle northeast on 12—hot, dull, and with heavy traffic. A few miles out, at Prato, turn right on the road to Fie and Siusi. Continue to Ortisei. Sharp grades, over 14 percent at times.

198

East on 242, past Selva, then east on 243. Wood carving centers in those two towns. You'll go through the Gardena Pass on the way to Corvara. Now north on 244 to La Villa and southeast to St. Cassiano. Pick up 48 east and ride over the Falzarego Pass to Cortina d'Ampezzo. A modern resort town, surrounded by "stage scenery" peaks, but expensive.

East to Misurina, a lovely lake resort, through Tre Croci Pass. Strong bikers can leave their gear at the cafe here and ride to the top of Tre Cime di Lavaredo for a tremendous view—several 16 percent grades here. Plan to hike a mile or so to the north side of the three spires. Misurina can also be used as a base to cycle north, past Carbonin, for another view of Tre Cime.

From Misurina, go south and east to Auronzo, Lozzo and Calalzo, passing a viewpoint over the lake. Continue to Venas, where you turn off the main road southwest to Forno. Ride west and south on 347 to Agordo. Canyon vistas here. North on 203 now to Cencenighe, then off the main highway north to Alleghe. It's built on a lake, with a promenade and benches fronting the water. Continue north on the same road to 48, and turn west.

Stay on 48 through Arabba and Pordoi Pass to the ski resort of Canazei. A couple of miles short of it, a road goes north to the Sella Pass. It's worth a detour to see the spectacular Dolomite formations. Back on 48, go to Pozza di Fassa, then turn right on 241 for a return to Bolzano. On the way, Carezza al Lago is worth seeing.

The tour can be extended with the side trips mentioned. All

roads are paved; the smallest may be hard dirt or gravel. Traffic is light on main roads in the mountains, except on weekends. The back roads have very few cars. There are bike shops in Bolzano and Cortina. German is spoken along 241, 48 and from Cortina northward, a reflection of the area's proximity to Austria.

Other side trips worth taking are: Picturesque Rocca Pietore and quiet Selva di Cadora, north of Alleghe; Falcade, a unique town with much character, west of Agordo; the Rolle Pass, southwest of Falcade, where you can see plunging granite slopes and take a scenic loop (partially dirt) for close-ups of rock formations. Bolzano itself is interesting, and it has good local breads and pastries. Don't miss the outdoor market.

MAPS, TERRAIN, TRAFFIC

The Italian Government Travel Office will provide the 1:800,000 Touring Club Italiano (TCI) map. Its adequacy will depend on where you're touring. If Tour 1, it will do, what with the limited number of roads available in that part of the country. For Tour 2, the Po Valley, and much of the center of Italy, you should have the appropriate sheets of the Touring Club Italiano's 1:200,000 series that cover the whole country. Those can be bought in Italy or from CTC.

For Tour 2, Michelin's 1:200,000 Northern Italy (with Switzerland) is cheaper. It can be bought for $2 in the United States.

The tourist office also has a pamphlet, "A Trip to Italy," which describes attractions in various parts of the country, through 18 suggested tours. It's heavy on architecture and history, but it does include good suggestions for what's significant.

Italy has a fair system of secondary roads, much better in the Po Valley and other flat areas than in the mountains. But even in the latter, traffic-free roads can be found, though at a cost of harder cycling.

Road surfaces are surprisingly good. Those in the north are superior to roads south of Naples. Avoid all state highways, those shown on the TCI map in red, which have heavy traffic. Although they usually have shoulders on which to ride safely, the fumes and heat of cars and trucks will be unpleasant. Main roads in the south, off-season, can be nearly empty, however.

The slot along the Italian Riviera gets especially heavy with traffic as summer approaches. If planning to cross the Appennines from that road into the Po Valley, by the way, cross at Genoa. It's the lowest spot in those mountains. It took me just a few hours to clear them, with no walking at all. The Lake Como region is also very crowded in summer.

Yellow-colored roads on maps are excellent, while white ones may be rough gravel. In all, Dave Miller liked Italy better than

France for its roads, saying that Italy's have better-engineered grades. He cycled the mountains in both countries. Margaret Logan thought that the best part of her route, from France to Italy, was between Bologna and Florence.

BEST CYCLING TIME

Italian climate is varied. Grey had hail one night in July while in the Dolomites. She said the weather was sunnier and warmer there in summer than in Austria, overall, though some days were cool. Occasionally it rained fiercely.

At the same time of the year, the south is oppressively hot. It's best cycled in spring and fall, in fact all but December to February, with that period of wet weather. There's more rain in the rest of Italy in fall than in spring.

A lowland city like Milan is just as hot in August as Naples. All but the northern mountains should be avoided in midsummer, because of both the heat and the tourists. Italy is the most popular goal of Americans and most Europeans during vacation time.

BIKE EQUIPMENT, RENTALS

200

Lots of good bike shops here. Parts are no problem, unless they involve English threads (bottom brackets, for example). Anything that breaks down can be repaired. Wide-range freewheels may be hard to find.

I've not heard of rentals in Italy. I believe it would be possible by individual arrangement at a bicycle shop, what with the number of good bikes sold in the country.

BIKE TRANSPORTATION

Trains will take bikes anywhere. A few bikers complained about them, saying that they invariably had arguments with personnel and had to watch that the bicycles got on the train. The procedures seemed haphazard.

Buses are supposed to take bikes, but that seems to depend on the mood and personal policy set by each driver. A couple of bike tourists also had a bit of trouble getting their bikes to the Rome airport, getting boxes and transporting them.

GENERAL
ENTERING, LEAVING, HASSLES

No visa needed, just a passport.

Thievery is common in big cities, but most of it is directed at the monied tourists. You may look poorer, but you'd still do well to watch your bike and its gear.

A woman biker will be harassed by Italian males. The kind of attention she gets can range from harmless banter to nasty incidents, as pointed out by Margaret Logan in *Happy Endings.* The attention will tend to be more benign if she has a male companion. My advice is that a woman not camp alone in the open.

LANGUAGE AND PEOPLE

English is widely spoken in cities and tourist centers. Except for those few who've lived or visited America or England, people don't know English in the hinterlands. German is common in the northern mountains.

Learn enough Italian to shop and order in restaurants. It's an easy language. A lot of hand gestures and body language is common among Italians; those can serve you well to communicate when words fail.

Italians are wonderful, friendly, full of bombast, and impulsive, tending to dramatize any ordinary occurrence, and given to emotion. Touring is never dull in Italy. But you may experience some suspicion and even mild hostility in remote villages, where outsiders are infrequent visitors.

201

It's a country where it helps to let the natives know you're from the States, with a flag or "U.S." printed somewhere on your bike. Ties with America are strong, and people will respond positively. You may even find yourself a guest in the home of someone who had worked in South Philadelphia or lived in California.

Street life is common, people sitting around in chairs and men playing cards. Except in the larger cities, on the other hand, leisure life seldom centers around a cafe where you can sit and pass the time, though a meal in a restaurant can be extended and outdoor restaurants are common in the south.

Many racing clubs, both Italian and foreign, train on roads in early spring. Ray Phelps and I were befriended by a Swedish club on the Riviera coast. They fed us and put us up overnight in their rented apartment.

OVERALL COSTS

If you stay in inexpensive hotels, pensions and *albergos,* and buy all meals, you'll spend up to $30 a day. Occasional stays indoors mixed with campgrounds brings costs closer to a $12 average. When you restrict yourself to camping and make the bulk of your meals yourself, you can get along very cheaply, as low as $7 a day. Although Italy has a reputation of being moderately expensive, that holds mostly for the conventional tourist. The country is, in fact, inexpensive for a biker on a shoestring budget.

Cheapest is the south, which is poverty stricken and offers tourists the most. It's not as rich in art and tourist offerings, but you may find the best cycling there.

ACCOMMODATIONS

A cheap double will be under $12. You do better in small towns than large ones, to as low as $7 and even less. Time your visits to big cities for midday, and ride on in late afternoon to adjoining towns for hotels or campgrounds.

There are somewhat less than 60 hostels in the country. That mode is undependable for bike touring: hostels are too far apart; they're clustered in the Po Valley, Lake Como and Naples; and the south and interior mountain towns have only a few.

At $2.50, the price is cheap. It includes all but kitchen and hot water use, which have nominal fees. In some of the more popular hostels, breakfast is mandatory and the price rises to about $3.75. It's still reasonable compared to northern countries.

Campgrounds are abundant, even near large cities or resorts. They're the most economical places to stay and in many ways the most convenient, since public transportation is almost always available to the cities. A tent with two costs $3.30, on the average.

Free camping on beaches is permitted, and it's easy enough to get permission to camp anywhere away from populated areas. That's especially true for the Calabria region and the rest of the south.

FOOD

Pasta and cycling are perfect mates. Their marriage has a sound basis in both economics and nutrition. If you concentrate on pasta dishes, you can eat well and cheaply, whether in restaurants or by cooking for yourself.

Not that you need go without protein. A judicious amount of chicken or seafood in a pasta dish will add taste and supply all the protein you need. Veal and beef are of poor quality. You need not have an endless fare of conventional spaghetti, either. There is enough variety in pastas and in the regional sauces to continually whet your appetite.

A modest *trattoria* in a large city will serve you a substantial fixed menu for $6. A mammoth pizza with the works will be $2. Meals in the south can cost half those in the north, and the atmosphere will be better. Hostels charge a maximum of $2.75 for a main meal.

ITALY

You can live almost on only cheeses, bread, fruit, the delectable cookies and wines. Conventional grocery items, fish, and seafoods are reasonable; the meals you make for yourself will be no more expensive—probably less—than at home.

Shop hours are curtailed by a long afternoon siesta, otherwise open 9:00 A.M. to 8:00 P.M. That varies, though. In the north the siesta is shorter or not observed. Shops are closed Sundays.

ADDRESSES AND FURTHER READING

Italian Government Travel Office
630 Fifth Avenue
New York, NY 10020
        and
360 Post Street, Suite 801
San Francisco, CA 94108

Luigi Barzini, *From Caesar to the Mafia* (La Salle, Ill.: Library Press, 1971). From the master limner of the Italian temperament, with love but unsparing. A proper sequel to *The Italians,* also excellent.

Michelin Green Guide, $7 in U.S.

203

NORWAY

24

BIKING MATTERS
SUGGESTED TOURS

TOUR 1. Bergen to North Cape. In 1979, Rosemary Smith and I bicycled from Stavanger to North Cape (Nordkapp), the most northern point in Europe to which it's possible to ride. We then left Norway for Finland. Lucy Grey and a woman friend covered much the same ground a month later. They flew back from Lakselv, some 100 miles south of the cape. A steamer or bus can also be taken back to Bodo or Bergen. There's no train that goes north of Bodo.

From Bergen to Nordkapp is over 1,500 road miles. We cycled all but about 370 miles, taking steamers twice in what we anticipated to be uninteresting country and where there were rough roads. It took us 27 cycling days at a moderate pace, although cold weather and rain often sapped our energy. At one stretch we had 10 days of daily rain.

Although this is a long tour, the pilgrimage to Nordkapp challenges all cyclists who visit Norway. Shorter parts of it can be ridden, of course, or it can be combined with tours of Sweden or Finland to make a whole summer of touring. In the south, variations are possible by using other side roads. Once past Trondheim, though, only one road goes north, unless you island hop. Norway, and especially this tour, is the most scenic country in Europe, notwithstanding the Alps.

Begin at Bergen with National 14, then N57. For a spectacular view of the Masfjorden, take the ferry from Saeyrasvag across the fjord, then a mail boat up the fjord to Solheim, set like a jewel between fjord and hills. You'll be almost alone on the boat. It carries no cars and only local people.

Rejoin N14 to Lavik, along the Sognefjord, and through Vadheim; then N14 through Forde and Bjorkelo to Stryn. Some climbing at Sande in that stretch of road and a long hill out of Bjorkelo, otherwise rolling hills. You can take a loop through Alesund from Stryn, rejoining the route at Molde.

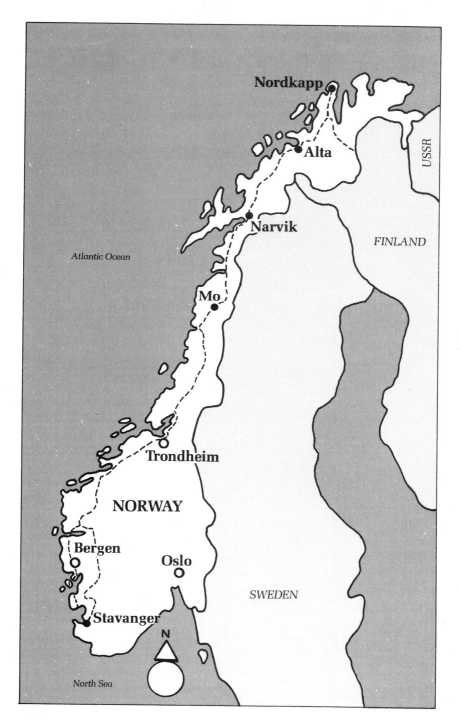

Connect with N60 to Stranda, then E69 and a ferry to Molde. Before Vestnes in that section are four tunnels—unlighted, cold, with water dripping from ceilings—and the road is broken and slimy with mud. There are another six or eight tunnels later on this route.

The tunnels are decidedly dangerous. If possible, cycle with a companion, both with front lights, and blinking lights in back. Better yet, try to get a lift through them.

Next, N66 to Kristiansund. We took a steamer here to Trondheim. Bring food with you. Otherwise, you'll pay over $2 for bread and ham on the boat. A bottle of middling beer will cost about the same.

Heavier traffic east on E6/E75 until E75 branches off to Sweden. Continue on E6 through Steinkjer into Mo. Except for the possibility of some island hopping in the Narvik and Tromso regions, it's E6 now all the way to Nordkapp. The terrain remains mostly rolling hills except for some hard climbing to the Arctic Circle, an awesome, high and barren plateau, and two stiff climbs before Krakmo.

About here you start seeing the sun for 24 hours a day. It skirts the horizon at first, but as you ride to the higher latitudes it gets no lower than about 15 degrees to the horizon.

The continuous light pervades your waking thoughts; you may find yourself pausing in midsentence at 10:00 P.M. and look up at the sun, still well up in the sky. Even at night you wake and walk aimlessly outside in the eerie quiet with wonder—another camper may be up too, staggering like a zombie in a Munch canvas.

The light is made shadowless and a curious pink-yellow, diffused by mountains and clouds. Everything seems suspended. For the next three weeks, well into Sweden, we were affected by its presence. When we started to have darkness again, it was like coming out of a dream.

Under this midnight sun, we took a steamer from Skjervoy, northeast of Tromso, to Honningsvag. Grey rode on through Alta to Hammerfest, where she also took a steamer to Honningsvag. She reported sections of dirt and rough road on that additional length of E6.

From the campground, 5 miles north of Honningsvag, to Nordkapp is 17 miles. All but the first mile is dirt, some of it powdery and impossible to cycle, otherwise rutted gravel (graders were leveling the road as we went up, so it's probably better later in the season). Speeding buses and taxis aggravate the cycling. It's mostly up.

Leave your gear at the camp to make it easier to cycle. We rode fully packed and regretted it. The 1,000-foot cliffs at the cape are often in fog and nothing may be seen for your effort. We were lucky to arrive in clear sunshine to view the sun circling the northern horizon.

There was no way to stake a tent into the barren rock, and so, after making a late supper, we bedded down in sleeping bags at 2:00 A.M. directly under the stars (under the sun, to be exact).

From Honningsvag a road leads to the Finnish border, through Lakselv. The surface is very bad the last 25 miles before Karasjok, soft dirt and gravel. No accommodations of any kind either, and voracious mosquitoes.

TOUR 2. Stavanger–Bergen–Stavanger. 500 miles (560 with side trips). A two- to three-week tour, it can also connect with the Nordkapp tour at Vadheim.

At Stavanger, take an initial side trip on the Lysefjord to Pulpit Rock; its backside is a dirt road. Ride through Tau on N13 to Sand, with some climbing. Fjaera (via Sandeid) on E76 to Odda, with more climbing, and along the Sorfjord to Voss.

Take a scenic side loop here along E68 to Gudvangen, a ferry to Flam and a train (snakes up a cliff to 3,000 feet in 12 miles) back to Voss; 10 miles of dirt on that loop. On N13 to Balestrand and a minor road to Vadheim. On N14 to Lavik and a return to Bergen as in Tour 1.

207

From Bergen continue south on N14 and minor roads through Stord Island, Haugesund, and Karmoy Island to Stavanger, taking a number of ferries along the route. Road is good and fairly level from Bergen to Stavanger, with occasional rolling hills. Scenery pleasant but not spectacular.

From Oslo, E6 to Trondheim and E18 to Stavanger are busy. N7 (Reindeer Road) from Oslo to Bergen is full of traffic. E68, northeast of Bergen, may be, too. Best to stay off these. The real scenery is at the junction of sea and mountains, anyhow.

MAPS, TERRAIN, TRAFFIC

The Scandinavian National Tourist Office provides a free 1:3,500,000 map of Scandinavia. It's useless for biking but it gives an overview of Norway, and its position relative to the surrounding countries. A 1:1,450,000 Tourist Map of Norway (Turistkart over Norge) shows a closer look, with main highway numbers indicated and some secondary roads identified, but only by line traces without numbers. It's free in some information offices of large cities in Norway. I couldn't get one in the stateside tourist office. The map may serve if you'll ride only larger highways, but not if you seek smaller roads.

Write to A/S Norske Esso for free copies of Norge Syd-Vest, scale 1:500,000; Norge, scale 1:1,000,000 in the south; or scale 1:1,500,000 in the north, whichever you need. They may not answer for a while; give them at least a month and a half

Excellent but expensive Cappelens Bil-Og Turistkart maps are sold throughout Norway at $8 each, 1:325,000 and 1:400,000 scales. They show locations of all accommodations, including camps and mountain huts. CTC sells them, too.

Also at CTC or bookstores in England are Geographia maps. Order from Complete Traveller in the United States. If you'll take in Sweden as well, their 1:800,000 Norway and Sweden is a good choice. About $6 in the United States. We liked it, although we thought the map heavy, large and bulky.

The Scandinavian National Tourist Office supplies "Vegdekkart," which indicates surfaces on major roads. The roads may prove to have rough surfaces in sections, even if maps indicate them as paved. Tunnels and mountain roads are especially bad, as repair work on them is difficult. Dirt roads are graded smooth and are packed hard. They're easy riding in dry weather, miserable when wet.

208 Roads are generally improved by paving. For example, a new bridge, built in 1980 at Storstraumen, between Olderdalen and Alta, eliminated 24 miles, mostly dirt, around the fjord, and its approaches are paved. Watch out for those "Norwegian miles," by the way. Your informers may be referring to their system in which 1 mile is about 6 of ours. We were caught a couple of times like that: "Oh yes, the campground is just 2 miles ahead," we'd be told. An hour later we struggled into it.

In spring, the land is saturated by water, melting from winter snows, and fed by frequent rains. It falls off slopes thousands of feet high—instant waterfalls each kilometer—and seems to spurt from the very ground itself, as if touched magically by Moses's staff. Streams become roaring torrents. If camping in the bush, you never want for fresh, safe water.

Only a small pocket of country around Oslo and along the southern shore to Mandal is flat. It's the least interesting part of Norway and is heavy with summer traffic. From Mandal to Stavanger is hillier and has better views, but the real spectacles are farther north. Roads are mostly rolling and not at all forbidding for moderate cycling, except for rank beginners. You'll need low gears, in the 20s, for the relentless number of hills, though.

Traffic is relatively heavy only around cities—Stavanger, Alesund, Trondheim, Narvik, Oslo, Bergen. Most of those have bikepaths leading to them. Roads are narrow, but cars are small and drivers courteous and patient.

BEST CYCLING TIME

We found it very cold around Narvik in mid-June, although it was pleasant when the sun shone in the afternoon. The tourist season is over before September, at which time it's quite cold again. "Give me strong kidneys tonight," prayed Ken Proctor during cold nights at that time, while bike camping in the Mo area with his wife, Jacque. If you sleep indoors, of course, the weather will seem much milder. Winds are mostly from the west and southwest.

The warm Gulf Stream washes the long Norwegian shore, and mountains condense moist air, so there's plenty of humidity and rain during any part of the cycling season. The north is drier and sunnier. Expect some rain during half the days of your stay. Pay special attention to rain gear, of course. When the sun does shine, you'll experience the clearest and purest air ever. You'll not get over its wonder.

BIKE EQUIPMENT, RENTALS

A/S Jonas Oglaend, a Norse bike manufacturer, will send you **209** information on bikes and availability of parts. Bike shops can be found everywhere. Fifty bike shops, for example, are north of the Arctic Circle, one even 20 miles south of Nordkapp, at Honningsvag. Many of the shops carry utility bikes, though. In small towns bike parts are found only in hardware or general stores. Ask around.

Parts and 27-inch tires for 10-speeds are in limited supply. You may have to ride a whole day to a large town to find any, in the north especially. Specialized tools for your bike should be taken along, though standard shop tools can be borrowed anywhere. Chains wear out fast, what with grit thrown into them and the frequent hill climbing. Both mine and Rosemary's had to be replaced after 1,200 miles into our tour from Amsterdam (about $7 each in Norway). It's easy enough to buy one, so don't bring a spare.

Repair facilities also are not that common, and are limited in what they can do. Tyler Folsom counldn't get a split cotterless crank replaced anywhere in Trondheim, for example, and he had to go to Oslo. Even there, he had trouble finding someone with the expertise and the needed parts.

Ask the Scandinavian National Tourist Office for "Cycling Vacations in Norway," which lists bike rental agencies. I never saw any bikes for rent and can't report on the type available. Ask also for a list of fixed-price bike tours, if those interest you.

BIKE TRANSPORTATION

Bikes on trains cost $2, regardless of distance. Check the bike into the baggage room a few hours ahead of time. No problem getting the bike to arrive at the same time as you. You'll have to take off your panniers and extras, and either carry those onto the train with you or pay extra if checked as baggage. A caution if sending a bike across the border to Sweden as unaccompanied freight (as when you might hitchhike, for example): the bike will be liable to excise duty (about $8) if it looks new.

Buses between cities have space for bikes, either in a back compartment or on outside racks. If they're full, of course, you might be out of luck. Unload baggage, as on trains.

Ferries are the easiest of all—just roll the loaded bike on and secure. No matter the lines of cars, you always get on a ferry with a bike. In fact, bikes and pedestrians go on first. Of a dozen times on ferries, we paid a nominal sum for the bikes only once. The rest of the time they were free; on steamers, also.

GENERAL

210

ENTERING, LEAVING, HASSLES

No visa required, but register at a police station if you stay longer than three months. No inoculations needed either. Customs is easy. There are some restrictions as to which foods you can bring in, but our experience was that entering and leaving the country was a simple matter of passport and a few friendly words.

LANGUAGE AND PEOPLE

A lot of English spoken, sometimes unexpectedly. In a remote village you may find a shop owner who has lived in England or America. The young are apt to be more fluent in English than older folk. It's taught in schools. A dictionary helps, though, if only to find the right words for grocery items you might want.

Norse reserve is often noted by writers and travelers. Once contact is made they're quite friendly and responsive, though they won't intrude on your privacy and won't be the first to make an overture.

There are only four million Norwegians in the length of 1,100 miles, a half-million in Oslo. Because of the low population density, you'd expect "wilderness" travel. You may find the opposite. Lucy Grey said, "My biggest disappointment was that it was so civilized. I wouldn't hesitate to take a child or teenager on any section of this trip."

NORWAY

Norway is indeed civilized. Although goods are expensive, they're made to last; cafeterias are immaculate and in good taste (utilitarian silverware looked like a design contest winner), and more music and art can be found in a small city like Bergen (a quarter-million people) than in many United States cities four times as large. While we were there, a Bergen music festival was going on, with famous musicians from all parts of the world. Even in the north, the local culture of the Lapps is unique and accomplished. Their colorful dress and craft artifacts are a delight to the eye.

OVERALL COSTS

The Scandinavian National Tourist Office will send you "Low-Cost Vacations in Scandinavia," which will give you an idea of typical prices for the current year. In 1979 I found it the most expensive country I ever cycled. My share of food and lodging averaged $10 a day, with a near-Spartan regimen. That included no restaurant meals, hotels or liquor. We bought no expensive meat or produce for cooking; we camped about half the time, many times free, and the rest of the days were in hostels.

Lucy Grey and her lady companion spent $20 apiece, but they stayed about a third of the time in hotels or cabins and the rest in hostels. They ate suppers in cafeterias, making most of their own breakfasts and lunches. Ian Davis spent $14.25 a day in the same year, staying in hostels and trying not to be extravagant. The Norwegian krone has hardly risen relative to the dollar in the past few years, but a constant inflation should raise rock-bottom costs to $12 a day, or higher, in 1981.

A minor but irritating cost is that of changing traveler's checks. You'll be charged from 40¢ to $1 for each check, regardless of the denomination. The fee, therefore, may come to 10 percent with a $10 check. There's usually a limit on total charges when changing a number of them at one time, from $2 to $4 tops. It's best to either change one large check or a very great many at one time.

Better yet, time your check cashing (and mail pickups) with arrivals in cities that have agency offices. Those are scarce. Thomas Cook has only one, in Oslo. Amex has offices in Oslo, Bergen, Stavanger, Tromso, and Trondheim. If you have U.S. or British currency, you won't be charged anything for the exchange to Norwegian.

Travelers over 70 get a 50 percent reduction on railroads, and a wife's boat or train ticket is reduced by half when traveling with her husband. Unwed couples can get this discount also; proof never seems to be asked for.

ACCOMMODATIONS

Hotels. Lucy and her companion paid from $20 to $50 each when they were forced to use a hotel. Motels cost about the same. Pensions *(pensjonat)* cost $14 to $22 each. Rooms in private homes *(husrom)* were from $6 to $10 each. Many *husroms* advertised by a sign along the road—rectangular with blue rim and an outline of black bed on white. Others were located by asking at a tourist office or hotel.

Cabins. Huts *(hytter)* are peculiar to Norway. A hut, with four bunks (double-deckers), cost $10 to $15, whether used by one or four persons. Even one or two others could probably sleep on the floor in sleeping bags, although it would crowd the small room. These are the best bargain by far when a group tours together. The huts are located by themselves, or in conjunction with a campground.

Huts have lights, an electric heater and hot plates, and mattresses and pillows. You supply sleeping bags, and you clean them up the next morning before leaving. They have no water inside, but there's usually a spigot nearby. A community building holds a kitchen, toilets, washroom and hot showers. Most of the *hytter* are within a mile or two of a store or cafe. They're located within an easy day's ride of each other, except in the far north where they become scarcer. They're also more expensive as you go north.

Huts we found especially pleasant were at: Lavik (overlooking the beautiful Sognefjord); Harran (good facilities, we got a reduction with a camping *carnet*); Majavatn, adjacent to hotel (most expensive at $14, but worth it, on a serene spot next to lake). All huts were at least satisfactory; none disappointed us.

Youth hostels. Get a guide from Norske Ungdomsherberger, if you haven't an IYH Handbook. Hostels are within an easy day's ride of each other in the south, but far apart north of Trondheim. Lucy sent her sleeping bag ahead to the Trondheim Youth Hostel for use in huts farther north. It saved carrying it up to that point.

Hostels are a mixed bag: useful for those not wanting to camp; reasonably priced—$3 to $8, the latter with a mandatory breakfast—in a high-priced country; but varied in what they offer, in conditions and in atmosphere. Those rated in a higher category in a hostel handbook are not necessarily better. Our worst one was rated highly and cost the most. Bike and property security is high in hostels.

Some hostels we stayed at were packed with noisy school kids, particularly before the end of the school year (May–June), when classes were taken on organized trips. Some had cramped bathrooms or no hot water. On the other hand, many had fabulous views, modern kitchens, and friendly wardens. Quite a few offered private rooms to couples, with no extra charge other than individual fee.

Among the best that we experienced were at: Stavanger (good view and facilities); Stryn (hard climb, but nice room and friendly); Hellesylt (huge kitchen and comfortable dining room, fabulous view); Levanger (pleasant, even had a washing machine); Bleiknesmo (charming); Voss (great facilities, though expensive); Balestrand (nice setting, good food); Andalsnes (small cozy rooms and sitting rooms, fabulous breakfast); Oslo (large but nice setting, expensive); Moss (new, small rooms, good kitchen).

The worst: Oystese (almost primitive, badly equipped kitchen); Eldalsosen (primitive, uninterested warden); Valldal (bare, kitchen not well equipped); Lillehammer (hotellike, expensive, terrible kitchen); Bergen Montana (up the side of a mountain, no kitchen, large and regimented); Kristiansund (no showers, poor kitchen); Krakma (cold water, primitive); Narvik (cold, expensive at $8 with a small breakfast, no security for bike); Karasjok (run down, no showers).

Camping is the only way to save money in Norway. You can camp free anywhere except near someone's home (within 500 feet) or on tilled ground. "Everyman's right," it's called, and it's the law. Only 4 percent of Norway's land is owned privately.

Up to mid-June the ground is soggy from rain and snow runoff, though, and it's hard to find a dry spot. You sink up to the ankles in the moss. At about that time, mosquitoes start breeding in earnest. And so, camping in the open is a bit of an ordeal, either early or later.

Commercial campgrounds may offer a respite from mosquitoes, sometimes because they're in a developed area that has less of them, or by providing a retreat indoors in a communal kitchen, dining room or recreation hall. Campgrounds almost always have adequate washrooms, usually superior to those in hostels.

A tent and two people are charged about $4, with an additional 40¢ each at pay showers. A camping *carnet* is required for entrance to camps, although it seldom gets you a discount of itself. Bike and foot campers are charged less than those in cars, however. The Norges Automobil Forbund (NAF) chain has a posted, multilanguage price list, which specifies lower prices for bikers. Many camp managers aren't familiar with it, and you should point it out to them. Try to get a copy of that list, the first time you see it, or copy down the information, and carry it with you for reference.

When tenting grounds are combined with huts, there's little

value in the latter since all the facilities are open to either mode. Unless it's raining or freezing, of course. "It's nice to hear the rain patter softly on a tent fly," I once said to Rosemary. "It's nicer to hear it against a window pane," she replied, less romantic about it than I.

A few comments on commercial camps in the north. Recommended: Setermoen Camp at Bardu (great facilities); Sagelvvatn (cheap at $2 for two, and scenic, although facilities are wanting); Honningsvag (good facilities but too many tour groups, overcrowding bathrooms and depleting hot water).

Not recommended: Hersletta, 13 miles north of Narvik (poor bathroom and tiny kitchen in a boiler room, shower $1); Stabburnsnes (shower $1 and cut off early in the evening). André Everett disliked Repvag (bucket toilets, an old potato cellar as washroom, cold water).

A list of camps is furnished by the Scandinavian National Tourist Office, and additional local sites are often listed in regional pamphlets at information offices in the country.

FOOD

Breakfast is too expensive at cafeterias for the amount that bikers need. Most hostels charge $3, which is included in the overall price if mandated. (All food, 1979 prices.) That breakfast includes adequate amounts of bread, cheese, cold cuts, beverage and an occasional egg or cereal. You can buy the ingredients yourself much more cheaply.

Lucy Grey found that hotels or private homes serve the best buy at about $5: an unlimited smorgasbord of orange juice, milk, buttermilk, tea, coffee, cereal, boiled eggs, 3 to 10 kinds of bread and crackers, two or more cheeses, two or more cold cuts that include ham, liver paté and varieties of pickled herring, pickles, strawberry preserves and orange marmalade. Also occasional sardines, shrimp, smoked salmon, and various fruit or aspic salads. The catch is that only guests can eat there, although I've read that some hotels will serve outsiders. The other catch is that you'll have to cycle afterward on a bloated stomach if you fill up with all the appealing fare.

It doesn't pay to eat a lunch indoors. Buy groceries for a picnic or snacks during the day. Norwegian bread is superb and cheap—60¢ for a loaf about 1¾ pound. Every region seems to add yet another delicious and wholesome version to a large national variety of breads. Bakeries (bakeri, or konditori) are everywhere; just follow the tantalizing, fresh-baked smell.

Cold cuts of meat are expensive, but cheese and butter are about the same as in the States. A cup of coffee costs up to $1.50 in a cafe. A few of them could eat up half your day's budget. Make your own, unless it's too cold outside and you want to come in to warm up. A beer is $2.70 for a good version, and hard liquor is out of sight, so don't attempt that to warm up.

Stores open at 8:00 or 9:00 A.M. and usually close at 5:00 P.M. (at 4:00 P.M. from mid-June through the summer), all during the week. Open mornings on Saturday. Everything is locked tight on Sunday except for kiosks, which stock some fruit and junk food.

An ordinary supper of meat, potatoes and vegetable in a hostel or cafeteria costs $5. A cafeteria may close by 7:00 P.M. Hostels have hours, too, and you may find the kitchen closed by the time you arrive. Restaurants stay open late and will charge $10 to $15. Smorgasbord is commonly offered and you can stuff yourself to make up that price.

Cooking for yourself is cheaper and the only sure way to fill up when biking. Most grocery items are higher than in the United States; hamburger cost us $3 and more a pound. Most meat is $4 a pound and higher. Fresh and frozen fish is cheap, though, at $1 to $1.50 a pound. As you go north, the choice of main meal ingredients gets limited. Frozen and precooked foods are more common in remote areas than fresh meats.

215

Rice, pasta and other packaged foods are reasonable. Vegetables, other than potatoes, turnips, and carrots (from California yet), can hardly be found. When available, they're very expensive—one fresh green pepper was priced at $1, a bunch of celery at $2.

Hostels and most campgrounds have community kitchens and cabins have hot plates, so you needn't bring a stove, unless you want to make coffee during the day. Stove fuel is available, either the S-200 gas cartridges or kerosene.

If you camp in the open, you'll have little problem finding water with which to cook. Pure water runs down the mountainsides everywhere, except in some of the plateaus, and small streams that flow from uninhabited areas are safe.

ADDRESSES AND FURTHER READING

Scandinavian National Tourist Office
75 Rockefeller Plaza
New York, NY 10019
          and
3600 Wilshire Boulevard
Los Angeles, CA 90010

A/S Norske Esso
Reklameavdelingen
Postboks 1369
Oslo V

Jonas Oglaend A/S
PO Box 115, Solavlien 3
N-4301 Sandnes

Cappelens Bi-Og Turistkart
J.W. Cappelens Forlag
Oslo

Edward Streeter, *Skoal Scandinavia* (New York: Harper & Row, 1952). Once over lightly about a car trip through Norway, Sweden, Denmark. Some nice observations about customs, institutions and terrain.

POLAND
25

BIKING MATTERS
SUGGESTED TOURS

Interesting areas exist in all parts of the country, and you can get a mix of attractions if you simply cycle in a two- or three-week circle in almost any direction. These two tours differ only in terrain, the one in the north being completely flat, the southern one going through some of the mountain area.

Because most roads in Poland lack road numbers, except on European E-numbers and the larger Polish highways, I indicate the routes mostly by towns or villages. You can make your own way between those on other roads, if you wish. You can't miss. Destinations are well indicated on the road signs, even if numbers don't appear. Hostels and campgrounds abound on both routes, and you won't lack for formal accommodations.

TOUR 1. Northern circle, about 670 miles and three weeks. It can be cut by about 200 miles and a week by skipping the lakes and returning directly to Warsaw from the Baltic.

Start at Warsaw. There's no easy way to get out of the capital; tough it to Borzecin, directly west, and then to Leszno and Sochaczew. Get a city map from the "It," the tourist office, or ask directions. Continue west to Gabin, Gostynin, Brzesc and Radziejow. Swing north here to Torun.

Visit a while in the old town of this historic city, the former home and workplace of Copernicus. Cycle north, but avoid E16. A number of minor roads can lead you to the Gdansk area on the Baltic, for example, through Chelmno, Skorcz and Starogard.

A cluster of medieval cities here on the Bay of Danzig offer swimming, music and cultural diversions. See and hear the organ at Oliva, for example, a fantastic horde of bronze angels and heralds moving about the organ pipes as the music plays. The Baltic region to the west contains near-empty beaches, sand dunes, and old fishing towns, if you want to take a side trip there.

ADVENTURE CYCLING IN EUROPE

Take the coastal road east out of Gdansk (not E81) for about 20 miles, then turn south on 173 to Malbork, an interesting town. Now east to Dzierzgon, Paslek, Orneta and Lidzbark Warminski, with a Gothic castle in the latter. Continue east to Kietrzyn and Gizycko. You are now in the midst of the Mazury, where a major part of the country's 10,000 lakes are situated.

Make way to Bialystok. You may take 190, which is not at all crowded in this empty eastern part of the country, near Russia. South of this city is the Bialowieza forest, where a third of the world's population of European bison are protected. Return west on any number of minor roads to Warsaw, through Siematycze and Wegrow, for example. Stay in Warsaw a few days, of course. It's charming, and rightfully called the Paris of the East.

TOUR 2. Carpathian Mountains, unspecified miles and time. The options of roads are more limited in this region. Although you can avoid the national highways, like T7 and 15, you'd be obliged to

take secondary roads that are traveled by campers and vacationers' cars. If you visit before the school season starts, or after it ends, there'll be considerably less traffic.

Start at Krakow, Poland's former capital and the most beautiful city in Poland. It's a favorite of young and old both, not only for its history but also for art, nightlife, and student atmosphere.

Meander south, in your own fashion and schedule, through the mountain towns and resorts (all reasonably priced for cabins and food, if you decide to lay over). Must stops are: Nowy Targ, Zakopane, and the Dunajac River, passing by Kroscienko, Stary Sacz and Nowy Sacz, all south and east of Krakow; and in the extreme southeast of the country, the Bieszczydy Mountains, in the Sanok and Lesko area.

MAPS, TERRAIN, TRAFFIC

The Polish National Tourist Office in the United States will send you an official 1:1,000,000 scale map if you ask for it. You won't find one in Poland. The map is detailed enough to show most of the ridable roads. Get one showing campground locations.

A contour map of the same scale is sold in the country. It has little purpose unless you plan to visit the extreme south, the only area with mountains. Some of the best scenery is there, not only in the area of Tour 2, but also in the southwest Sudetens. The word, Poland, means field, and most of your cycling will be on the flat, or at worst in gently swelling hills with grades of a few percent.

Stay off the main roads as much as possible, at least in mid-summer, when both vacationing Poles and foreigners glut them. What are shown as secondary roads on the map have good to excellent surfaces, and they contain little traffic. Even "other roads" compare favorably with most of America's smaller highways; they're asphalted and have the advantage of being almost empty, except for cattle, horse-drawn farm carts and utility bicycles. Poland is the only country I know that warns unabashedly in its motor travel booklet: "During week ends, roads may be locally used for strolling."

Portions of many roads in the western part of the country (formerly German) and those through the old, medieval cities are cobbled. They've been left that way for the sake of draft horses that are still used, though roads that are used heavily by cars have been covered over with asphalt. The cobbles may help give footing to horses, but they're rough on bicyclists' backsides. About the only relief is to ride on sidewalks, or find parallel streets in towns. Watch for streetcar tracks in the cities, too. Americans who have never encountered those kind of rim-catching traps can be in for a sudden, nasty fall.

BEST CYCLING TIME

Spring comes somewhat late and April can be cold. Summer is pleasant, with only a few hot days. In the north, nights and some days in August are already cold. The rest of the country stays warm through September, and even into October. Fall seems to be driest, and you may get some, but not excessive, rain at any time.

In late summer a stiff wind comes from the west along the Baltic, sometimes for days on end. It's best to plan cycling with it. Winds in the rest of the country are variable. The quality of air in the country, especially in the lakes region of the northeast, is as pure as in Scandinavia.

BIKE EQUIPMENT, RENTALS

Bike stores are hard to recognize, especially in small towns. From the outside they may look like junk shops or empty stores. Unlike our stores, theirs don't advertise the wares by putting them in the windows. You're more apt to see a few plants there and a couple of sleeping cats.

220

The word for bicycle is *rower* (from the first English bikes in the country long ago, which were a Rover brand). It should be printed somewhere on the outside of the shop, but don't count on it. You'll know it's a bike shop inside, though. Parts are strewn everywhere, and customers compete for floor space with parked bikes waiting for repairs.

You might get what you need, depending on what it is and the clerk's success in finding it in the hundreds of randomly placed boxes. Poland makes few parts that would screw into, or otherwise mate with, the usual 10-speed, such as a wheel spindle or a freewheel. But they'll have universal things like brake shoes, cables, and even derailleurs. You might have to adapt those; cut down spokes, jerry-build attachments for a carrier, or knot the end of a cable to hold it in your shift lever. As with other Eastern European countries, it's safest to bring spares with you instead of taking a chance.

Camping equipment is generally the heavy, utility kind that motor campers use. Quality sleeping bags and tents aren't to be found at all. Mine have always been a source of wonder to other campers. Not found either are other camping items and bike accessories that are taken for granted in the States—compact stoves, plastic tubes, panniers, bike shoes. No bike rentals at all.

BIKE TRANSPORTATION

Bikes are carried on trains for ridiculously low prices, ranging from 24¢ for up to 20 miles, to $1.50 for distances over 185 miles. Those prices are based on the official rate of exchange. On a black market basis, they would be a third of that (see later discussion of the black market). Bicycles are not allowed on buses, there being no room for them.

GENERAL
ENTERING, LEAVING, HASSLES

Quite simple to enter, since you're obliged to have a visa and to preexchange money for each day of it at a given rate (check with travel agent for the current rate); the authorities are thus assured that you won't go broke and become a ward of the state, and that you'll spend a minimum in the country.

If you decide to stay longer, you need only go to any police station before your visa expires, and change the appropriate amount of money for each day of extension. You'll get it on the spot.

You might be searched when you leave the country. That's **221** unpredictable. If you abide by customs regulations, approximately, you need not be concerned. The guards aren't strict. It's difficult to take too many goods out of the country, in any case. There's little to buy in Poland of great worth, and your panniers have limited room.

An awful bureaucracy will slow you everywhere, from buying something in a shop to getting documents. A few years ago, shop clerks still used an abacus to count; they entered each sale by hand into a huge ledger, as well as into the modern cash register on the counter. Happily that's past, and they trust the register today, but the spirit lives on. No orderly queues—people mob the counters as clerks shuffle about lackadaisically, or gossip together. A postal clerk may close the window in your face when it's time for her break, after you've stood in line for 15 minutes. You have to move to the next line.

It's better in small towns and villages, where shops are less crowded, and where you can even get into a conversation with the proprietor.

Your unconventional look, on a pack-laden bike, may bring some stares but never any difficulties. Backpacking youth from all of Eastern Europe—some are quite wild looking—flock to Poland for vagabond vacations. The country has the freest atmosphere of the Eastern Bloc.

No one will follow you—a near impossibility on a bike anyhow—and you'll see few police or soldiers about. The police you do see aren't armed, except with a small billy. They're cordial and helpful. Crime is low-key in Poland; family quarrels and drunkenness are the usual thing. You can walk the streets at 2:00 A.M. without fear.

If you cycle at night, have a light. Tyler Folsom, the around-the-world cyclist, was stopped by police for not having one. The only encounter I ever had with police, in two trips to the country, was for the same reason. I was cautioned in 1971 by a policeman to get a light—"for your own sake," he said almost apologetically—as I rode in the middle of an empty Warsaw street one early morning.

Watch yourself in dealing with black market entrepreneurs, especially on the street. Entrapment is not uncommon. If you indulge, do so with a family, a shop owner, or someone you meet, stay with a bit, and feel you can trust.

Although I've had petty pilfering off the bike, I've left it unattended dozens of times without too much concern. Still, as anywhere else in the world, it's best to park the bike in large cities near the window of a cafe or shop, where you can watch it from the inside.

LANGUAGE AND PEOPLE

222

What do you do with a language that has words like *czterdziestodziewieciokrotnego?* (It means 49-year-old.) Polish is difficult for those not born into it. Although it's consistent in pronunciation, as in Spanish, it's as highly inflected as German. But if you learn a few words, it'll be appreciated.

Better yet, point out the phrase in a handbook closest to what you want to express, when you're stuck. You'll be the delight of the people you question; they'll scramble over each other to help. Bring the phrase book with you; I couldn't find one, or a Polish-English dictionary, anywhere in Poland in 1979. English language guides are available, though. They're quite helpful.

The second most useful language is German, mostly in the western part. Those past invaders have returned, spearheaded by recreational vehicles rather than tanks, as before. The Poles made ready this time, learning German and catering to their tourist needs.

English is only spoken in the largest cities like Warsaw and Krakow by young students and leftover aristocrats, now disowned and down on their luck. French, which used to be the gentry's language also, is not known anymore except in the older hotels.

Poles are steeped in their past. They'll show you monuments and reconstructed buildings and insist you visit the grim reminders of World War II—the crematoriums of Oswiecim (Auschwitz), Treblinka and Majdenek, and the site of mass executions at Palmiry

Cemetery. See those if you have the stomach for it. I didn't.

A strong and sentimental feeling for the land is another national characteristic. I once told an old caretaker in a campground that my mother emigrated to the United States when she was a very young girl. He was visibly moved, his eyes pregnant with tears, at the thought that she may never return to her native land. He put a large handful of dirt in a bag, handed it to me and said, "Here, give this bit of Poland to your mother."

There's a lot to experience other than sentiment and tradition: folk art and crafts, world-renowned posters, excellent symphony orchestras and opera companies, coffee-shop life, and simply meeting and talking to people. That's easy to do. At the slightest excuse they'll try to communicate with you, more so when they discover you're from the States. Americans are their favorite foreigners.

A young spirit pervades today's Poland. What with the slaughter of one-sixth of its population during the war—six million died—and a lot of babies since, most people are under 30. Tastes are Western, with pop music and clothing styles modeled to America's.

OVERALL COSTS

Prices in Poland are probably the lowest in Europe. There's a **223** frustrating catch to it, though: you're obliged to prechange—pay in advance, in effect—from $7 to $12 for each day of your visa (usually with a travel agent in the States, getting a voucher for dollars that will be converted to Polish zlotys when you get to the Polish border).

The rate depends on whether you're a regular tourist, under 26, a student, or a person of Polish origin, the last converting at the $7 rate. It's easy enough to claim the latter, incidentally; even if your name is O'Reilly, for example, you can say that your grandmother on your mother's side came from Poland at the turn of the century. The travel agent making the exchange won't dispute you, and who knows? Maybe she did.

At the $7 figure, you'll still have a hard time spending your money if you camp and don't live high on the hog. When Folsom rode through the country in 1977, he spent $4.50 a day. I experienced the same costs in 1979. The balance of my zlotys was spent on gifts.

Costs are fixed and held constant by the state. Poles have resisted food price raises for years with demonstrations and strikes. Campground fees are also fairly constant, but hotels used by foreigners go up steadily. If you avoid those, your costs should stay low.

Most consumer goods are shoddy, the clothes and manufactured articles for everyday use. The best are in Pewex shops, government stores where they're sold only for foreign currency. You can buy foreign luxury items there, too, such as American whiskey and cigarettes.

Arts and crafts of good quality—amber jewelry, handmade rugs, crocheted and embroidered articles, silver—are bargains. Buy at the government Cepelia or Desa shops. The various Polish vodkas, some of the best in the world, are cheap. You can buy them in any grocery shop.

You're restricted to $35 worth of goods that you can take out of the country without paying duty. That's not watched carefully. You can avoid that possibility by sending purchases out piecemeal, as you buy them. Duty has to be paid on certain goods, regardless of amount of purchase. Check with the customs people in the post office before you buy expensive items.

Travel on streetcars and buses is ridiculously cheap—under a nickel within cities—and service is extensive. You need not ride your bike unless you want to. Every village can be reached by bus. You can cross the whole country for less than $10 on a train.

All costs quoted in this chapter are based on the official rate, the one at which you'll be exchanging money for visa purposes. On the pervasive black market, anyone will give you from three to four times as many zlotys for a dollar as the state does. But since you can hardly spend the money you were first obliged to change, there is little point to buying more zlotys unless you want to live like a king during your stay.

There are two economies in Poland, in fact—the official one and the black market. I didn't meet one Polish citizen who wasn't involved in the latter in some way. Foreign money is bought as a hedge against inflation and to buy foreign goods in the Pewex shops. In that, the government aids and abets the black market by selling those goods to anyone with foreign money, no questions asked. Dollars or francs will also get Polish citizens cars at once, while those with Polish currency must wait a long time.

When you're ready to leave, you may still have zlotys. They aren't likely to exchange them for dollars at the border, no matter the assurance you may receive from agents in the United States. You can either give the money away or deposit it for the next visit to Poland. It's a good time to stock up, instead, on cheap provisions if you're headed for Sweden or some other expensive country.

ACCOMMODATIONS

Hotels range from $70 for a deluxe double at a Hilton type to $3 each for a room shared by two to three others. A private single will be about $6. Rooms at the more expensive hotels will be all you're likely to find in big cities, at least in the summer season.

Besides being expensive, hotels seldom have a secure place to park bicycles. They're not prepared for foreigners traveling that way. The cheaper ones have no elevators. You'd be obliged to carry your bike and luggage a few flights of stairs. The room will be small, unless you've paid a fortune for it; a bike will be hard to fit in. Besides, the management may not even let you take the dirty thing into the room.

Hostels offer more security, unless bike parking is outside. The majority are situated in schools, though, and there's usually a locked room in which bikes are kept. Hostels in big cities are crowded, but you can usually get in if you're there at the door at 5:00 P.M. when they open, or before they close at 10:00 A.M. In smaller cities and towns, no problem.

Polish hostels are cheap. The highest category charges $1.40 for the first night and progressively less for additional nights. On the third, you pay half. Hostels in Krakow and Warsaw cost more. There are no showers in hostels converted from schools during the summer, the majority of those in the country. There's warm water, anyhow, and you can take a sink bath.

Beds are packed together closely in large city hostels. The width of a backpack may fit between them, but they're often closer. What hostels lack in space, many make up in atmosphere and location. Torun's, for example, sits in a 500-year-old building in the old city wall, convenient to all points of interest in the old town.

Kitchens are fair—better than in Mediterranean countries and worse than in Scandinavia. School hostels have no kitchens. They are also only open during vacations, ending in mid-August.

Camping in some of the 100 campgrounds in Poland is pleasant, unless you're undergoing streaks of wet weather and cold. Camps are open in May or June and they close by the end of September. There are three categories, only the lowest (number 3) without hot showers. The others vary in quality but have the basics. A suggestion: bring a spare handle or a pair of pliers into the shower with you; you'll need something to work the controls, as Poles often steal the handles. Bring a sink stopper, too. They're not supplied. A campsite costs about the same as the average hostel.

Security is good. Campgrounds are used by Polish families on an outing or vacation, and your neighbors soon start looking out for you if you smile at them and say a few words. You can leave everything to their care without worry. Not that potential thieves are commonplace. Most other campers are young couples, who have no opportunity for privacy in crowded and shared city apartments.

225

Category 1 campgrounds have restaurants, which provide a convenient place to socialize with the natives. In contrast, most people you meet at hostels are other foreigners. In hotels, you meet virtually no one.

Campgrounds rent cabins reasonably, also, but they're hard to find unless you reserve ahead of time. Get help from an information office; have them call ahead if you can schedule your arrival.

Besides the paying campgrounds, you can also camp in any of the 500 free *parkingi,* or roadside bivouacs. Those were set up as rest stops for motorized vacationers, but Poles use them for overnight camping. They're primitive, generally without water. You'll have to bring that in from the nearest home, sometimes a couple of miles away, or beg it from other campers. The only things provided at the sites are roofed eating areas, with tables, outhouses and wastebaskets, but you do have a cleared area to pitch a tent, or you can sleep under the roof in case of rain.

You can camp in the open easily. Woods cover more than a fourth of Poland, and nature preserves—flora and fauna—are distributed throughout.

If you succeed in communicating your wishes, you might camp in someone's field or backyard. No one will refuse you, and you're apt to be invited inside the house for some socializing. The peasant is suspicious of strangers, but he's also humanly curious. If there's communication, he won't be able to resist finding out something about you. Should that happen, expect a mixture of very primitive living with modernism. Lighting may be one bare bulb with a pull cord in the middle of the room, and there may be an outhouse, but a brand-new color television is likely to sit in the center of the living room.

As far as I know, there are no laundromats in Poland. A resident of Warsaw told me that he thought he saw one once in that city, but he wasn't sure. It was probably a conventional laundry. Unless you stay in a city a long time to wait for that slow and uncertain service, you'd better wash your own clothes.

FOOD

Shops are open from 8:00 or 9:00 A.M. to 7:00 P.M. Dairy products are plentiful, while meat is scarce. If you attempt to cook for yourself, you'll not succeed in buying any beef or veal at all, the pork will be inferior, and even cold cuts and *kielbasa* (Polish sausage) are hard to find. You'll not penetrate the mass of people waiting outside the meat stores, anyhow. But fish and chicken can be found easily, cheaply and without waiting.

Greens and fruit are available only in season. Buy from farmers along the road. Costs of food are unbelievably low: a pound of excellent rye bread, 18¢; a pound of soft cheese, 55¢; a large bottle of jam, 20¢. But what with low restaurant prices, it hardly pays to carry food, except for emergencies.

A dish of stuffed cabbage costs 54¢; *kielbasa* and bread, 70¢; *kielbasa* in a *bigos* (a stew with cabbage), 50¢; a trout with a complete meal, $1 in a fancy restaurant; a cod fillet, 50¢; and crepes three for 15¢, with jam. Potatoes are served with just about everything. With cabbage, they seem to make up half the Poles' diet. As a change, try them as potato pancakes, which are quite good.

If you arrive too late at a cafe, it may have only one or two meal choices left. That happens by about 7:00 P.M. An evening's lot is cooked and when it's sold, that's it. But the bar section of the restaurant has a display case with refrigerated dishes of herring, chicken, deviled eggs and *kielbasa,* which can always fill you.

There's little lingering in restaurants. That's reserved for the drinking places. At the popular coffee house *(kawiarnia)* and the wine hall *(winiarnia),* a drink and a dainty cake can be stretched out for an hour. A cup of coffee at 60¢ was the most expensive drink I found, but a glass of tea cost a tenth of that. Beer prices were somewhere in between.

227

More to the taste of laborers and farm workers is the crowded beer-joint *(piwiarnia),* where the talk is 15 decibels higher than normal, and the atmosphere so thick that you can cut it.

You'll find no disposable gas cartridges of any kind in the country, should you plan to use a stove. Motorized campers use heavy butane-propane bottles that they refill at gas stations. A denatured alcohol is sold in grocery stores, about 40¢ for 8 ounces. "Express," a refined benzine, is sold in chemical stores, 25¢ a pint.

ADDRESSES AND FURTHER READING

Polish National Tourist Office
500 Fifth Avenue
New York, NY 10036
    and
333 North Michigan Avenue
Chicago, IL 60601

PTTK, Cycle Touring Commission
Senatorska 11
00-075 Warsaw
    Ask for information leaflet for foreign cyclists, and any specific questions about cycling.

ADVENTURE CYCLING IN EUROPE

Adam Bajcar, *Poland* (Polonia Publishing House, Warsaw, latest year). A Polish "Green Guide" that tells what to see, old and modern, the hotels, tourist hostels and campgrounds in each locality. A dozen city maps help you get around, and a short introduction reviews some history and offers useful travel information.

PORTUGAL
26

BIKING MATTERS
SUGGESTED TOURS

Portugal is the cycling backwater of Western Europe. Few Americans and not many Europeans cycle there. A small country and not advertised much, it wouldn't seem to hold advantages for the bike tourist. It's out of the way and there are stronger competitors for tourists in the Spanish cities to the east.

And yet, it's just this relative remoteness that keeps it largely unspoiled, and which promises a different kind of touring experience. I offer two tours, which can be combined for a total of 850 miles and up to four weeks of touring.

TOUR 1. The first is an easy to moderate 515 miles, at its longest, in the less mountainous and more popular south. It can take two easy weeks.

Start in Lisbon. Take a ferry, west of the bridge to Trafaria, across the river Tagus (Tejo). Bikes are not permitted on the bridge. Ride south to Costa de Caparica and east on 10-1 until you come to 10 at Corroios. Now south to Setubal and across the river to Outao, where you cycle on 263-1 to Comporta. There, pick up 261 all the way to Santiago do Cacem.

Great view of a castle here. You'll go over fairly even ground, with some rolling hills, passing groves of cork and eucalyptus trees. Small villages, with white houses that are outlined in blue resemble children's blocks. Occasional donkey carts will pass, and you'll see windmills on hills.

See another castle and a fishing village by riding southwest on 261-3 to Sines. Leave it on 120-1 and pick up 120 at Tanganheira. Stay on that road to Alfambras, with possible side trips to beaches on the Atlantic along the way. You'll not see the ocean from the road, otherwise.

You can now take either 268 to Sagres, at the extreme southwest tip of Europe, or ride 125 to Lagos, on the Algarve coast. This area is great during the winter off-season, but is crowded other

229

Atlantic Ocean

PORTUGAL

Aveiro

Figueira
da Foz
Coimbra

Guarda

230

Tomar

Santarem

Lisbon

Setubal

Evora

SPAIN

Santiago
do Cacem
Beja

N

Lagos

times. Parts of it have developed greatly in the last few years but not as much as in Spanish beach areas. In spite of many golf courses and tennis courts, it's largely native in character.

Follow the coast east on 125, rough in spots, to the Spanish border. Go north on 122. A castle to see in Castro Marim, and another in Mertola. North on 265 to Serpa, and 260 west to Beja. Now north on 18 about 7 miles, where you take a left fork onto 258-1 to Cuba, and then Alvito. There, take 257 north to Viana do Alentejo, and farther north on 254 to the walled city of Evora. Lots of interests and sights here.

Ride 114 west-northwest to Coruche, and 11-3 to Salvaterra de Magos. Return to Lisbon on 118 south, 10 west across the river, and south to the airport.

Except for the region between Beja and the coast, you'll not experience any hard riding.

Tour 2. There are more mountains and rougher roads on this tour, north of Lisbon. About 335 miles, and 10 days to 2 weeks.

Retrace the end of Tour 1 from the airport to Salvaterra. Continue on 118 upriver to just past Chamusca, where you cross over it on 243 to Golega. Go north on 365, then 110, through Tomar to Coimbra. Lots of ups and downs, and you'll be on a main highway, but secondary roads in this region are pretty rough. Many attractions in Coimbra.

Turn west on 111-1 a few miles to Geria, where you turn north on 234-1 to Cantanhede. Pick up 335 north to the old town of Aveiro. It's in the center of a large natural park, which extends south almost all the way to Lisbon.

Ride 109 or parallel park roads south. Tarry a while at Figueira da Foz, picturesque and with tourist attractions. Return to the main highway at Leiria. Take 1 a few miles south to Batalha. Avoid 1 the rest of the way to Lisbon by riding 362 to Santarem. Next, take 3 until the Tagus, where you pick up 10 to the Lisbon airport.

A dozen miles north of Coimbra, 234 and 16 can be taken to Guarda and farther north for some real cycling challenges. You'd have to be in great shape and have super-low gears for that part of Portugal.

MAPS, TERRAIN, TRAFFIC

The Michelin 990, which covers Portugal and Spain 1:1,000,000, can be used. Better is the Michelin 1:500,000. Best is the 1:550,000 map distributed free by the Automobile Club of Portugal. Ask them or the Portuguese National Tourist Office for a copy. The tourist office will also send you various city maps if you ask for them.

Roads are quite good, considering the poor economy of Portugal. Asphalt is common on most main roads and even the secondary ones, south of Lisbon. In the north, minor roads are rough in long stretches. But you're liable to come across some gravel or hard dirt, and occasional road repair almost anywhere. Cobblestone surfaces are usual in villages, towns and across old bridges.

The countryside is simply lovely, even along main highways. You'll not see the advertising and kitsch of other countries' tourist areas. Fishing villages are authentic, carts are painted colorfully and donkeys' harnesses are crafted lovingly—all genuine native work, not for the benefit of tourists. Village bars and cafes exude atmosphere. A cycling paradise.

Traffic is light, even on main roads. It's best to stay off them along the coast, when you can, to avoid trucks. My experience has been that drivers were courteous, though I've heard of some wild ones.

BEST CYCLING TIME

In the area of Tour 1, you can cycle with shorts and T-shirt during a winter's sunny afternoon. Average highs from December to February, in the south, are about 60°F. Nights will be cold and you'll have cool rain some days, but you'll think it's spring, overall. During January, the Algarve region is filled with almond blossoms, believe it or not.

232

Wait a month longer before cycling north of Lisbon. It's considerably colder and it rains more there. There's an average yearly difference of 15°F. between Porto, in the north, and the Algarve coast. The difference is even greater for the northeast, with its mountains. The northern parts are best cycled in early summer, while the south is quite hot.

If you plan to tour all of the country, cycle south at the end of February or beginning of March and finish a few weeks later in the north. You'll also avoid the early spring arrivals of tourists in both places. Or combine the southern tour with a visit to Seville and Cordoba in Spain.

Winds seem to be variable. In February, I had more winds from the north than from other directions.

BIKE EQUIPMENT, RENTALS

Outside of Lisbon, there's little in the way of equipment. I saw a good shop in the capital, on Bua Jose Estevao. The street is only two or three blocks long and the shop is easy to find. It had a Bianci and other quality 10-speeds. In other cities and towns, you may find some bike parts in motorcycle shops.

Three-speeds are available in large cities and they might be hired from bike shops by individual arrangement. But there's no country-wide bike hiring program, and the practice is not common to an individual shop, as the one in the capital.

BIKE TRANSPORTATION

Both trains and buses take bikes. Service is slow on both, and the train network is limited. A group of ten or more can get a discount on the train.

GENERAL
ENTERING, LEAVING, HASSLES

Passports, no visas, no hassles. I've always felt secure in my possessions, especially in villages. There are some approaches and whistles from men toward women bikers, especially in larger towns, but it's not as persistent or aggressive as in Italy.

LANGUAGE AND PEOPLE

Almost no English is spoken, even in many shops in Lisbon—not **233** in the bike shop that I visited, and where foreigners seldom come. Portuguese looks like Spanish, but its different pronunciation and general sound masks the resemblance. At least it does for me. You'll have to work at the language to be understood, if you know Spanish. French may be more easily understood by the educated than English, especially among older Portuguese.

The people are some of the gentlest I've known anywhere. I never saw any harshness, though some people were reserved to the point of coldness. As with many Spanish, the natives have a natural bearing and dignity. The impression is stronger for the somber black dresses that women wear, including long stockings and a fedora type of hat, in black also.

Still, when you're in need of help or simply wish to communicate, the native responds readily. Whether it's information or repair of a bike, people will go all out to aid you. Bikers remarked on it. "Some of the friendliest people in Europe," said Tyler Folsom of the people he met.

OVERALL COSTS

You can probably live on an average of $7 a day or less. I've not had recent data from bikers and can only estimate, based on other sources.

The Portuguese escondo has kept steady in the last few years, relative to the U.S. dollar, but inflation has been high. But I'd guess it still remains one of the cheapest countries in Western Europe.

ACCOMMODATIONS

It's easy to find a double for under $7. Showers may cost 40¢ extra each. Breakfasts are sometimes included. Two couples can even rent a villa for as little as $70 a week out of season. Prices are posted in rooms, but those are the maximums. You may be able to negotiate for a lower price if tourists are scarce and it's the off-season.

There are only 13 hostels in Portugal, 3 of them in the Lisbon area. Cost is $1.40 for those over 30, $1.15 for those under 30. That even includes the hire of sheets. No charge for tent camping. All but 3 hostels have kitchens. A fee of 10¢ a day is taken for kitchen privileges.

Hostels are so far apart—on the order of 100 miles—that they are impractical for your entire tour. If you don't stop at hotels or pensions, you can use some of the 70 campgrounds. Unfortunately, many of those are grouped around tourist cities; 15 are in the Lisbon area, for example, and 6 around Aveiro. Few can be found in the interior.

Some camps have lavish facilities, including restaurants, super-markets and swimming pools. Judy Glading wrote that one in Lisbon even had a hairdresser! Hot water, of course. Most have some food provisions and people may come around to sell bread, fruit and other food items. Send to the Directorate General of Tourism for a booklet.

Open camping is legal anywhere, and you may have to resort to that if away from civilization. Ordinarily, though, why do it when you pay so little for accommodations?

FOOD

Meals are reasonable to cheap. You can get a decent fish or meat meal in a city for $3.50 and pay half that in small towns.

Pork and chicken are the most common meats, and fresh fish and exotic seafood are staples. *Caldo verde,* a "green soup" of potato and cabbage, is popular. It's a filling snack and costs 25¢. Every region has a version of fish stew or a fish and meat casserole. Hostels sell meals at $1.60 and breakfast at 50¢.

A restaurant or cafe out in the country may be unmarked. Peek in when you see locals walking in and out of a house frequently. If you see tables and a bar, you'll know you're in the right place.

Fruit is ripe and inexpensive. Oranges cost 25¢ a pound and

234

figs a bit more than twice that. *Cornpal,* a fruit drink, is sold in cans. It's not a carbonated concoction, but the real thing. Great for energy pickups.

Picnic lunches are a delight, and are inexpensive: cheese, canned fish, sardines and other seafoods, and bread. Wash them down with a green wine like *vinho verde,* a Mateus rosé, or other local wines.

Fish is the best bet when cooking for yourself. You can buy it fresh almost anywhere. Fried, or made into a stew with vegetables, it can be your main food staple.

Shop hours are interrupted by the usual two-hour Mediterranean siesta, but stores stay open until about 7:00 P.M., Monday to Friday. Camping Gaz cartridges are sold.

ADDRESSES AND FURTHER READING

Portuguese National Tourist Office
548 Fifth Avenue
New York, NY 10036
and
1 Park Plaza, Suite 1305
3250 Wilshire Boulevard
Los Angeles, CA 90010

235

Directorate General of Tourism
Av. Antonio Augusto de Aguaiar 86
Lisbon

Automovel Club de Portugal (Automobile Club of Portugal)
Rua Rosa Araujo 24
Lisbon

Emily Kimbrough, *Pleasure by the Busload* (New York: Harper & Row, 1961). A somewhat bubbly but entertaining account of a trip through the Portuguese hinterlands by a well-known travel writer.

Michelin Green Guide, $7 in U.S.

ROMANIA
27

BIKING MATTERS
SUGGESTED TOURS

The first tour was taken by Don Lemmon, much of the second by Gerard van der Veer. Both tours were found satisfactory.

TOUR 1. Transylvania, Oradea to Bucharest; 380 miles, ten days. Arrive in Oradea by train from Budapest, Hungary. At 178 miles away, it's the nearest large city with an international airport. Or you can take a local flight from Bucharest to Oradea.

Your entire ride will be on E15, east and southeast to the capital. It's almost completely in the mountains, though river valleys are followed most of the way. Grades are gradual and long.

Roads are excellent. Lemmon says they're better than those in his home state of Pennsylvania. Very little truck traffic and drivers are respectful of bikers. They'd wait behind you on a curve for a clear road before passing, for example. Lemmon preferred them to their American counterparts.

TOUR 2. Oradea loop; 390 miles, two weeks. You can combine this tour with Tour 1 or take it by itself if you're touring eastern Hungary. It goes through parts seldom visited by foreigners. The southern half of the route is oriented more for visitors. It has a number of inns, motels, resorts and campgrounds along the road. The part north of E15 has almost no accommodations geared to tourists; you'll have to depend on the local situation, on the few existing campgrounds, and on open camping.

Take 19 north out of Oradea and through Satu Mare to the village of Livada. It's all a flat plain on the side of mountains, and a quiet road. Ride 1c southeast to Baia Mare. Van der Veer continued on 19 instead, cycling a loop along the USSR border, through Sighetu Marmatiei to Baia Mare. But he advises against that loop, saying the roads were very bad.

From Baia Mare go through Satulung and Dej on 1c to Cluj. The road is mostly flat along river valleys. Take E15 southeast to

Turda, and then ride upriver on 75 to Cimpeni. A long climb to Nucet, and then downriver on 76 to Oradea.

MAPS, TERRAIN, TRAFFIC

The 1:1,250,000 map issued free by the Romanian National Tourist Office shows hardly fewer usable roads than either the two Ravensteins—1:1,160,000 and 1:1,000,000—or the Geographia 1:1,000,000. Those cost from $4 to $6 at Complete Traveller. The Ravensteins and Geographia are combined with Bulgaria.

Buy a map before entering Europe, as neither Romania nor adjoining countries have any.

The central and northern parts of Romania are covered with mountains. The broadest plain is in the south along the Danube. In those southern farmlands, a countless string of backward villages lines secondary roads, such as 6 and 3. Few accommodations are available in them.

From Turnu-Severin to Bucharest, E94 is in poor shape and is filled with trucks and construction equipment. Although I took that road some years ago and the surface may have improved since, the traffic most certainly hasn't. I'd advise not to take it.

The northern and central parts of Romania remain the best touring areas. They have striking scenery, monasteries, and folk

237

craft villages. The Black Sea coast is full of resorts, of limited interest unless you just want to swim. Unlike in Bulgaria and Hungary, no roads are forbidden to bikers in Romania.

Main roads and many secondary ones are well paved. Small ones along borders, those through the most rugged mountains, and the farm roads of the south can be in awful shape. They're macadam surfaced, a base of crushed rock that is satisfactory when new or well maintained. When not, the roads become horribly rutted and potholed. In wet weather, the clayey mud becomes an adhesive. I had to chop mud that was built up between fork and wheel with a screwdriver in order to ride at all. Much cobblestone found in villages and towns.

Except for the trucks on E94, there's little traffic in Romania. On Lemmon's and van der Veer's routes, it was sparse. Secondary roads see mostly farm wagons and livestock.

BEST CYCLING TIME

June to August is hot. You can freeze in April, if you chance on a cold spell. Early May is safer to start, and September is a good touring time. Most rain falls in June. Traffic picks up a bit in the summer along the Black Sea, but it's a minor concern elsewhere during any month.

238

BIKE EQUIPMENT, RENTALS

I needed a rim and was able to buy a Russian 700c in Bucharest. Only tires of that size were available at the cycle shop, though the rims were erroneously stamped as taking 27-inch tires. I saw no other bike parts that would be useful on my bike. Lemmon talked to a group of club riders with good machines. They said that one of them who'd be traveling to the West would always return with parts for all. It was their only source of quality components.

It's doubtful if any kind of bicycles are rented anywhere in the country.

BIKE TRANSPORTATION

The chances of getting a bike on a plane for an in-country flight are very good. In that respect, Lemmon found all of Eastern European bureaucracy reasonable and informal. You'll pay extra for the bike since there's a weight limit on baggage.

Van der Veer took a train to Holland from Cluj, so trains will take bikes. I have no information about bikes on buses, but there's a kind of informal citizens' system of transport. Private cars and trucks pick up passengers for a small fee. One may take your bike if it has room.

Stand on the highway and flag down a vehicle. The amount to pay is negotiated simply. State your destination and let the driver write the fee on a piece of paper. If you agree, get in. If not, wave him on.

GENERAL
ENTERING, LEAVING, HASSLES

Passport and a visa are needed. The visa is issued either at the border or in the United States. The latter is better. You have to change a minimum of $10 a day to get a visa, or prepay for accommodations.

I received no reports of harassment of any kind, nor of border difficulties.

Kids pester for cigarettes and chewing gum on the road. They're not obnoxious or nasty as some of those in eastern Turkey, but Gypsies may try to pilfer things off your bike. It happened to me. Pass your shock cords through loops on sleeping bag sacks and don't keep removable items under them. Threaten any would-be thieves with *milicia*, Romanian for police. They seem to be in terror of the word.

239

LANGUAGE AND PEOPLE

Romanian is seemingly close to Italian when you see it written, and you can catch some words if you know it or Spanish. But Romanian also contains words from Slav languages. There are four dialects in the country, different enough to cause difficulty in understanding even for Romanians.

French is taught in schools and German is spoken in the north, but English is hardly known. The tourist offices are of little help. Most are prepared for Slav or German visitors, not English. Outside of Bucharest, don't expect to be understood in English.

The people are outgoing, effusive like their Latin cousins rather than reserved like some of their Slav neighbors. Both Lemmon and van der Veer commented on it, and that was also my impression. Van der Veer noted that many middle class citizens with money and interest in the West approach you for Western goods, such as jeans, cigarettes, lighters, nylon stockings and ballpoint pens.

When I had to replace my bent rim, I found everyone sympathetic and helpful. They took me to a home-industry type of iron-monger who gave me aid and an offer of supper and an overnight stay. There was no question of it. The village felt responsible for me and my problem.

OVERALL COSTS

You'll live well on the $10 minimum exchange if you stick to camping instead of indoor stays. When planning to camp, those costs can be prepaid. The Romanian Automobile Club coupons you buy will satisfy prepayment and no minimum exchange will be needed. Check with the tourist office on how to buy the vouchers.

Banks are open mornings, and hotels and tourist offices change money 8:00 A.M. to 8:00 P.M. Any money left over will be reconverted, given that it's in excess of the minimum per day and that you have receipts for its exchange. You may run into an official not too familiar with that practice; keep any printed matter stemming from Romania that states the principle. If some trouble arises, show it to the border personnel to convince them of it.

The black market will give you an exchange rate twice the official one, or more, but it's risky. You might be cheated or turned in.

ACCOMMODATIONS

Hotel prices are fixed by the state, according to category. The lowest listed by the tourist office in 1980 cost $17 double and $13.25 single in Bucharest. There are cheaper hotels, but they'll try to send you to the most expensive. Nothing malicious in that; they believe Americans want the best.

240

Hotels in small cities and towns cost less, as low as $12 double, $9 single. You'll not get one of those unless you book ahead or chance on it. Prices are 20 percent lower off-season.

Motels along the highway can be found for about $3 a person, more in popular places. Make arrangements on the spot. The tourist office can arrange for a room in a private home. Romanians are expressly forbidden to take you into their homes unofficially, though they do. At least it has happened to me.

No hostels are listed in the IYH Handbook, but they do exist. They cater to youth and officially serve only groups, and they have built-in socialistic propaganda in their organized programs. The arrangements don't seem useful to bike tourists, but you might be interested in seeing what is offered in the way of a short stay. Ask the tourist office for a copy of "Holidays for Youth." Prices seem very reasonable.

Campgrounds are located along main roads and in a few mountain resort areas. The tourist office doesn't tell the prices, seemingly not encouraging those inexpensive accommodations. A bungalow in a campground costs about $6 for two, which suggests tent camping must be quite cheap.

As in all Eastern European countries, and in many Western

ones too, camping in the open is not allowed officially. Natives do camp and there's no reason why anyone would challenge you, unless you run into some kind of official trouble. Best to stay out of sight, of course. That's easy to do in wooded mountain areas, but most of the plains have no woods. You'd have to plan to stay at campgrounds there. Asking a farmer for permission to camp on his land wouldn't be fair to him. The tent would be too obvious and your illegal stay would get him and you in trouble.

FOOD

Romania is one of the poorest European countries in which to eat. Restaurants in towns are dismal affairs, drab in decoration and with crude tables and chairs. Food is plain, mostly soups, cabbage and poor-quality meat, though meals are cheap. The best restaurant in a small town will serve a substantial meal for $3.50. In the simple bar-restaurants you pay half that or less.

Shopping for food is a horror. Stores have long hours, some well into the evening, but outside of the capital there's little to buy. Most communities are self-sufficient, and they have no need to carry much food.

Canned goods are limited and cost about the same as in the United States. In a town, a store may have one kind of canned meat, two kinds of jam, sauerkraut, olives, dried soup, and not much else. The meat is generally fatty and gristly. Except in season, there's no fruit except one or two kinds in canned form.

241

Dark bread is good and cheap. Excellent salami is the best thing that can be bought in the country. With jam, that can form your lunches. You may also buy eggs and vegetables from farmers. Bring a phrase book to let them know what you're looking for.

You're really better off to eat your main meals in restaurants. I made a practice of filling up every time I found a good place to eat, even though I had eaten an hour or two earlier. Still, keep some emergency canned or freeze-dried goods just in case. Bring those in from a neighboring country or from home.

ADDRESSES AND FURTHER READING

Romanian National Tourist Office
573 Third Avenue
New York, NY 10016

Romanian Automobile Club (ACR)
1 Bucharest
27 Nikos Beloiannis St

ADVENTURE CYCLING IN EUROPE

Juliana G. Pilon, *Notes from the Other Side of the Night* (South Bend, Ind.: Regnery/Gateway, 1979). An emigrant, the author returns for a visit and comments on the daily life in a Communist system. Best of the lot about this country.

242

SPAIN
28

BIKING MATTERS
SUGGESTED TOURS

TOUR 1. Madrid–Granada–Seville–Cordoba: the great cities. About 510 miles and two weeks, more with longer visits in cities.

Madrid is a few miles north of the geographic center of the Iberian peninsula. Roads radiate from it like a spider's web. This route is one of the strands that leads to the south, the must place for any traveler to Spain. But in spite of attracting tourists like flies, these cities overwhelm them with their history and beauty. The first part of the tour, to Granada, was provided by Donald Tomlin, who cycled it in 1978.

Because of the lack of many secondary roads fit for cycling, you're confined pretty much to a direct route. Take 401 from the capital to Toledo, then C400 until it joins N4 at Madridejos.

At Toledo, you could continue on N401, instead, to Ciudad Real. It's worth a visit for its Gothic cathedral. You can then join N4 by cycling on C415 to Valdepenas.

At Bailen, leave N4 and cycle south on N323 to Granada. West on N342 and N334 leads to Seville. From there, take N4 east to Cordoba. C431 can be taken instead of N4, but it has some bad stretches just before Cordoba.

From Granada, you can head south through Otivar to Almunecar and the beaches of the Costa del Sol. Or cycle C340 and C335 to Malaga, and from there to Seville on N334. You'll not like the Costa del Sol, however, unless you enjoy a Miami Beach kind of development. Trains can be taken from any of these destinations to Madrid.

Tomlin said that the road from Madrid to Bailen was good, and N323 to Granada poor to fair. The balance of road to Almunecar was excellent. Traffic on his route varied—he went in July—from heavy to hardly any. He had a low development of 22 inches and didn't have to walk any hills, but he did have to work to make some of them.

243

ADVENTURE CYCLING IN EUROPE

TOUR 2. Southern Pyrenees and Andorra to Barcelona. About 520 miles, two to three weeks, depending on pace.

This tour was contributed by Tibor Pollerman, an American living in London. It's a fairly difficult ride, and you should be in good touring shape. You'll bike a number of high passes and climbs, but gradients won't exceed 10 percent. All roads are asphalted, though some are bumpy because of larger, imbedded stones (rated as good, below). Traffic is very light, with only some congestion near Barcelona.

Start at Irun, a dozen miles east of San Sebastian. Get to it by train from Paris, via Bayonne, or take a ferry from Plymouth, England, to Santader, and take a train or cycle east to Irun. You can also take a train from Madrid, in which case get off at Pamplona, 55 miles south of Irun.

From Irun take C133 and N121 to Pamplona on an excellent road. North of that city, an unnumbered road goes east to Aoiz, then north to Arive, and east to Escaroz. Six miles farther north, turn southeast to Isaba, south to Roncal and east to Anso. Now

south until you meet N240. East on it and then C134 to Jaca. Still excellent roads.

Stay on C134 to Sabinanigo, 8 miles north to Biescas, and east on C140 to Broto on a good road. Ride southeast on C138 to Ainsa and east on C140 on excellent roads. C139 north to Castejon de Sos is a good road. Now southeast on C144 through Pont de Suert and C147 to Tremp, both excellent roads. East from here to Coll de Nargo, a good road.

At Coll, you can save about 75 miles and a lot of hard climbing by going directly to Barcelona on C1313 south, then southeast on C1410. Otherwise, continue Pollerman's route northeast to Andorra and south to Barcelona on excellent roads.

Take C1313 north into Andorra and join C145 and then N20, the latter actually in France. Ride south on it through Puigcerda into a twisty N152 to Ripoli. Continue all the way to Barcelona. Take a train there to almost anywhere, or cycle on the coastal roads to France or southern Spain.

MAPS, TERRAIN, TRAFFIC

The map provided by the tourist office is hardly better than a sketch; it's useless for cycling. General plans of four cities are on it, though, and it does show the locations of mountains.

The Michelin 99, 1:1,000,000, contains the principal secondary roads. Many of these are unsurfaced, so revelations of more roads on a map of larger scale may be of doubtful value.

In any case, only northern Spain and coastal areas are covered in more detail, in the 2 Michelin 1:400,000, the 13 Firestone Hispania, and the 3 Mair maps, the last two series in 1:200,000 scale. CTC sells the Firestones at $2.25 each, and the American Map Company the Mairs at $3.25.

No tour you can devise in Spain will be all on flat land, unless it's limited to a short stretch along one of the coastal areas or solely in La Mancha country, south of Madrid. But even on the coast, you soon bump into sharp hills, such as in the foothills of the Sierra Nevada between Malaga and Ameria on the Costa del Sol. Spain's mountain ranges have a habit of spilling right into the ocean.

The feel of that kind of cycling was graphically put by Judy Glading: "The road drops off to dizzy depths on one side, and rises in a sheer wall on the other. You can look down on the tops of mountains and villages a mile distant, atop another hill . . . Along the coast you could go five kilometers, and look over and see the point you left an hour before only 50 feet away."

Spain fascinates and satisfies the general tourist. It offers Moorish palaces and Gaudi's architectural fantasies; Goya, Picasso, and Altamira's cave paintings; wild scenery and placid vineyards; small, sun-bleached villages, and crowded, narrow alleys in old cities. What it lacks for the cyclist is a good system of paved secondary roads. The only areas where they're relatively abundant are in Castile and Mancha.

Nevertheless, you can avoid main roads in many parts by flanking loops, usually through hills and over rougher surfaces. These options, in spite of discomfort, are the more satisfactory as a cycling strategy. They take you into tourist-free villages, and they offer the real Spain.

Road surfaces can be horrid. Unexpected stretches of repair work pile up traffic and make you walk. Once we came upon a German cyclist on top of a hill, sitting by the side of a torn-up road. "Miseria," he murmured weakly as we pushed our bikes past him and his heavy utility bike.

Holes on downhills are a frequent worry. Where roads are in excellent condition is where you'll find the bulk of the traffic. But there are surprises. A minor road can be both excellent and traffic free, as in Pollerman's Tour 2. Of course, you pay for that pleasure in harder pedaling.

BEST CYCLING TIME

The climate varies greatly. The mountains, the effects of surrounding water, and the lack of humidity in the central plateau result in a subtropical region in one area, and a pleasantly dry mountain village a hundred miles away. The only generality that can be said for the mainland is that it's too hot in summer for any extended trip by bicycle, except for the northern coast where it's cooler. The high monthly temperatures there average in the mid-seventies.

Early spring, starting even in March, offers great cycling on the southern coast. That month is also free of the hordes of motorized tourists that descend from the north a month or two later. Midspring is better for the inland regions of the south, the northern regions and the eastern beaches.

Fall is good everywhere. You can even cycle comfortably in early winter between Malaga and Alicante, at which time the crowds diminish. It may be cold camping some nights then, however, and the shorter days will make dull evenings in the dark. December high and low averages there are 64 and 50, the same as in March. The cycling season in Spain is long.

Rain is scarce in late spring and the summer months, but that depends on the part of the country. The northern coast tends to be moist a good part of the time, and the Mediterranean coast had a lot of rain in late winter and early spring, when I was there.

BIKE EQUIPMENT, RENTALS

Most bike parts can be found in the largest cities. In spite of backwardness in many parts of the economy, Zeus bike components are made in the country. Bike racing is an enthusiastic sport. Tires sold are 700c size, so bring spares if you have 27-inch. If you don't need a part that specifically has to fit an English thread, you'll not want for replacements.

I've never heard of anyone renting a bike in Spain. If it's possible, it's doubtful that anything but a 1-speed can be found.

BIKE TRANSPORTATION

No problems whatsoever on trains, as long as the one you're on has a baggage car and won't make transfers. Otherwise, bring the bike in a day early (or wait). There's no charge. No bikes taken on buses.

GENERAL
ENTERING, LEAVING, HASSLES

No visa, just a passport.

In the Franco days, there was some harassment of long-hairs, except on the Costa del Sol and other relaxed, coastal areas. Today, attitudes are easier, but relative formality still reigns in the matter of dress. Off the beach, it's considered disrespectful to walk around in shorts, women and men both. Custom should also be observed in churches, where women should have some sort of head cover and not expose expanses of flesh.

Machismo is rampant in Spain, but it's benign compared to Turkey or Italy. Men are persistent but romantic in pursuing women. They clap as a woman cycles by. Not many Spanish women cycle; I saw only young teenagers, on banana-seat bikes, in large cities and recreation areas.

You'll get catcalls wearing a helmet, but Spanish drivers were reported to be courteous. Lock your bike and remove pumps and other easily removable items in cities like Madrid and Barcelona. I always felt trustful of people in villages.

LANGUAGE AND PEOPLE

You may have studied Spanish and considered yourself proficient enough to get by. You then hear someone talking in a bar in Barcelona or Bilbao and can't make out any of the conversation.

Don't downgrade your ability; they're probably talking in Catalan or Basque, separate languages from Spanish.

But even your new-world Spanish may be somewhat inadequate to the Castillian form, and to local accents. You'll have to get attuned to the slight changes in pronunciation.

English is scarce in out-of-the-way places, but common in the tourist traps. If you rely on it, you'll not communicate with the Spanish. In places like Torremolinos, on the southern coast, I was hard put to find a Spaniard, in fact. The coast was full of Scandinavians and English, not to mention the Germans, who are most everywhere in Europe where there's a road. All those foreigners speak English, of sorts, and you won't be wanting for conversation.

The siesta impression of Spaniards is off the mark. They have a sense of balance, as far as pace is concerned, but they're hardly an easygoing people. I saw energy and industry everywhere— forever cleaning in cafes and working hard in the fields—and got a distinctly opposite impression. That's true especially in the north, where the climate is more conducive to extra vigor.

Dignity is also a distinguishing feature. No matter the job or situation, a Spaniard has a sense of bearing and strength of character that's notable. All cyclists commented on the friendliness and consideration of the people that they met.

248

OVERALL COSTS

Gone are the days when you could get along on $4 a day in Spain, with a double room for $1 and a much better one for $2. Now you'll pay twice that and more. But it's still one of the best bargains in Europe.

The bikers who've been there recently (1978–79) spent $10 a day with stays in hotels (shared) or campgrounds for half the time, and open camping the rest. Most ate in restaurants or cafes, with just picnic lunches and snacks bought in grocery stores. If they cooked meals and camped more, the daily average would have been closer to $7 a day, and even much less with total reliance on open camping and cooking.

The peseta has remained constant with the dollar in the past couple of years, but inflation has driven prices up. Expect to spend from $8.50 to $12 a day under the above conditions.

If you want to save money, stay away from tourist centers and the coastal areas. Those are not only higher in hotel and food prices, but it's more difficult to find free camping in the midst of the development.

A 50 percent reduction is given those 65 and over for train trips longer than 60 miles. Banks are open 9:00 A.M. to 2:00 P.M., an hour less on Saturdays. Don't exchange all your money when you first enter. Ask other travelers for places that will give you the best rates. They differ. Exchange fees are reasonable.

ACCOMMODATIONS

A one-star double room costs $17, with breakfast. One-star *hostals* and pensions cost half that, but you can even find double rooms for $5. Showers are extra. Tyler Folsom paid $1.55 for his half of a double in Port Bou in 1978, about the same as at the hostel. Singles are about two-thirds of doubles. An occasional hotel may not let a man and woman share a room if they're not married.

Hostels are about $2 each. Full pension for a day is $7; if your tour includes only hostels, your overall daily cost can be just that amount, or a little more.

Close to 90 hostels are listed in the IYH Handbook. They're distributed fairly evenly, but since Spain is a large country there may be as much as 175 miles between two of them. To depend only on hostels, you'd have to choose your route carefully.

Preference is given to those 25 and younger, though I've not seen that enforced. No family rooms are offered in Spanish hostels. Most require a breakfast to be bought at 65¢. Few of them have kitchens.

249

Hundreds of campgrounds exist, but only a few dozen are located away from the coast. Even those are bunched around the large cities. You can't depend on them solely for accommodations.

Most camps have the usual amenities. The better ones have hot showers. Provision stores are well stocked and are open even on Sunday and into the evening. Many camps stay open all year. Some have bungalows. Costs are reasonable, a top price of $5 for two people with a tent. A camping *carnet* is needed.

Free camping is officially forbidden near towns, rivers, beaches and other developed land. I've not had any problems with camping in the open, even near populated areas. I usually made an effort to stay away from direct sight of the highway, though.

FOOD

Spanish food is delicious and restaurant prices are cheap to reasonable. A *menu de la casa,* a full meal with wine, starts at about $3 in a cafeteria, or $4.50 in a good restaurant. Two *paella Valenciana* dinners—chicken, ham, sausage, shrimp, fish, in rice—with table wine will cost less than $4.50. Table wine alone costs 70¢ a liter, and good sherry $2.25. A serving of *tapas,* clams, anchovies or other snacks, costs $1.

Away from tourist areas, meals are even cheaper. Portions are generous, and you'll fill up. Sometimes you'll walk into a place advertised outside as a restaurant and might find yourself in a bar. Look again; the restaurant is probably up the stairs, on the other side of the bar.

You can cook for yourself, but there's some difficulty in finding a full range of ingredients in villages. Fresh and delicious produce and fruit is abundant and cheap, though; a vegetarian's delight.

A long siesta in the afternoon should be accounted for when shopping. Food shops stay open into the evening, to about 8:00 P.M.

Stream water is doubtful; boil it, outside of high mountains. Many villages have safe drinking water springs in their center. Because it's so cheap, Spain should be enjoyed. Other than picnic lunches and a lot of fruit snacks, I prefer to eat in modest restaurants most of the time.

ADDRESSES AND FURTHER READING

Spanish National Tourist Office
665 Fifth Avenue
New York, NY 10022
and
209 Post Street, Suite 710
San Francisco, CA 94108

Federacion Espanola de Ciclismo
Ferraz 16
Madrid

This bike club may answer your inquiries (in Spanish). They did mine, but I wrote in relation to this guide.

Michelin Green Guide, $7 in U.S.

James Michener, *Iberia: Spanish Travels and Reflections* (New York: Random House, 1968). Ten leading cities, and all about customs, art and people. By the popular author, also an aficionado of Spanish ways.

A NOTE ON ANDORRA

Tibor Pollerman found Andorra disappointing in that it was very commercialized: "After riding through the Spanish Pyrenees, it seemed like entering Las Vegas, with duty-free shops everywhere selling cameras, perfumes, liquor, and so forth. But after leaving the town of Andorra, the scenery was beautiful and the

250

accomplishment of climbing more than a mile up is worth it."

He used a Firestone Hispania map (Pirineo Oriental T-24, 1:200,000). The road through Andorra is much wider than the Spanish and French connecting roads. He found the traffic slight. There are no trains in Andorra. Both Spanish and French are spoken, though the native language is Catalan. Spanish or French currency can be used.

251

SWEDEN
29

BIKING MATTERS
SUGGESTED TOURS

TOUR 1. Lapland, 520 to 550 miles, about two weeks, a tour that goes through vast expanses of forests and mountains. The route is paved all the way, unless you take some detours on small, connecting roads. You'll climb hills throughout until you reach the eastern leg, along the Finnish border.

Start at Lulea, which has an airport and is on E4 on the northeast coast. Take National 97 to Boden and Jokkmokk (Arctic Circle here). All upriver, gradually, into high country. Continue N97 to junction of N98. Some climbs on way to Svappavaara. You'll be in the heart of Lapp country. A connection with Norway can be made by following N98 to Kiruna, where the road stops, and taking the train to Narvik.

Take County 395 to Vittangi and follow downriver to Pajala. Join C400 and ride the Torne Alv (river) to the coast at Sangis. Or to Harapanda, using N99. On E4 back to Lulea for about 65 miles (or 85 from Harapanda), but much of that main road travel can be relieved with loops of secondary roads. In any case, E4 is not bad; it has a good shoulder and bikepaths in built-up areas, although it's noisy with traffic and smells of exhaust.

The farthest distance between either campgrounds or youth hostels is 68 miles; settlements where food can be bought are within a half-day's ride at most. During the last leg, along the Finnish border, cross over the river at a number of points for cheaper Finnish food or accommodations.

TOUR 2. Southern provinces, about 335 miles. A mixture of Baltic seashore, farms and woods, it can take up to two weeks if you loiter or take side trips. Flat along the shore and some benign hills inland.

Start at Ystad (Malmo, 40 miles west, has an airport), at the southern tip of Sweden. Ride N10 and C103 to Simrishamn. Rejoin N10, then C118 to Ahus and Rinkaby. Side road east to Solvesborg,

SWEDEN

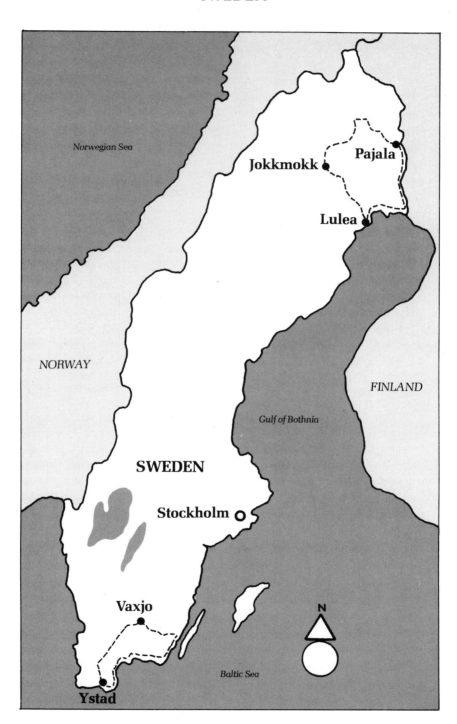

N15 along coast all the way to Kalmar. N15 can get busy at the height of the season, and you'll find less traffic by taking N29 north at Karlshamn and C120 east at Tingsryd. Visit Oland Island, opposite Kalmar, for a day or two of riding.

From Kalmar west on N25 to Vaxjo; this area has the Kosta, Boda and Orrefors glassworks, where you can view the making of that renowned Swedish product. Southwest on N23 to Osby and a return south on 20 to Ystad. A ferry goes twice a day to Poland from this historic, old port town.

The Swedish Cyclists' Touring Club schedules a score of tours in all parts of the country. Get information from local tourist offices or write to them in Stockholm.

MAPS, TERRAIN, TRAFFIC

The free Scandinavian National Tourist Office map, 1:3,500,000 Scandinavia, serves only to show Sweden's position relative to its neighbors. That office will also send an OK Motoring in Sweden map, 1:1,200,000, that may be satisfactory if you're not interested in the smallest roads, usually graveled. The map does show symbols for the locations of camping sites and historic spots.

254   The Geographia 1:800,000 Norway and Sweden, although expensive and bulky, is a good choice if you'll visit both countries. You can buy it from CTC, or in United States or English bookstores.

The nine sheets of G.L.A. "Turist Kartan Svenska" maps, 1:300,000, are most detailed. They show topography and walking routes, hostels and campsites, and are probably too detailed for the bike tourist unless he wants to explore a small area in depth.

Write to the Tourist Department of the Swedish Embassy for a map of "Road Conditions on National Main Roads and the County Roads." As in the rest of Scandinavia, roads are narrow. Surfaces are excellent on roads marked as paved. Gravel roads are difficult for narrow tires; take those only if you have 1⅜-inch tires, or wider.

Urban areas have cycle paths, which are compulsory where they accompany the road. They're well marked coming into towns, but not so going out. You can get lost; make a practice of looking back at the signs that lead into town to insure you're still on the path. If in doubt, use the motorway. Should the police stop you, they'll at least be able to direct you to the cycle path.

Sweden has soft contours all along its shores, with hills only well inland and in the north. Those areas are also well forested, the coastal areas being mostly in farms.

Only three roads, from Sundsvall, Umea and Skelleftea (all on the coast), lead through the mountains into Norway. E78 in the extreme north just skirts Sweden, on its way from Finland to Norway.

The countryside is very pleasant, with wildflowers all along the roads. Very little garbage is seen. In spring and early summer you can pick wild strawberries, blueberries and raspberries almost everywhere. In August, mushrooms and other berries can be picked.

BEST CYCLING TIME

A short spring and fall make May to September the practical range of cycling time. About 60°F. is the average daily maximum during those two months in Stockholm. In the north, cut that time by a month on each end. June is the best month, since it precedes school dismissal, and has the most light in the day (24 hours near Finland). July is the worst, with most traffic on the roads.

Most rain falls in August, with July and September having less, and May and June being the driest. Rain comes in showers and doesn't last long. In a month of cycling we had only a few days of rain, and that mostly during the late afternoon and night. We did have one awful downpour for half the day, but that was unusual. The air is always fresh, although there are signs of pollution near large cities and a stench in towns with paper mills.

255

BIKE EQUIPMENT, RENTALS

We sent 27-inch tires on ahead as replacements, and were surprised to find when we got there that those sizes were stocked in bike stores. We were told that was a recent development. There were also many good quality components—derailleurs, freewheels, chains. Parts availability has improved in the last few years, and more and better equipment is coming in all the time, according to Goran Lundstrom of Spanga, our informant and new-found friend.

Rentals are common in all cities. Quality varies, but you can find an adequate bike for casual riding, at least.

BIKE TRANSPORTATION

You'll either have to check the bike into the train station two days ahead of time or wait a day for it to arrive after you get to your destination. Buses may carry bikes, but generally not in built-up regions as around Stockholm.

If you stay in the capital a few days, you're better off to use the subway instead of using the bike to see the sights. A pass can be bought for $7 (at the station or a newsstand) that allows unlimited travel for three days.

GENERAL
ENTERING, LEAVING, HASSLES

Just a passport if coming in by air or sea, not even a passport check when cycling in from an adjoining country. Visa if for more than three months. No in-country problems of any kind.

LANGUAGE AND PEOPLE

Much English is spoken. Other languages seem to be rare, except for German in camps and restaurants. Swedish pronunciation is strange—the "a" in Lulea, for example, is pronounced like an "o"—and even though a Swede may speak English, he won't understand place names and Swedish words unless you pronounce them correctly. Get a small dictionary.

Swedes are things-oriented, resembling Americans. This is essentially a socialist country. It has superior social services—infant mortality is the lowest in the world, for example—and its per capita income is consistently among the highest. The general affluence is reflected in its consumption habits.

Department stores are full of quality goods and there's a mania for boats both on the seashore and in the inland lakes areas. Swedes love the outdoors. They sail and take walks in the mountains. Men and women know how to relax and enjoy the good life; it's common to see a car pull over at midday near a clearing in the woods, a table set up with chairs, and coffee made on a Primus stove. The sight is striking, the man reading the morning paper and the woman serving, or vice versa, under tall pines in the forest.

Like Norwegians, Swedes tend not to intrude on your privacy until an overture is made. Then, they're quite friendly. But don't expect to be invited into a home easily.

OVERALL COSTS

We spent $10 each for daily living, the same as in Norway. However, we seldom camped for free and that inflated the average somewhat. With more open camping and cooking for yourself, I'd judge $9.50 to $11 a day to be a reasonable cost for 1981.

"Low Cost Vacationing in Scandinavia," from the Scandinavian National Tourist Office, lists the less expensive hotels, ways to beat meal prices, and inexpensive diversions in the larger cities. Their "Youth Travels in Sweden" is also valuable for savings and services available for the young. Visitors 67 and older pay half-price on trains and Stockholm buses.

You'll be charged a fixed fee of about $2 for cashing traveler's

256

checks in banks, also for exchanges of American money in amounts larger than about $12. Exchange a large sum at a time.

ACCOMMODATIONS

A few hotels can be found starting at $12 single, $17 double, in small towns; more usual for a room without bath is $16 and $22 and up. Stockholm and the largest cities will charge twice that and more.

A room for two in a private home costs as low as $12, half again more in big cities. The tourist office that books it for you charges another $2. It comes to little more than what two would pay in a hostel, if at the low rate, and it could be more pleasant. A private home in the midst of a city is often a problem for bike storing, though. It may have to be left locked on the street when the rentor doesn't want it inside or if he has no cellar space. The room may not have cooking privileges either, another disadvantage.

Unlike in Norway, the prices of youth hostels—$3.75 to $5.50—don't include a mandatory breakfast. We didn't use many hostels in Sweden. The few we tried were full or crowded. One turned us out into the rain, being full of long-term residents, although we were allowed first to make a supper in its kitchen.

A group of six can rent a chalet in a campground for $18. Two will have to sleep on the floor, since it'll have four beds. A chalet is much like a Norwegian *hytter,* with a hot plate for cooking and beds without linen.

Over 500 formal campgrounds are scattered throughout the country. They often don't open until mid-June, but caretakers are accommodating; they may not charge anything and will even open washrooms for you. Camp locations are given in the National Tourist Office's "Camping in Sweden."

A tent site costs from $2.75 to $6, based on one tent to the site. We found that you can occasionally argue the point that bikes take less room than cars and get a discount. There are kitchens and sometimes dining areas. Showers are often included; when not, you pay a reasonable 25¢ each.

Campgrounds are officially rated from one to three stars, but their quality is seldom correlated to either cost or category. We found seaside camps generally bad and costly, and highly rated officially. Although 95 square yards are theoretically allotted per site, in practice the grounds were jammed with caravans and we were hard put to find enough space for bikes and tent.

Some random judgments on camps—Recommended: Lulea (good facilities, crowded in caravan area but not in a separate tenting area); Ava Havsbad (good facilities, next to lake, quiet, well laid out); Bergeforden (excellent facilities, very crowded but not on edges, where caravans couldn't go); Sandarne, Steno camp (crowded and not enough showers, but good kitchen and pleasant site); Bjorklinge (although primitive facilities, sauna and shower were good, quiet and uncrowded); Bergkvara (on an island, good kitchen and showers, plenty of room); Borga (beautiful). The Sjalevad camp, just south of Ornskoldsvik, doesn't charge anything for bicyclists. The owners told us they believe in bike travel, though they don't do it themselves.

Not recommended: Byske (overcharged for the facilities provided, showers hopeless, very crowded); Umea (small kitchen, bad facilities, shower's hot water ran out); Furuvik (a sardine tin, kitchen OK but not showers, laundry room locked up); Soderkoping (completely hopeless); Ahus (poor facilities, no character).

"Everyman's right" allows camping in the open, as in Norway.

FOOD

Forget smorgasbord, unless you're extremely hungry and think you'll get your money's worth. It's not a bargain otherwise; at the kind of fancy restaurant that you see in typical travel literature, it can cost as much as $25. A poor man's "breakfast smorgasbord" can be usually bought for about $3.50 at railroad cafeterias of large cities, and in Stockholm's Central Station you can even get all-you-can-eat buffet lunches or supper for $7; treat yourself occasionally to this reasonable facsimile.

258

Meals, from $4.50 to $6.75 even in cafeterias, are relatively the greatest expense in Sweden for active bikers. The best bargain is a restaurant with a sign saying "servering." It offers *husmanskost*, or home cooking, is more representative of the country's cuisine, and a lunch costs from $3.50 to $7. But the only way to save money is by cooking for yourself, or at least filling up on store-bought, ready-to-eat cold foods.

Shop at Domus or Konsum stores. Hours are 9:00 A.M. to 5:30 P.M., Saturdays half-days. Prices (1979) are decidedly higher than in the United States: (per pound) coffee, $4; meat, $2.50 to $6; hamburger meat, $3 and more; frozen vegetables, $1.80 to $2.75; cheese, $2.50 to $5.

Strawberries in season were $1 a quart; at the end of the season, $3. The first fresh peas in spring brought $2.65 a pound; they're considered a delicacy and were bought up fast. Smoked eel in a delicatessen cost $1.80 each (delicious and should be tasted).

Bread is $1.20 a pound. It's wrapped, spongy and sweet. The only decent bread is bought fresh from a bakery *(konditori)* ; ask for *osotat,* the word for nonsweet or slightly sweet. The *konditori* also serve coffee and pastry.

A cup of coffee costs up to $1, but a refill will be half or less. A 10-ounce bottle of weakish beer (class 2, Vikt) costs about $1; in the supermarket it's 75¢. Liquor is extremely expensive and is sold only in government stores. It's a wonder how the country can have a drinking problem.

S-200 gas cartridges for cooking stoves are common. So is alcohol in convenient small containers, if you have that kind of stove. A refined kerosene, with hardly any smell, is called "white *fotogen*" and is cheap, at about 25¢ a pint in bulk from Gulf gas stations.

ADDRESSES AND FURTHER READING

Scandinavian National Tourist Office
75 Rockefeller Plaza
New York, NY 10019
and
3600 Wilshire Boulevard
Los Angeles, CA 90010

259

Cykel & Mopedframjandet (Cyclists' Touring Club)
Stora Nygatan 41-43
103 12 Stockholm 2

Toni Scheiders, *Sweden* (New York: Hill & Wang, 1959). Timeless photos to whet your appetite for this country.

Paul B. Austin, *On Being Swedish* (Miami, Fla.: Univ. of Miami Press, 1970). The Swedish character told by an Englishman living there. What's behind Sweden's society, its history, manners and art.

SWITZERLAND
30

BIKING MATTERS
SUGGESTED TOURS

TOUR 1. Geneva to Zurich; 320 or more miles, depending on roads taken. About two weeks with layovers, flat or rolling country and easy cycling.

Leave Geneva either on 1 or over minor roads to the north, through Le Grand Saconnex, Versonnex and Divonne les Bains, for example. Head northeast. Dozens of easy, minor roads are possible between the area of Lausanne and Bern. A good route is through Romont and Fribourg.

If you use the SRB-Radwanderwege tour booklet, you can follow established bicycle trails for many portions of this tour. The Kummerly & Frey Switzerland for Leisure map also indicates those trails and others in a general way (see section on Maps, Terrain, Traffic for more discussion of this).

From Bern go northwest to Biel, or northeast to Kirchberg, Langenthal and Olten. Either way, there are more bike trails. Continue to Zurich. Cycle a broad sweep around Lake Zurich, making use of trails and minor roads, and return to Zurich.

This entire tour, although pleasant, provides no Alpine scenery. You'll hardly realize you're in Switzerland. For mountain scenery, keep riding east at the eastern end of Lake Zurich on 8 to Wattwil, and 16 to Gams until you reach the Rhine Valley. The way will be more difficult. More bike trails in the valley, leading south to Chur and north almost to Bregenz, Austria.

Connect at the latter with the cross-Austria tour. Traffic on E17 between Austria and St. Gallen is heavy; if you come that way, take minor roads north of E17.

TOUR 2. Rhone Valley, Geneva to Bern; an easy to moderate 240 to 250 miles. It takes a week or ten days, and is the most painless tour you can take of high Alps. Side trips, as mentioned below, can lengthen the tour and double the time.

Leave Geneva on 1 and ride the northern side of the lake to

Lausanne. Connect with 9 and continue along the lake. Lovely views in all directions. Go past St. Maurice a few miles, and cross the river to the village of Collonges.

Follow the river on the secondary road to its north, through Fully and on to Laytron, just before Chamoson. Cross to Riddes, on the south side of the river. Cycle up the river, recross it at Aproz, and ride through Sion.

You'll have rejoined 9 at Sion, but leave it immediately and ride on the southern side of the river to Bramois and Granges. Here, consider taking a side road north, up to Montana. A cable car ride from it to the heights of Bellalui is a must.

Otherwise, continue on the secondary road to Sierre, where you rejoin 9. Stay on it until Visp. A 22-mile side trip south to Zermatt and the Matterhorn is a good possibility here.

From Visp go to Brig. Leave 9 and take 19. The climbing increases from Brig to Gletsch, gradually for the most part. The latter town faces the source of the river, the blue Rhone Glacier. You'll face a stiff climb on 6 to the top of the 6,700-foot Grimsel Pass, but a bus assist can be used instead.

Once over the pass, it's all downhill and flat land to Meiringen. Just before this town, a road (11) goes east to the Susten Pass. If **261**

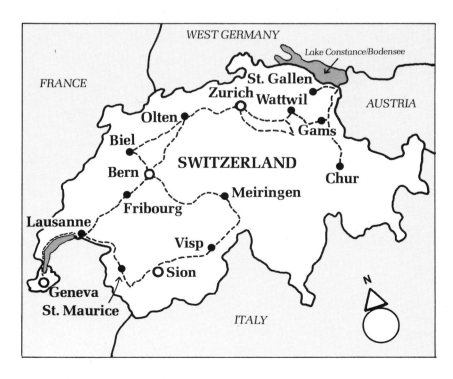

Grimsel wasn't enough for you, you can tackle this one's 6,900 feet. The pass is a favorite challenge to Swiss cyclists.

The route stays on 6 through Brienz and Interlaken. Keep to the north side of Thuner See through Thun and into Bern. Ann Conklin found 6, on the south side of the lake, to be narrow and full of heavy traffic.

Brienz is a woodcarving center and has a steam cog-railway to the top of Brienzer Rothorn. Interlaken is good for a lengthy lay-over. A day ticket on the Thuner See ships is fantasia-land and one of the best deals in Switzerland—get on and off the boat anywhere along the lake all day long. Other attractions are rail trips up the mountains, and a cable car to the Schilthorn, one of the greatest panorama views in all Switzerland.

At Bern, connect with Tour 1, in either direction, or take a train back to Geneva.

MAPS, TERRAIN, TRAFFIC

There's an embarrassment of riches in the number of maps for this small country, literally a thousand to choose from. The Swiss Federal Topographical Service (Eidgenossische Landestopographie) prints most of them, ranging from a 1:25,000 series of 364 sheets to an overall 1:500,000 map. In between those scales are other series: 1:50,000, 1:100,000, 1:200,000 and 1:300,000. As in the United States Geodetic Survey series, contours are shown on all of these.

The maps cost about $4 each sheet and can be bought by mail from the Alfred Barth Company. Send for a key.

There are others. Kummerly & Frey offers a few: a 1:250,000 that's the official Swiss Auto Club map, for $6 in Switzerland; a 1:300,000 Switzerland For Leisure at $6.75; a 1:500,000 Camping map distributed by the Swiss National Tourist Office for free; and a 1:600,000 Swiss Youth Hostel Guide, free from the tourist office also. The YH map shows only railways, motorcoach and trolleybus lines, and the location of hostels. B. Dalton may sell Kummerly & Frey maps in the United States.

And more: Geographia 1:400,000 at $6, and the Ravenstein pocket map 1:505,000 at $4, both from Complete Traveller; and the Michelin 1:400,000 at $3 from Michelin in the States. Also, sold at the tourist office in the United States: Hallwag 1:300,000 at $5.75; Hallwag Central Switzerland Hiking Map 1:100,000 at $5.75; and two other hiking maps 1:200,000 at $3.75. The same office sells the *Michelin Green Guide* for $6, a valuable adjunct to your travel literature for Switzerland. Other Swiss maps with smaller scales exist, but they're not worth consideration.

262

SWITZERLAND

What to choose among these riches? You can indeed spend a fortune on them. Send for the ones you get free, of course. Then, for more useful detail, it depends on how much of the country you'll ride and in what fashion.

Indy Altersheim, who lives in Baar and bicycles in all parts of the country, contributed the suggested tours and most of the details in this chapter, and much of the writing itself. He suggests the Kummerly & Frey 1:250,000, or the appropriate sections of the four 1:200,000 Topographical series. The latter maps give a better idea of hills, with their contour lines. For passes and climbs in the Alps, he says that you can even consider a few sections of the 1:25,000 series, which show contours at each 20 meters and enable a biker to judge the steepness of each climb.

Another map that should be considered by bikers is the Kummerly & Frey Leisure 1:300,000. It indicates bicycle trails, as mentioned in Tour 1, admittedly in a crude fashion with its small scale. Their approximate locations are shown, nevertheless, and the map can be used in conjunction with a booklet that shows over 40 of those trails in detail. It's the SRB Radwanderwege, and it's free from the Swiss Bike and Motorbike Club (Schweizer Rad- und Motorfahrer Bund). The booklet is in German, but it doesn't matter; the map sketches are plain enough, and the trails are marked.

The Kummerly & Frey Leisure map indicates other interests: locations of hostels, campgrounds, walking trails and swimming pools, as well as the usual road information and tourist attractions. If you have time, by the way, definitely schedule some days for hiking the well-marked footpaths above mountain roads, which are indicated on that map or other hiking maps.

Everyone knows that Switzerland means mountains. What is less known is that there's a 30-mile-wide plateau running southwest to northeast, from Lausanne on Lake Geneva to the eastern end of Lake Constance. That wide path is not flat, certainly, but the hills are no more formidable than those of western Massachusetts or southern Ohio. The suggested Tour 1 goes through this region.

Short stretches of fairly level road are found elsewhere, too, in river valleys and around the numerous lakes. Trains can be taken between those, and it's possible to enjoy a pleasant tour across the entire country without undue strain.

There are those, however, who see Switzerland as mountain cycling and who want to experience the real Alps, south of that plateau. Whether for robust exercise or as an ego trip, there is plenty of opportunity to find that kind of cycling. It needs little searching of maps. Choose almost any secondary road that zigzags, preferably one with a green line running alongside it, which shows that it's scenic.

Altersheim says that those Americans who cycle mountain passes are usually on the popular Simplon or Gotthard. Few, if any, attempt the lesser known Fluela, Albula, Julien or Klausen. Just be careful on those steep, long downgrades and hairpin curves, and pay attention to riding techniques, brakes, tires and general condition of the bike. Incidentally, when you're advised that a given section of a road or a pass has a "maximum gradient" of 13 percent, that maximum may be just a short stretch, and the rest will be a more normal 10 percent or less.

Roads are almost never bad, and are usually good to excellent. In late spring and early summer, a stone and oil treatment of their surfaces can cause small, sharp stones and troublesome sticky oil. Sometimes you may run into cobblestone or brick surfaces in towns. And some remote passes may have a short stretch of stone at the top. Otherwise, surfaces are among the best in Europe.

Most wider valleys have parallel side roads with reduced traffic. Autobahns, which prohibit bicycles, have those side roads generally. Traffic is worst on main highways that lead to resort areas on weekends and July to August. Try also to avoid riding on weekends through any passes, local or major. Major passes with bike-prohibited main roads or tunnels have an "old road," well maintained and with much of the traffic siphoned off by the throughway. The bike route is much tougher, of course.

264

BEST CYCLING TIME

September or early October is best, June next, and July and August the worst. The chief factor is the influx of tourists during the summer.

The weather is also best and the safest in the fall. It's the clearest and has the least chill in the wind. The earliest time that it's warm enough for cycling, at lower altitudes, can be mid-April, but it depends on the arrival of spring weather. At all times of the year, the mountains can get cold. Bring along some long johns, a sweater and gloves, as a precaution.

Passes often don't open to traffic until late May or early June. They usually close in October. See the Camping maps issued by the tourist office for closing dates and for heights and maximum gradients of specific passes.

BIKE EQUIPMENT, RENTALS

Most Swiss ride on light bikes for conditioning or race training. Components for those kinds of bikes are widely available. Wide-range freewheels and derailleurs for touring are a gray area, and it's likely you'll find parts based on the Italian bike model, instead. However, suitable parts can be obtained quickly by mail through a cooperative bike shop. A phone-call order usually brings delivery in 24 hours or the same day. Best to bring critical spares with you, especially if on a tight schedule. But 27 X 1¼-inch tires are the general rule in Switzerland.

Most railroad stations rent 3-speeds at their baggage counters. They're satisfactory in the valleys and around resort cities, of course, but not for extended touring in hills. With a rail ticket, the bike rents for about $6.50 the first day, $5 a day thereafter. Bikes can be dropped off at any other station.

A 10-speed with fairly high gears likely (lowest development about 38 inches) can be rented from a bike shop at about $6.50 a day, $19 a week, $44 for three weeks. Altersheim suspects that bike shops rent only in the larger resort areas, and not throughout the country. A half-dozen cycle centers have been opened by the Swiss Touring Club. They rent bikes and each center publishes a brochure describing local bike routes. Ask the touring office for a fact sheet.

BIKE TRANSPORTATION

265

Not only is it easy to bring bikes with you on trains, but you can readily send baggage or the bicycle ahead, and either pedal up mountains without the weight or hike a mountain trail, for a change. This convenience is especially valuable when you come to tough and crowded passes.

Buses are liberal in carrying bikes or forwarding baggage, but you may be restricted by circumstances. If there's rail service, you're obliged to use it instead of the bus. Buses load bikes last, and when they're full with other luggage you're out of luck. You lose out, also, when the bus is small and has limited capacity. Sometimes, getting the bike on depends on the bus driver's good humor, though that's denied by officials. Your luggage can be sent, in any case.

A further complication is that the bus travels between post offices, which hold the luggage. Those are closed on Saturday afternoons and Sundays. Your unaccompanied luggage may be left at a restaurant or hotel, or somewhere else. On such days, ask beforehand where you can expect to find it.

Unaccompanied luggage can be forwarded by either train or bus for a flat rate of $4 per piece, up to 66 pounds and regardless of distance. Strap the panniers together, and put the whole lot into a garbage bag to make it one piece and avoid the extra charge.

Bikes cost the same. With a passenger ticket the luggage goes free, but the bike costs $1.35.

At peak times, register luggage and bike early, preferably the day before you wish to pick it up. That's satisfactory if you stay indoors and hold on to some basic necessities for that night, but not if you send your tent and sleeping bag ahead. Be sure to account for those items when you want to camp.

Ask the tourist office for a copy of "Holidays in Switzerland by Rail, Boat, Postal Motor Coach." It's published by the Swiss Federal Railways, and it includes a map that shows railway and bus routes for the entire country. Also included are special rates.

GENERAL
ENTERING, LEAVING, HASSLES

Passport needed, no visa.

There's no antagonism toward bikers at all in Switzerland, except in a peculiar and minor way, which was pointed out by Altersheim. Fitness cycling is big there, and riders take it seriously. If you overtake a Swiss biker on the road, he's apt to get mad. But if he passes you, he'll probably not even acknowledge your presence; you'll be beneath notice.

In a reversal of the usual American attitudes, the Swiss consider the pedestrian has the right of way on the road over any vehicle. The biker has that same right vis-á-vis motor vehicles (but don't push your luck, advises Altersheim).

The law is taken literally when it comes to bikes that strike pedestrians—and cars that hit bikes, of course. It goes hard on bikers that do, and fines can be given right on the spot, automatically and ruthlessly. Follow safety rules and ride single file. Give hand signals too, or you might be in for an unpleasant surprise from an official.

LANGUAGE AND PEOPLE

English is commonly spoken by the educated everywhere, and certainly by all officials and the tourist oriented. French, German and Italian are native in the parts adjoining those countries and many people are bilingual or even multilingual.

Questionnaire correspondents said the Swiss were courteous but not especially friendly. They seemed amused by the laden bikes, being more accustomed to racers than bike tourists.

The Swiss are characteristically efficient and ordered. Altersheim says they're also as hard headed and contrary as New Englanders.

With that combination of traits, it's not a country to run afoul of the law, though it's one in which you should feel quite safe. Still, bikes do get stolen and they should be locked when left out. Some people said they took bikes into their rooms; others weren't allowed to. Ann Conklin reported that an AYH leader lost over $5,000 in traveler's checks when the day pack in which he kept them was stolen at a train station.

OVERALL COSTS

Stiff prices, with Scandinavia the highest in Europe, are the real deterrent to a long bike holiday here. Unless you're flush and want comfort, you had better forget about any kind of hotel and depend on camping. Same with food. Make your own meals or eat only in hostels if on a budget.

A few bike tourists who were there in 1978, and who camped or hosteled and cooked their own meals, spent from $10 to $15 a day. Another couple of bikers who used hotels occasionally and ate in restaurants infrequently spent from $20 to $30 a day. Accounting for some inflation and loss of the dollar's worth, it would seem difficult to tour Switzerland for less than about $16 at the most frugal in 1981.

267

Bank hours are 8:30 A.M. to 4:30 P.M. Monday to Friday, closed weekends. Money is exchanged at larger railroad stations and airports until 10:00 P.M. each day.

ACCOMMODATIONS

A *New York Times* travel article reported in 1979 that a few hotels could be found in Zurich during the low season for less than $30 a couple. A few more were under $35. Those accounted for only some 100 beds in the city, and are no indication what is available ordinarily.

Some of the less visited towns did have rooms at those prices, where a double could even be had under $20 in out-of-the-way inns and taverns. Rooms in pensions or private homes are usually lower than inns. Check for those at local tourist offices.

But the majority of hotels listed in the Swiss Hotel Guide are higher than $33. Send for the latest issue of that booklet from the tourist office, as well as a hostel guide and map.

Swiss hostels cost from $2.75 to $4.75 a person, local taxes not included. Cost for cooking is extra too, and some require a sleeping sheet be hired for $1. They're still the best indoor bargain in this country.

But hostels are very crowded for that reason. You're advised to make reservations, certainly during July and August. Youths up to

25 have priority at peak times, too. Those factors may make it difficult to use them. Camping on the premises is not allowed, in case hostels are full.

Almost 100 hostels are distributed evenly in all regions. If you're traveling in the off-season, or with solid reservations, it's possible to plan around them for your entire tour.

Discounts and low-cost accommodations are offered students and youths. Ask the tourist office for "Student Lodgings at University Cities."

Recommended hostels were: Bern (good facilities, though packed together); Soluthurn-St. Niklaus (comfortable, big lawn for relaxation); St. Gallen (great dinner); Zermatt (good showers and kitchen, breathtaking view of Matterhorn); Faulensee (super meals); Luzern (very clean, good cafeteria); Crocifisso-Lugano (swimming pool); Zurich (clean, hot water); St. Moritz-Bad (one of the best anywhere); Grinderwald (open fire, atmosphere, though mattresses on floor).

Thumbs down on: Interlaken-Bonigen (regimented—go to Balmer's Hostel instead); Geneva (cramped kitchen, murky dining room); Basel (kitchen underequipped, cool wardens).

268   Of the 450 campgrounds in the country, 330 are shown on the Camping map. Get it from the tourist office. The camps are located mostly in the popular tourist places and along highways. They can get very crowded in those areas, such as around Luzern and Lugano.

Only camps classified as Category 1 have warm showers as a rule; that may limit your choice of nightly stays. You may have to plan to use camps in conjunction with hostels or pensions.

Food stores are usually on the premises or nearby. Washers and dryers are found in very few camps; in fact, laundromats are reportedly nearly unavailable anywhere.

Costs include: fees per person, from 60¢ to $4.25, according to category; an extra tent or "lot" fee; and a small visitors' tax. A camp with a shower can easily total more than a hostel. A 5 to 10 percent discount is given with a *carnet,* though, and some camps charge less pre- and post-season.

Free camping in the countryside is forbidden, and could be arbitrarily enforced. Don't try it unless you have permission from someone on private property, or if you're in the wild and are absolutely certain the law won't see you. A few bike tourists wrote that farmers allowed them to camp readily.

If you do camp in the open, don't use stream water. The fountains in villages are safe and so is tapwater, but don't use farm springs or troughs. Mineral water is not all that available either. It's usually sold only in large stores in towns or cities.

FOOD

Multicourse meals range from $3 to $10 in the cheapest restaurant that was listed in the hotel guide, but the average will be higher in most places. A modest restaurant in a back street can serve lunch starting at about $5 and dinner a couple of dollars more. What you pay depends to some extent on what you have and how hungry you are, of course. A rule of thumb is to allow 50 percent or more than at home, for either meals or grocery food.

Altersheim suggests you ask for the bill as you are served your last item in a restaurant if you're in a hurry. Otherwise, you'll wait 15 minutes after you're ready to go.

Hostels that serve meals ask in the vicinity of $1.80 for breakfast and $3 for dinner. A snack of a sandwich can cost just $1, and bakeries have tables where you can munch on pastries and rolls. They aren't cheap, and a cup of coffee to go with the goodies costs $1. Domestic beer is good and reasonable, but liquor is horribly expensive. A small U.S.-type cocktail will be $6. One saving grace: federal law says tipping is not necessary.

Grocery stores are open 7:30 A.M. to noon and 1:30 to 6:30 P.M., Saturday up to 4:00 P.M. They're closed Sundays and most are on Monday mornings, also. Watch for Swiss holidays. There are many, they vary from region to region, and they can sneak up on you. Everything except hotels, restaurants, some gas stations and transportation is locked tight.

The best grocery prices are in chain stores such as Migro, Coop, Volg, Denner and Usego. Some items like milk, bread and potatoes cost the same or less than in the States, but most are more expensive, some twice as much. It's still cheaper than eating in restaurants. Grocery stores are abundant in valleys, but you may ride for hours to find one in the mountains.

S-200 and C-200 butane cartridges are sold at about $1 in camping stores. Kerosene can't be bought in gas stations. It comes bottled in either nonprescription drugstores or pharmacies, at least in the German-speaking part of Switzerland. I have no information for the other regions.

ADDRESSES AND FURTHER READING

Swiss National Tourist Office
Swiss Center
608 Fifth Avenue
New York, NY 10020
and
250 Stockton Street
San Francisco, CA 94108

Schweizer Rad- und Motorfahrer Bund
Schaffhausenstr. 272
8057 Zurich

Alfred Barth Co.
Bahnhofstr. 94
8023 Zurich

Christopher Hughes, *Switzerland* (New York: Praeger, 1975). A clever and entertaining definitive description of the Swiss in all aspects, social, political and cultural.

Michelin Green Guide, $6.

B. Dalton bookstores sell some Kummerly & Frey maps in the U.S. Inquire locally or of the New York City store at 666 Fifth Avenue.

TURKEY
31

BIKING MATTERS
SUGGESTED TOURS

Turkey offers adventure touring. It's not quite Asia, though most of it lies within that continent. Nor is it Europe, even if it's been part of NATO and is listed by many almanacs among European countries.

Neither of these two tours is easy, though the first includes some fairly level cycling near Istanbul and Izmir. The second includes hard climbs, up to 12 percent. It was sent to me by Douglas Watson, an American who lives and works on the southern coast. Major portions of this chapter were made possible from data that he contributed.

TOUR 1. Istanbul to Izmir; about 410 miles and two weeks. Make your way from the Istanbul airport or from the city to Yesilkoy, a few miles to the southwest of Istanbul. Cycle west to Silivri, then Corlu. Turn south a dozen miles to road 18. Turn west to Tekirdag, an interesting city with many restaurants and places to stock up on groceries.

Continue west on 18. Don't make the mistake of trying the road southwest to Murefte. The maps show it "not passable by motor vehicles." In 1978, Tyler Folsom and Venita Plazewski found it not passable by bike, either. On 18 there's a long climb to Malkara, and still more hills south to Sarkoy, on the Sea of Marmara. Avoid going on E24, from Kesan south, on which traffic from Greece and Bulgaria travels.

The riding is easier now, west to Gelibolu. Cross on a ferry to Lapseki. The hills return with a vengeance southwest to Canakkale, and beyond it to Enzine. On the way to the latter note a sign showing the way to Hisarlik, a few miles west off the road. See the ancient ruins of Troy here. At Altinoluk the road plunges to the sea; it will be easy riding the rest of the way along the coast.

Stay on 6 to Izmir, through Ayvacik, Edremit and Bergama. The last is the site of ancient Pergamon, with impressive ruins. Road **271** surfaces are generally good throughout this route, though they have no shoulders most of the way and loose shell chips form the banks.

Izmir is a mix of old and new. Its old quarter is much less blatant and more relaxed than Istanbul's. Choose a native hotel for atmosphere. Return to Istanbul by train or boat, or a combination. A train can be taken to Bandirma, north of Izmir on the Marmara, and a ferry from there to Istanbul, across the sea. Fare is about $5.40 a person, for each leg of the journey.

Istanbul is full of sights and excitement. It's probably the most cosmopolitan city in Europe, mixing the Orient with the West. It's literally divided between the two, half in Europe and the other half in Asia across the Bosporus, the narrow strait that separates the continents. Stay in the old section, near the Topkapi Palace, to be in tune with the city.

This tour can be changed to a 335-mile Marmara Sea loop by taking 2 east from Lapseki to Bursa, then hugging the coast to Izmir and returning to Istanbul. If you go that way, avoid both 1 and E5 from Izmir on the west. Those roads are heavy with truck traffic and cars. Ride on the road that parallels them to the north, through Samandira. The roads around the Marmara are not easier than the one to Izmir, and they're even busier during the tourist season.

272

Tour 2. Mediterranean coast, Adana to Antalya; about 375 miles, easy to difficult, about two weeks. Start at either end. A ferry runs between Antalya and Mersin, some 40 miles west of Adana. It

costs about $10 and the schedule changes about once a week, so check it out before you leave on your trip.

From Adana to Mersin is a flat ride. Continue on E5 to Tarsus, with its historic sites, where you pick up E24. Lots of hotels at Mersin, all of which welcome bikes. Or camp on the beach. The best fish in this part of Turkey is here; have it at the Liman Lokantasi. Going west to Selifke, there'll be some rolling hills. Stay at a Mobil campground or pass the town and use a hotel at Tasucu or Bogsak.

Beyond Tasucu and into Anamur, you'll have winding, switch-back climbs. Watch the downgrades, which are sharp and danger-ous. Halfway is an unnamed restaurant with good kebab. Anamur is divided politically and Watson says he felt uncomfortable there.

More hills now, and in worse shape. At one place the road becomes a small strip, and at a few places the edges are crumbled away. Dangerous—watch the trucks. A number of motels at Alanya; Sun Hotel on the beach is a good one. Very friendly people.

Beyond Alanya the road is fairly easy, with some rolling hills. Stop at Manvgat to see the waterfall, and buy some ice-cold water-melon there.

When you get to Antalya, you're back in civilization. Best hotel is Otel Antalya, but it's expensive. Many others there, though. A good restaurant is Gaziantepli Develi Isletmeleri. If you're thinking of cycling around the peninsula on 30, be warned that it's very rough; you'll walk a lot of it.

The trip can be extended on the Adana end by taking either or both of two loops. The first is 60 miles around the Seyhan Dam Lake, on the western side, using a paved road to Catalan. Go back to Adana on the eastern side, which is unpaved. You compete with camels and sheep on it. Watch out for sheep dogs. The second ride, about 120 miles, goes to Kosan and back through Ceyhan.

Another good touring area is the Black Sea coast. It's not easy riding, either—there's a 2,500-foot climb west of Espiye in less than a dozen miles, for example. Many of the towns are somewhat inland in a higher altitude, to which the road rises. The roads are not very smooth, either. But Folsom says the hotels and living costs are cheap, the traffic light and the scenery good. Boats go regularly between Istanbul and Black Sea cities.

MAPS, TERRAIN, TRAFFIC

The Turkish Tourism and Information Office issues a free 1:1,850,000 map, as well as one for Istanbul. The only map with a larger scale that's sold in the United States is a Geographia 1:1,500,000, at Complete Traveller for $6. Bert and Dinnie Nieuwenhuis were able to buy a 1:850,000 Shell map in-country.

The tourist office map is a 1979 version and it shows all the paved roads in the countryside, other than around big cities. Half the main roads on that map are gravel or macadam, an accurate indication of the state of roads in Turkey. Those with the worst engineering and maintenance are in the mountain areas of the north, northeast and at the Iranian border. In the latter area, many roads are described as not passable.

Most roads are narrow. They don't have shoulders in the usual sense, the largest ones simply being a bit wider. But there's no glass on them. Watson says he didn't have one flat from that source in two years—and he rides tubulars!

Turkey can be likened to an oval serving dish turned upside down. The center is a long plateau, with a gradual rise to the east. The slopes of the dish are all mountainous and the roads through them few and formidable.

The scenery, on the other hand, is strikingly beautiful. A view of a sunset from a pass, across a hundred miles of ridges, is wondrous and memorable; it's a great place to camp or to contemplate. The coasts are green, the interior brown.

There's less traffic the farther east you go. On the road east of Bingol I sometimes saw scarcely a dozen vehicles a day, most of them tourist cars and vans.

274

E5, from the Bulgarian border to Ankara, is heavy with cars and trucks. It's dangerous in the Istanbul area. Turks like to lean on their horns as they pass, many claxons or obnoxious multitones.

Trucks spew acrid diesel fumes. At the end of the day you're black. From Istanbul to the capital, take the tougher but less crowded highway 1. Traffic on the shore roads along the Aegean Sea is light most of the time, moderate near Izmir.

BEST CYCLING TIME

The Black Sea mountain passes can have snow in mid-May, but the coast itself is warm enough for touring at that time. The Mediterranean coast has the same weather as Greece, and a tour can be started as early as February. Racing starts there in March. Fall weather is good until October in the south, and through September in other parts.

Summer on the plateau in the interior is extremely hot and dry. But in the high altitude of the extreme east, it can be cool in July. I slept under a blanket a few nights in a hotel in Van that month.

I had no rain during June and July, from Ankara to the Iranian border; I hardly saw clouds for those two months, in fact. The rainy season in the south starts in October and ends in March.

Winds were variable in my experience, stronger in the afternoon than morning. As I rode east, their direction was more pronounced from that direction. Prevailing winds on the southern coast are from the south.

BIKE EQUIPMENT, RENTALS

The Nieuwenhuis pair were able to buy 27 X 1¼-inch tires in Istanbul, but they're not usually available. To get those or 700c's surely, you'll have to know someone in a bike club. Bring your own.

Limited bike parts are available in the country, according to Watson, but they're very expensive. Import duty on parts runs high. I paid 50 percent, based on the parts' value plus value added because of airmail fees. Altogether, it cost me some 75 percent of the parts' worth. It can be as high as 100 percent. A black market in bike parts exists among bike club members.

If you take the second tour, visit Bisiklt Mamircisi at Cinarli Mahallesi, 120 Sokak no. 5, Adana. Muhittin Kondu, who runs it, is a bicycle repairman who worked with the Turkish national bike team. He'll be friendly and helpful.

BIKE TRANSPORTATION

Airlines in-country don't take bikes. Trains do, with no problems. So will boats all along the shores.

275

Buses and shared taxis, the *dolmus,* run between small towns and villages. They'll carry anything, from chicken crates to bikes. Fares seem to be informally imposed, though I suppose they must be standardized to some extent.

GENERAL
ENTERING, LEAVING, HASSLES

Passport, no visa. Your bike will be registered in your passport when you enter. It's expected that you won't sell the bike and they do check it carefully when you leave.

Turkey has had instability for years, reflected in occasional antagonism to foreigners. There have been kidnappings of Westerners and even a few killings. To my knowledge, all those were motivated politically. When Americans were involved, they were soldiers, diplomats or multinational employees.

That point—that terrorism is selective—was made in an article in the *New York Times* Travel Section, May 4, 1980, by Marvine Howe, chief of its Ankara bureau. The United States consulate, it was pointed out, had no record of any American visitors being attacked or injured in 1979, and the few foreign visitors in past years who were harmed were victims of common crime, the kind that can happen anywhere in the world. The article concluded that terrorists simply do not target tourists.

You'll see paramilitary police patrolling highways and bridges, and the regular army has a deliberate presence in the country at large. The tent camps of both are often seen in the east, especially. I often stayed with them when I felt insecure in the open.

Watson apparently had no problems during his two years of cycling in the south, but he advises avoidance of night travel, in any case. I had trouble only in the east, where kids threw stones at me or teenagers tried to shake me down for money. In western Turkey, people were as friendly or more so than in the rest of Europe. In fact, more Turks invited me into their homes and bought me drink and food in cafes than in the civilized West.

All bets are off when a Turkish man pursues a Western woman. He's macho personified. The easier public manner convinces the Turk that she's a potential lover.

I remember once when I was having a roadside picnic with two English women who stopped their car to talk to me. Three Turks stopped their car soon after; they openly courted the women, ignoring my presence completely. Only after the women left, did they address me: "You speak their language well, and they were friendly to you. Why did you let them get away?" They couldn't understand my inaction.

I observed and heard more about that kind of attention, some of it nasty and threatening. This is one country that a woman biker should certainly not cycle alone. Veronica Scargill recommends that women should keep arms and legs covered.

Turkish drivers, usually truckers, have played "chicken" with me on the road. Other bikers reported this, too, and it's best to avoid the through highways in the western part.

Dogs are another threat. They run in packs and seem to have no owners. In the country, a sheep dog may attack if it thinks you a threat to the flock, or if goaded by shepherds. Watson says he's heard of rabies in his area, around Adana.

LANGUAGE AND PEOPLE

I hope I haven't put off potential bike tourists from visiting Turkey with the above cautions. I liked the Turks and I had some of my best people-to-people experiences there. I found them friendly, helpful and wonderful hosts.

Turks are known for hospitality. They'll shower you with attention, and are hurt if you refuse it. They're polite, with graceful manners, but proud, too; they stiffen to an insult or slight. Respect

TURKEY

is shown guests, and the same is expected in turn.

Not that Turks don't have idiosyncracies. They're very curious, for example. In a near-empty cafe, a man will come to your table and ask permission to sit. Shortly, he's looking over your shoulder as you write your notes or read your soft-cover. A few minutes later, you're in conversation.

That curiosity sometimes leads to problems with your equipment. Invariably, Turks will want to try out your bike. If you let one do it, others will line up to take a turn. It's a matter of pride to be able to ride it, never mind that they grind your gears shifting it.

When I left my bike for any time, I always checked out the controls in case someone fiddled with them. Often a young man would simply take off on my bike right in front of me, without preamble. He wasn't trying to steal it; he simply couldn't resist trying it out.

The curiosity also led to endless questions about why I was cycle touring: "Can't you afford to hire a car?" They couldn't understand why I'd want to ride up a hill when for 25¢ I could hire a taxi to take me to the top. Sometimes they lost all patience with my explanations and packed my bike on top of a limousine-taxi, their compliments, with instructions for the driver to let me off at **277** the summit.

And yet, bike racing is popular enough in Turkey. A stage race, the International Tour of the Mediterranean, has taken place for the past 12 years. It's usually in early April. If interested, write the sponsoring cycling federation, TBMF, for details. That organization also sponsors bike racing clubs in Istanbul, Ankara, Izmir and Adana.

A custom that may take you aback is the practice of men walking hand in hand in public. They're not lovers, but good friends. It's an accepted way of showing it. At the same time, men and women—even married couples—don't demonstrate affection in public. It's in poor taste. When you travel with a mate, abide by their custom, and save your cuddling for the boudoir.

A few educated natives in a given town may speak English. If you spend any time in it at all, they'll soon seek you out. More commonly, nobody out of a whole village will speak English. German is by far the more common second language everywhere.

Turkish is not difficult. Its pronunciation is consistent and fairly simple, and so is the grammar. You can learn a few phrases and the words for food, numbers and functions easily enough. The time and effort are well invested, for the appreciation that it'll bring from the natives and the added understanding of what's going on around you.

OVERALL COSTS

In 1974 I spent $4 a day in Turkey, camping free and staying at occasional hotels. I ate all food in cafes.

Surprisingly, reports from latter-day bikers show that living costs have risen but little since. Apparently, a bike tourist could have gotten along on $5 a day in 1979. In 1981, make that about $6.50. That's rock bottom, of course, camping out and sharing costs with a companion when in an occasional hotel. Turkey has to be the cheapest country in which to tour, other than Eastern Europe.

Part of the explanation is that the Turkish lira has been devalued to such an extent since my visit that it offset a rise in prices, to a large degree. Another devaluation is due, at the time of this writing. Tourism has also declined since the Cyprus invasion and because of the more recent reports of violence. Bargain prices are the result.

Some recommendations: avoid street black marketeers; they will palm your dollars as they ostensibly inspect them for genuineness, or they'll cheat you in the exchange. You'll get no bargains; remember W. C. Fields's advice. Ask at a bank if they charge a fee for exchanging money. Some don't. Banks are open all day Monday to Friday, except for lunch.

You'll be charged double when you visit a museum, ruin, or church with a camera. If it's small, keep it in your pocket or handbag. You should pay for it when you intend to take pictures, of course. Topkapi Palace in Istanbul and many other attractions are half-price on Wednesdays.

All boat fares to Greek islands are way out of line, the overcharge being for taxes from both sides. Neither country considers this unfair; neither encourages tourists to visit the other.

Bargaining is a way of life in Turkey. The natives think it's half the fun of shopping. Practice it for pleasure and economy.

ACCOMMODATIONS

Cheap hotels in Istanbul's old section cost about $5. A first-class hotel throughout the country is $12 to $13. For a second-class double, subtract about $3 (all accommodations, 1980 prices).

In the country you pay less. The rooms are usually without a bath, which will be down the hall and sometimes on another floor. In small towns and remote areas, hotels may have no showers at all. Check on this first. I usually took my bike into the room, but often the room clerk allowed me to lock it near his desk; things are very informal in Turkish hotels.

You can always try to bargain. I often asked for a less desirable room at a lower price. The room came out to be about the same, but the excuse allowed the clerk to save face in case the bargaining became a difficult test of wills. At some country hotels in the east I was allowed to pitch a tent on the hotel grounds for a nominal cost or for free.

The National Organization of Turkish Youth will send you a list of Turkish hostels. There were some two dozen when I sent for it last. You won't find them listed in the IYH Handbook.

The hostels are mostly in schools within towns. They're open when students are on vacation, during July and August, though a few are open longer. The ones I stayed at were all dorm types. Hardly anyone was ever in them. They had showers, though with no hot water. A cold shower in the height of the hot day satisfied me.

Bike security was excellent, and the locations were convenient to the town or they were near some stores. Hostels had no kitchens. They cost about $1.50 each person.

With oil shortages and higher fuel prices, many accommodations offer no hot water or they limit it to a few hours in the day. A Turkish bath *(hamam)* can be taken instead. Most towns have 1; Istanbul has 120. A visit will cost you under a dollar. It's more than just a bath, of course, being a ritual of steaming, scrubbing, massaging and relaxing. Try it once, anyhow.

279

Only about 20 campgrounds are listed in the tourist literature, all along tourist routes and near large cities or resorts. Costs are $2.80 to $4 for two persons in a tent. Showers are normally cold.

An informal arrangement of camping at a gas station, motel or restaurant is common. These facilities are often combined. A stay on the grass in back of them enables you to use the toilets and sinks, and you can sip tea and relax in the cafe.

I was never charged at one of these "camps," it being understood that I'd buy a meal in the cafe. A few of these places have expanded into a kind of campground, by installing showers, staking a level field in back for tents, and charging fees.

Camping in the open is common. Beaches are popular in shore areas, and I used fruit tree groves and woods without any kind of interference. Sometimes someone would come over to see what I was doing and would bring me fruit or nuts.

I was more apprehensive as I rode farther east, and I asked permission to camp near a house or in *jandarma* camps, those police who patrol eastern Turkey. No one bothered me in any way in western Turkey, and I always felt secure there.

FOOD

Great eating—I believe Turkish food preparation among the best. The emphasis is on small dishes of vegetables and meat specialties that you combine into a meal. Even a small restaurant may have 20 pots of food in view across a counter to the kitchen, as well as a number of refrigerated hors d'oeuvres in a display case.

When you enter, the custom is to look into the pots, smell, and evaluate. Then tell the waiter what you'd like. He'll bring it to you. It's the simplest kind of ordering, and you preview the food.

A meal of assorted dishes and a bit of *raki,* the licorice-based liqueur, will cost no more than $3 in a modest country restaurant. But you pay less—on the order of $1—for simpler meals of kebabs and bread, or a few *dolmas,* vegetables such as peppers or egg-plant stuffed with rice, pine nuts and currants. A filling bowl of soup or a large yogurt is about 30¢ (all food, 1981 prices).

Tea costs just pennies a glass. Coffee is quite expensive, though, and Cokes cost 30¢. Wine is good. A fifth starts at well under $1.

Cooking for yourself is a bit of a problem in remote areas, where stores carry limited groceries. The best practice is to shop in towns. Their shops are well stocked. Small stores specialize in breads or sweets, yogurts, vegetables and meat, just as in France. They're open late, to 7:00 P.M. and some even to 9:00 P.M., Monday to Saturday.

280 Cold cuts of meat, and a tasty white cheese of curds, cost a little over $1 a pound. Tomatoes are 30¢ a pound, and most other vegetables from 30¢ to 65¢. Lettuce and squash are as little as 12¢ a pound.

Fruit such as cherries and strawberries are 50¢ a pound, and plums, apples and apricots in season half that or less. Nuts are cheap. Per pound: peanuts, $1.50, pistachios, $1.80, hazelnuts, 75¢. Mix them with dried fruit and you have a scrumptious gorp.

ADDRESSES AND FURTHER READING

Turkish Tourism and Information Office
821 United Nations Plaza
New York, NY 10017

General Consulate of Turkey
1901 Avenue of the Stars, Suite 1145
Los Angeles, CA 90067
(serves as an information office)

National Organization of Turkish Youth
Ordu Ca Yesil Tulumbasok, 41
Aksaray, Istanbul

TURKEY

Halil Kilicoglu, Chairman Foreign Affairs
Turkiye Bisiklet ve Motosiklet Federasyoru (TBMF)
Ulus Ishani, B-Blok
Ulus, Ankara

Nancy Phelan, *Welcome the Wayfarer* (New York: St. Martin's Press, 1965). The author's travels in Turkey. Her descriptions and experiences are just as I saw it in this exciting and strange country; the book brought it all back vividly.

Tom Brosnahan, *Turkey on $10 and $15 a day: 1979–80* or later edition (New York: Frommer-Pasmantier, 1980). A man who worked and traveled there, and who knows the country well. One of the better country guides.

32

ENGLAND, WALES, SCOTLAND, NORTHERN IRELAND

ENGLAND

BIKING MATTERS
SUGGESTED TOURS

The United Kingdom—England, Wales, Scotland, Northern Ireland—is the easiest place in Europe for which to plan a bike tour. Not only does it have an obvious advantage of a familiar language, but there is more cycling information about that relatively small area of land than anywhere else.

Information about cycling routes is so abundant that I feel there is little point in trying to compete by suggesting any specific routes in this section. After a century of bicycling on their island, the British are the most authoritative sources.

The most plenteous source is the Cyclists' Touring Club. For a $15-a-year membership, you get the advantage of the superlative services of the CTC Touring Department. The services are listed briefly in a sheet they'll send you. For Britain, they include such publications as Touring Area Notes; the Byway Network, a collection of routes along back roads and country lanes; Map Routes, for selected regions; and other information sheets.

Start your membership with a request for a generalized map and description of the specific area that you're interested in. Ask for the leaflet, "Cycling in the British Isles," at the same time. The map you'll get will have many bike routes already outlined.

UNITED KINGDOM

These will enable you to identify and send for the appropriate route sheets.

As part of membership, you get the compact CTC Handbook. It's a gold mine of touring data, some for Europe generally, but

most for Britain. Listed are transportation details, an extensive accommodations section, including recommended B&B addresses, repair and cycle shops, and local information officers of the club, with their addresses.

Should you need further information to make up a tour, you can write again or stop at the CTC office for consultation, before starting. A number of nonprofit, organized tours are also possible through the CTC, but those must be arranged for well ahead of time.

At the London office of the CTC Travel Shop, you're able to buy printed material—maps and books like the *CTC Guide to Cycling in Britain and Ireland,* and *Bike and Hike: 60 Tours around Great Britain and Ireland,* J. Sidney Jones, 1977 (about $4). You can also arrange for public transport and low-cost bike insurance with them.

A subscription to *Cycletouring* magazine comes with membership as well. It prints free "Companions Wanted" notices, in which you might want to advertise for a fellow biker, or respond to one. The magazine has numerous articles about touring in Britain, as well as on the Continent, and it's a further source of bike touring ideas.

284 Should you prefer not to join the CTC, you can still get bike tours for nominal sums (about 50¢ each, or free) from a number of places: British Tourist Authority's (BTA) "Britain on Two Wheels"; the East Anglia Tourist Board's "The Broads Holiday Map"; Countryside Commission's "Cycle Hire in the Peak District," and "Rent-a-Bike in Stoke," both with route maps; and informal tour sheets provided by many bike rental shops.

Britain is well represented by touring stories, with routes, in *Bicycling,* the former *Bike World,* and *American Wheelmen* magazines, and in various United States bicycle touring books. Bonnie Wong's Touring Exchange service contains a couple of tours in Scotland, for a nominal handling charge. All these tours, numbering in the hundreds, give you a wide choice for a trip.

A regional sightseeing guide will enrich your appreciation of the countryside. A number of them are sold by the British Travel Bookshop in the United States. Send for their list.

MAPS, TERRAIN, TRAFFIC

The Bartholomew 1:100,000 National maps, some 60 for all of Britain, cost about $2 each. They are the best compromise for small areas of interest. Three or four will allow concentration on the small, unmarked by-roads that make English cycling so characteristic and delightful.

Your alternatives are the 1:50,000 Ordnance Survey series, over 200 sheets at $3 each, or the nine Ordnance Survey maps,

1:250,000 scale, at $2 each. You'd need too many of the former and you'd fast run out of the maps as you ride. They're too detailed for the average bike tourist.

The second, smaller-scale maps could be satisfactory if your riding style is less leisurely, or when you want to see more of the country by taking the somewhat larger highways, those designated by "A" and three-digit numbers, or the secondary roads, marked "B," with following numbers.

An Ordnance Survey Route Planning Map 1:625,000, at $3, is useful for routing large distances. Any of these maps are available at CTC or bookstores. Costs to ship overseas are 50 percent extra. It might be hard to find maps outside of large cities, so bring them before touring.

Most of England is gently rolling countryside, when it's not flat. The only hills of any note are in the moors of the southwest, and the Shropshire, Hereford and Cotswold hills, toward Wales. Also in the north, the North York Moors and the Pennines. The highest elevations are in the lake district of the Cumbrian Mountains in the extreme northwest; they contain the most rugged riding. Since England is so varied in topography and is fairly small in area, a route from easy to difficult can be easily mapped out.

285

Road surfaces are excellent. Local and "B" roads are narrow and winding, and hillier, than "A" roads. A compass comes in handy on cloudy days, when you can lose your sense of direction with all the turns. Plan to travel hill country at the end of the tour, getting into shape on flatter areas.

Most roads have no shoulders, though "A" roads often have paths alongside. In hills, it's better to use newer "B" roads to avoid 10 to 20 percent grades of older and minor roads; in flatter regions, local roads are adequate.

There's an incredible number of unsurfaced trails and public footpaths on which you can cycle. Some go long distances. CTC will supply information on those. So will the Countryside Commission.

Some 2,000 miles of towpaths lead along rivers and canals. You need a permit to cycle on them (55¢ for a year), available from the British Waterways Board or the Paddington Traffic Office. Some paths are privately owned and vary in regulation of use.

The variety of terrain and the beauty of the countryside is a surprise to many tourists, who think of the island as packed with people and grimy industrial cities. Some of the latter are in the western midlands, to be sure. That's the least interesting part. For the rest, you may start with seashore on a given morning, meander among moors at noon, and end in wooded hills by evening.

Though drivers are courteous, traffic is heavy in the south, even on many of the "B" roads. Retreat to the local roads in that case. The general area of East Anglia, northeast of London, and the hills northeast of Newcastle Upon Tyne have the least traffic.

BEST CYCLING TIME

The average daily high temperature from May to September differs by less than 10 degrees, from 62°F. in May to 71°F. in July. The average humidity in the same period climbs from 73 to 80 percent. Days of rain average about the same throughout, 12 or 13 days in a month. It's a wet place, but with a reasonably uniform summer temperature.

When I asked an English friend when he'd suggest I visit, in order to see the most sunshine in England, he joked: "It could be almost anytime; last year it was between 2:00 and 4:00 P.M. on July 21st."

Because of England's high latitude, almost completely above that of France, it stays light longer into the evening during the summer, and you can get a lot of time on the road. However, the nature of the roads—villages every few miles, many places of interest, lots of hills and curves on many—works against much daily mileage. But that's not the kind of country it is.

286

BIKE EQUIPMENT, RENTALS

Though you'd think there would be no problems in servicing a bike, you'll find that few cycle shops out of the large cities and university towns carry parts for a 10-speed. As on the Continent, the bulk of bikes used by natives are utility types. Bring spares if mostly out in the wilds. If cycling close to cities, no problems except for some bike tools, which are hard to find. Gary Conrad reported that he couldn't find a metric allen key for a stem in three days of looking, as an example.

Hundreds of bike mechanics—"repairers"—are listed in the CTC Handbook, but many of those stock parts and they work on 1- and 3-speed bicycles. Besides, they're often busy with a backlog of local work. In the quiet English countryside, life is slower and easier than in the bustling American society; don't expect the shopowner to get as excited as you when a breakdown occurs, and when you feel that you need immediate attention. To avoid laying over a few days, be prepared to fix your own.

Bike rentals are satisfactory and widespread. The best are shops in London and the largest cities, where you can get a 10-speed and accessories. Otherwise, it's 3-speeds.

A bike hire scheme was organized by the Countryside Commission, in conjunction with the IYH and the CTC, in which a few hostels rent bikes. You need return the bike to any of the hostels in the scheme.

"Britain on Two Wheels" and the other leaflets cited in the section on Suggested Tours list shops that rent bikes in various parts of Britain. The Countryside Commission provides further information as well. Some British shops advertise in *Bicycling* magazine; they cater to Americans by providing 10-speeds.

BIKE TRANSPORTATION

Bikes are carried free with you on trains, subject to room in the baggage car. The exceptions are the high-speed trains and special ones, which may charge up to half the ticket price. Service is excellent and efficient, and you needn't be concerned about scheduling. You load your own bike. Buses don't seem to be used much.

GENERAL
ENTERING, LEAVING, HASSLES

No problems; just a passport.

Personal property is respected and security is high. Your presence on a bike is hardly noted.

LANGUAGE AND PEOPLE

Despite a common language, Americans may find it hard to cut through some of the local British accents. You may have more trouble communicating in northeastern England, in Tyneside, for example, than you would in France when using your high school French. Be understanding. After all, they were speaking that way before there was an America.

The British are supposed to be reserved, but all my questionnaire correspondents said that they were warmly received everywhere, and that people went out of their way to help with routes, shopping and any unexpected problems. The packed bikes helped break the ice, especially with rural people who didn't come in contact with many tourists. At campgrounds, English families will adopt you, feeding tea and goodies.

OVERALL COSTS

Most biking correspondents reported spending from $10 to $15 a day. But only Gary Conrad camped in the open, about half the time. Staying with relatives another quarter of the time, his daily expenses were only $4 a day in 1978. The others either stayed in hostels, a few formal campgrounds, or in B&Bs, or in some combination. Had they done some camping, they thought they'd have lowered costs a few dollars.

Most also ate in cafes, making their own lunches and some breakfasts. Meals were considered expensive, and cooking more for themselves would have cut costs further. On a strict budget, and using formal campgrounds and other accommodations occasionally, I'd guess that a person could live reasonably on $8 to $10 a day in England in 1981.

If you stay a few weeks in the country, you can open a special account in a bank and draw money against it, instead of carrying it in traveler's checks. The latter are exchanged at favorable rates at banks for about a $1 service charge.

ACCOMMODATIONS

The cheapest single in a small town will cost about $14. A double is twice as much. With some searching, you can find a double room in London, with breakfast, for $40. A railway hotel is cheaper; if it doesn't have room for a bike, you can leave it in a baggage room overnight.

288

The unique British accommodation idea, the bed and breakfast, is a better choice if you're the indoor sort. B&Bs range from $9 to $15 apiece, and include a substantial breakfast—eggs and bacon, cereal, the whole bit. They can be in a private home that puts up guests or at a fairly large establishment that looks almost like a hotel. But hotels they're not; you're usually expected to leave during the day, if you're staying over, and some don't even include a bath. A supper can be had at a number of them if you order ahead.

Lists of B&Bs are found in the BTA's "B&B in Britain," from local touring information centers, or in a guidebook like *Let's Go, Britain and Ireland* (see Appendix I). The CTC Handbook contains 50 pages of B&Bs in small print; these are accommodations that were selected on members' recommendations.

Hundreds of other excellent B&Bs exist, which are not listed anywhere. You can find them easily enough; they'll have signs outside. Prices are not fixed, so ask before you take a room. Bike security is good, with indoor lock-up the rule.

Hostels are the other popular choice of bikers in Britain. They're cheap, at somewhat over $3.50 for the highest category, but rules are somewhat petty and constricting: a strict curfew, Mickey Mouse clean-up work at many, release in the morning held up until inspection is passed. A few hostels have camping, which avoids some of the regimentation. Meals are provided if ordered in advance.

Various day-off closings during the week or for a time during vacations may occur in certain hostels. Take note of it before counting on a given stop. Correspondents said they never saw anyone turned away because of overcrowding. No one complained of any hostels. Breakfasts in them were reported to be "horrible," though, and some people were nervous about bike security, the bikes being left out in sheds or on the porch.

For a possibility to stay occasional nights with cycling hosts, get in touch with Leigh Howlett's Cyclists' Mutual Put-U-Up Scheme; see Appendix D. Young people are accommodated at university hostels, YMCAs and YWCAs. Those are described in "Youth Accommodation," free from the BTA.

The BTA also prints "Camping and Caravan Sites," about $4, which lists almost 2,000 places in the United Kingdom. Buy it in the United States from the British Travel Bookshop or British Gifts. The Association of Cycle and Lightweight Campers will also provide information, as will the Camping Club of Great Britain and Ireland, which has a list of over 2,500 sites. To be assisted by the latter, you must have a camping *carnet* (available from CTC), discussed in Chapter 1, in the section on Useful Associations, and Appendix C. However, *carnets* are not required at any commercial campgrounds, as they are in other parts of Europe.

289

Write also to the Forestry Commission for its leaflet, "Camping and Caravan Sites," and to the London Tourist Board for its list of sites within a radius of 30 miles around London. Information about campgrounds can be gotten from local information centers, too; some towns operate their own municipal sites, as do occasional inns and gas stations, and local farmers will take in tents as a side business.

Camp features range from near-posh, with dance hall and game room, to simple clearings in remote areas, though the latter may have showers. Most camps with the lavish conveniences are in seaside areas.

In spite of seemingly ample facilities, camping doesn't seem to be popular among British cyclists. It may be because of the island's wet climate, or a stronger tradition of hosteling. But it won't be considered odd if you ask to camp in a field or woods on someone's property. A farmer may charge a little, about $1 to pitch a tent. You'll generally find it harder to find a free site in built-up, farming regions than in pasture lands and mountains.

FOOD

You won't miss very much if you don't sample some British food in restaurants, though you might like to try some specialties like kidney pie, Yorkshire pudding with beef, or fish and chips. Restaurants can be expensive, but a pub lunch of chicken and chips or beef pie will be under $3.50.

You might want to drink a few of the many kinds of British beers in a pub, but don't feel obliged to. They serve nonalcoholic beverages, and they allow minors to enter.

A fish and chips shop will sell you a filling snack for $1.75; Hot Pot food places serve inexpensive dishes for about $1.75, and you can buy a Ploughman's sandwich in a pub for the same price. The best bargains for filling up are in ethnic restaurants in the cities—Pakistani, Indian, Italian, Greek.

Hours may be inconvenient. Pubs open in late morning and serve lunch for a couple of hours, then close until tea-time at about 4:00 P.M. Closing time is 10:30 P.M. Sunday hours are shorter, or the pub may be closed.

A variety of food is sold in grocery stores and small–town markets. Local cheeses and bread are delicious and make a good lunch staple. Pilchards, a canned fish, was recommended as a source of cheap protein by one bike tourist. Produce is fresh and of good quality. Food shops are usually open all day, from 9:00 A.M. to **290** 5:30 P.M. during the week.

If you cook for yourself, bring either an S-200 gas cartridge stove or one for kerosene (paraffin). White gas is unheard of.

ADDRESSES AND FURTHER READING

Association of Cycle and Lightweight Campers
30 Napier Way, Wembley
London

British Cycling Federation
Touring Bureau, 3 Moor Lane
Lancaster

British Gifts
PO Box 26558
Los Angeles, CA 90026

British Tourist Authority (BTA)
680 Fifth Avenue
New York, NY 10019
        and
612 South Flower
Los Angeles, CA 90017

UNITED KINGDOM

British Tourist Authority (BTA)
64 St. James Street
SW1A 1NF, London

The British Travel Bookshop, Ltd.
680 Fifth Avenue
New York, NY 10019

British Waterways Board
Estate Office, Willow Grange
Church Road, Watford
Hertfordshire WD1 3QA

Camping Club of Great Britain and Ireland
11 Grosvenor Place
London SW1W 0EY

Countryside Commission
John Dower House, Crescent Place
Cheltenham, Gloucestershire GL50 3RA

CTC Travel, Ltd.
13 Spring Street
London W2 3RA

Cyclists' Touring Club (CTC)
Cotterell House, 69 Meadrow
Godalming, Surrey GU7 3HS

East Anglia Tourist Board
14 Museum Street
Ipswich, Suffolk

Forestry Commission
231 Corstorphine Road
Edinburgh, Scotland EH12 7AT

London Tourist Board
4 Grosvenor Gardens, Victoria
London SW1W 0DU

Paddington Traffic Office
Delamere Terrace, Paddington
London W2

Angus Wilson, intr, Edwin Smith, photos, *England* (Views, 1971). A picture book that shows the country's glories, past and present. Comments by Wilson on life and values of the people.

WALES

BIKING MATTERS
SUGGESTED TOURS

See England.

MAPS, TERRAIN, TRAFFIC

See England for maps.

Wales is hilly throughout, though not formidable by bike tourists' accounts. Its highest mountain is under 3,600 feet, and roads are seldom above 1,500 feet. The problem is with the grades in the central region, which often are 20 percent or more. Since traffic along the borders of Wales is heavy, you'd be frequently on those interior roads, which are less busy. But Wales is only 140 miles from north to south, and less than 100 miles wide, so you can choose your routes and take your time.

The countryside is beautiful, and it can be as wild as Scotland's, if you stay away from the built-up area in the south-southeast. Quiet valleys, fishing villages along the coast, and photogenic mountains make Wales a unique experience.

Many roads are very narrow. Watch yourself especially on curved downhills. Traffic on these is light, though.

BEST CYCLING TIME

It gets warm later than in England—May to June—so early summer is best. Otherwise, as in England.

BIKE EQUIPMENT, RENTALS

See England for general information.

The CTC Handbook lists only seven recommended repairers for all of Wales. There are few bike shops with parts for 10-speeds. On the other hand, the country is so small that it's simple to get on a train and travel to Birmingham or to London in quick time.

BIKE TRANSPORTATION

As in England.

You may find yourself far from a railroad line. In that case, you

292

might be able to reach it by local bus, if you take the bike apart and make a compact package of it.

GENERAL
ENTERING, LEAVING, HASSLES

Same as England.

Gary Conrad said it was bad for hay fever sufferers, with an incredible amount of pollen. Its count drops in late summer or fall.

LANGUAGE AND PEOPLE

Welsh has equality with English, but English is spoken everywhere. Welsh culture, language and song are strong in the people's everyday lives.

OVERALL COSTS

About the same as in England.

ACCOMMODATIONS

Tourism is on the upswing in Wales and the number of B&Bs increases steadily. A local tourist information office will have a copy of "Where to Stay in Wales" for about $1.

Hostels are as thick in Wales as in England. Same rules and prices apply. The Pwll Deri hostel, though hard to find, is worth a stay for the sunset along cliffs and sea.

Send for "Touring, Caravan and Camping Sites" from the Wales Tourist Board. Cost for a site is low; you may get little for it, though, varying from just a place for a tent to basic services.

Free camping sites are sometimes hard to find, but farmers will let you stay on their land readily. Offer to pay.

FOOD

Except for regional difference in dishes, same as in England. A lot of the food is fried in heavy fats.

ADDRESSES AND FURTHER READING

Wales Tourist Board
Llandaff, Cardiff CFS 2YZ
South Wales

See also England for other organizations.

R. M. Lockly, *Wales* (New York: Hastings House, 1966). Seventeen tours by which the author talks about the country. Good illustrations.

SCOTLAND

BIKING MATTERS
SUGGESTED TOURS

See England.

MAPS, TERRAIN, TRAFFIC

The 1:250,000 Ordnance maps contain enough detail for most cycling. Eight of them cover Scotland.

The country is very rugged, the more so as you go north. It has very few flat areas, the most vast being on the North Sea coast around Aberdeen. Come with low gears and be ready for a slow pace.

Another good reason for cycling slowly is to take in the wild beauty of the countryside. The upper third of Scotland, the region split off from the main body by a line of lochs, is especially unique— bare, exposed to winds, and brooding. Bike tourists who cycled there tend to get rhapsodic describing it.

Roads are fewer in number here, and even "A" numbered ones can be narrow and steep. Surfaces are good to excellent, some potholes on minor roads but almost no debris or glass. There are more roads in the south, but traffic picks up, too.

The islands of the Outer Hebrides are worth a visit if you have the time; the Island of Skye is more readily accessible and can be circled on a good road. It does have long, tough hills, though.

BEST CYCLING TIME

A colder region here means that your cycling months are fewer. The best compromise is probably in June, before schools let out. But even a trip in July or August can be filled with cold, driving rain.

Except for the eastern shore and the south, Scotland is wetter than England, and is unpredictable. Its winds are usually strong, and they can be fierce any time.

BIKE EQUIPMENT, RENTALS

See England for general information.

Considerably fewer shops are here than in England, and mostly in cities. There's less of everything and little chance of spare parts you'd need. The CTC Handbook lists only about 18 repairers for all of Scotland. You'll have to do your own. Carry spares.

The Scottish Tourist Board issues "Bicycle Hire in Scotland."

Bikes are rented in about 30 cities and towns. Cost varies and averages $3.50 a day. The bikes are recreation types, and many shops require that bikes be returned daily.

BIKE TRANSPORTATION

See England.

No trains on Sunday. Bikes are not carried on buses: Jennie Yancey was told they do take them out of season. Several ferries a day run to most of the islands, and they take bikes.

GENERAL

ENTERING, LEAVING, HASSLES

See England.

LANGUAGE AND PEOPLE

Accents are different from those in England, and you may have the same minor difficulties being understood.

OVERALL COSTS

Somewhat higher than in England, about $15 a day staying in B&Bs and eating in public places.

ACCOMMODATIONS

Hostels and B&Bs are sparser than in England and are farther apart, though plentiful enough for nightly stays. The far north and the Isle of Lewis have fewer settlements and amenities. With less chance to sleep indoors in those regions, you'll have to depend to a greater degree on tenting. It will cut your costs somewhat, but will be more unpleasant if you run into foul weather.

No hostels allow camping. Prices and rules are the same as in England. Meals are provided at only a few.

Many campgrounds and private homes offer caravans (campers or trailers) for rent. Very nice change, and you can cook your meals in them, too. About $5.75 a night.

Free camping is allowed, with permission where it's possible to find the owner. Yancey found the ground too soggy for camping. Boil the water from streams. Sheep are everywhere and may contaminate it.

FOOD

Restaurant meals are $10 to $12 a person. Fish and chips and fast food places are scarce in the highlands.

No problem with provisions or pubs in the central and southern parts, but in the north you'll have to carry ample emergency supplies. Shops are closed Sundays.

ADDRESSES AND FURTHER READING

Scottish Tourist Board
23 Ravelston Terrace
Edinburgh, EH4 3EU

See also England for other organizations.

Eric Linklater, *Scotland* (Upper Darby, Pa.: Studio, 1968). An introduction that is geographically oriented. Beautiful photos, getting the feel of the land.

NORTHERN IRELAND

296   Many people shy away from visiting Northern Ireland because of the unrest. I've been assured by former residents, in the United States, and one or two intrepid bikers that the country is perfectly safe for bikers, as long as Belfast and Londonderry are avoided. One biker who has cycled there, on the other hand, wrote that I should not encourage people to visit there. The Northern Ireland Tourist Board seems to want tourists to come. I simply present what I could find out about cycling conditions.

You can come from Scotland by ferry to Larne, north of Belfast. Ferries from England land in Belfast, also. You can ride up from Ireland in the south too, of course, as did the Staffords (see Ireland).

For suggested routes, see England. Write to the National Tourist Board, River House, 48 High Street, Belfast BT1 2DS for a free copy of the Ordnance Survey 1:250,000 map. It's detailed enough for your use, and it shows camping and caravaning sites. On the reverse side, the tourist board shows a couple of suggested routes, and describes places of interest.

Or write to CTC for a Bartholomew Sheet 1 Antrim/Donegal, with the same scale.

The tourist office will also send you a list of places to stay, a pamphlet on bike rentals, and a suggested tour from Raleigh bicycles. Nine B&Bs are listed in the CTC Handbook, and only two repairers, one of them in Belfast. Bike transportation shouldn't be relied on.

UNITED KINGDOM

Accommodations are limited, but do exist; only a trickle of tourists come. The IYH Handbook includes a dozen hostels for Northern Ireland. Price is just $1.75. No meals are provided at them. Camping is not encouraged officially, but a couple of bike tourists reported camping in the open without event.

YUGOSLAVIA
33

BIKING MATTERS
SUGGESTED TOUR

Slovenia and Croatia; 565 miles, three weeks (two for stronger bikers). In a rugged country, this tour keeps climbs down to a minimum. The sharpest grades are no more than 15 percent, and the road surfaces are mostly good to excellent. Roads are almost all minor.

Inevitably, you'll come across a few stretches of coarse stone or dirt. I tried to keep those to a minimum, but road repair can happen anywhere and you'll have to accept some bad roads to cycle in Yugoslavia. Part of this tour was cycled by Walter ten Hoeve, and I was on some of the roads also.

Start in Trieste or Zagreb. Or you can connect later in the tour from Austria or Hungary. There's an awful climb out of Trieste on 6 to Ljubljana. To avoid it, I have this circular loop go counterclockwise, in a direction that is more gradual overall.

Cross the Italian-Yugoslav frontier onto 2a. Ride about 10 miles to the village of Podgrad. Turn left to Ilirska Bistrica. Cross 6c there, and climb on the same minor road you were on, through Leskova Dolina to Bloska Polica. Turn east to the village of Zlebic, then north about 7 miles. Look for a small road along a stream. It goes through Videm to Krka—a climb here. The road was poor macadam a few years ago, but it may have improved now.

An excellent road leads east to Novo Mesto. Turn south and climb up 4 to Metlika and Karvolac. Stay on 4 south and east to Glina. Turn northeast, off 4, to Petrinia, then southeast through Kostajnica to Dubica. A parallel road just to the north, through Sunja, can be taken if you want to avoid going over a mountain.

From Dubica cross the Sava River and highway E94, to Novska. Turn northwest to Kutina; from here to Zagreb is easy riding. Go north along minor roads to Bjelovar. You'll pass through such villages as Garesnica, Hercegovac and Pavlovac. Along the way, you can take 9 north to connect with Hungary. From Bjelovar the road goes directly west to Zagreb. Stop in the city for an interesting visit.

Ride west a bit, across 1b and the river, to Zapresic. Continue west almost to Brezice, and turn right to Bizeljsko. Stay on the same road to Celje. Now turn south to Lasko and west to Zagorje. Keep on the road south of the Sava River through Litija to Ljubljana, a great fun city.

Ride the parallel road to 6, on its west, to Postajna. Use 6 to Trieste. Be careful going down a long hill to this city; stop along the way for a great view of the Adriatic.

MAPS, TERRAIN, TRAFFIC

Maps sent free by the Yugoslav National Tourist Office are useless for bike travel. The Auto-Moto Zveza Slovennije, 1:850,000, can be bought in Yugoslavia. It shows roads down to the smallest unpaved ones in the mountains, and lacks detail only in those that are near large cities and in the few flat areas of the country. What's important to bikers, it has good markings for degrees of uphills through the mountains. Pick your way more easily with their aid. Auto-Moto sells large-scale regional maps also, about $2.

Complete Traveller sells a Geographia 1:800,000 for $6. Mair puts out three 1:200,000 maps of the Dalmation coast; you can buy them for $3.25 each from the American Map Company. It also

299

sells a BMC 1:500,000 for $5. Aral karte 1:600,000 can be bought at gas stations, too.

Cycling in Yugoslavia is rough, if you stay off the throughways. Roads shown in orange on the Auto-Moto map are asphalted. Those in yellow are macadam, a base of broken and crushed stone and dirt. When kept in repair, macadam roads are acceptable for cycling, albeit slow and bumpy with high-pressure tires. When their surfaces are broken, they're awful. You have to pick your way around potholes and boulders that thrust out of the ground, and you take chances of breaking an axle when going fast. Downhill runs are dangerous. Roads shown white (and yellow ones that are shown as narrow) are likely to be the worst, since they serve as connections of small villages or they pass through the most formidable mountains.

Additionally, roads get even worse the farther southeast you travel, close to Greece and Albania. The tourist office can give you a copy of a map that shows the current condition of roads. I've sent for a copy a few times and never received it, but it may have been the wrong time of the year. Try in spring before you leave.

But there are often surprises, good and bad, in spite of what's shown on the map. A minor road suddenly is asphalted in the middle of nowhere, while a main one may be disrupted with repair work or may not have been repaired for years. You have to be ready to improvise your route.

In towns cobblestones are frequent. Cities have dangerous trolley tracks that can catch wheels.

Stay off the E94 tourist slot from Ljubljana to Belgrade or off E27 on the Adriatic, and you'll see some of the most spectacular and wild country in Europe. Each day, in spite of bad roads and hard climbs, you'll be overwhelmed by sights of deep gorges and craggy peaks, unspoiled woods—Yugoslavia is one-third forest and three-quarters mountains—solitary monasteries, and isolated villages.

Grading is upward of 30 percent in places, and at least one daily climb of 10 to 15 percent is common. The tour I suggested is as mild as you can find, away from the river valleys or the coast.

The amount of traffic is inverse to cycling difficulty, with small roads being almost empty and through roads like E27 and E94 heavy. Truck traffic is bad on main roads. Off-season, however, the Dalmation coast has less tourists and cycling is pleasant.

Many highways are forbidden to cyclists. Police stopped me on E5, south of Belgrade, and escorted me off the road. You're allowed on sections of it west of the capital and the main road beyond Nis to Bulgaria can be cycled, too.

Bikes are forbidden on the main streets of Belgrade. I walked those and cycled when traffic thinned. Tunnels can be encountered in the mountains. Bring front lights and a blinking back light, and use care.

BEST CYCLING TIME

The Adriatic coast resembles the rest of the Mediterranean in climate; cycling can easily start in April, and even in mid-March. In the rest of the country you can freeze in April, more so if accompanied by the rain that is common then. Early May is a safer time to start.

The mountains can be pleasant in summer, while lower altitudes are hot. Fall is probably the safest time to plan a tour, in September when tourists have thinned. The chance of rain is fairly even throughout the season, with late fall being the most likely time.

BIKE EQUIPMENT, RENTALS

I saw Karrimor bike panniers and a few accessories in a combination sport-bike shop in Ljubljana. The best bikes they had were Czech Favorits, of medium quality and limited range of gears. Components for those were available. I saw no other bike supplies while I was in the country, but I imagine Belgrade had a bike shop, too. Alan Bubna visited several bike shops, where he saw 27 X 1¼-inch tires for sale.

301

It's doubtful if there's even a 3-speed for hire in the country. A request of the tourist office about bike matters brought a reply that Yugoslavia is not prepared for bike touring and does not encourage it.

If you mail in any bicycle equipment, be prepared to pay customs duty on it.

BIKE TRANSPORTATION

Trains take bikes. If you're going a long way, with transfers, see that bikes are changed. If not, do it yourself. There may be a long wait for the next train. A couple of tourists complained of this.

GENERAL
ENTERING, LEAVING, HASSLES

Americans need visas and passports. A visa is issued at the border, but you'll avoid delays if you get one at home from the consulate.

Although there is no minimum daily exchange of money required, you may have a bit of a hassle with a border guard. I've been asked to show some proof of support. I showed traveler's checks. The sight of a bike and a suggestion of Gypsy life in the guard's mind may have been the problem.

In-country, you're not bothered. I had one incident along the Danube opposite Romania, when I was seen photographing at the water's edge. An army officer stopped on the highway and admonished me, though the area was empty of houses or anything but the river itself.

In the Moslem south, women will be subject to harassment from macho-oriented males. Use the same care you would in the Middle East, never being alone and avoiding provocation. You'll have enough of a task fending off suitors without further stimulating them with revealing dress.

Piet de Jong cautioned that it's important to identify oneself as a non–German if speaking that language. People haven't forgotten World War II.

LANGUAGE AND PEOPLE

If you know any Slav language, some verbal or written communication is possible. The Cyrillic alphabet may throw you if you're not familiar with it. Signs and menus may be printed in it in Serbia, even in the more cosmopolitan Belgrade.

English is known by some young people, mostly along the Adriatic and in big cities. Most English will be spoken to you by other travelers, rather than natives. In some of the smaller towns, even tourist agencies may not have anyone who can speak any but a native tongue.

German is much more useful. A few of the young people speak some French or Italian, also. Russian is the only major language not used at all.

Yugoslavia has more diversity in people and culture than any other European country I know. Since it's a relatively new nation, a union of diverse Balkan states that were distinct previously, you'll see marked differences when passing from one region to another. The dress, language, religion, and the very look of people changes. You're never bored.

There's much interest in America; the young will engage you in political discussion, on which they're very keen. There are many influences from the West—Pepsi Cola, pop music, Western-style TV ads, luxury goods, small-scale private enterprise—and a casual, informal society is closer to the United States than to the rest of Eastern Europe. People are optimistic and gay. Nightlife is lively, especially in taverns on weekends, a contrast to the proper and somber small towns in Austria or Germany.

There's a serious side. Social idealism is strong in the young, and you may be surprised by attacks on the capitalist system. They'll talk with facts: Western newspapers are sold, and many TV programs are from the BBC or other Western countries. Yugoslavs are free to travel in the West. They'll not be arguing from an isolated, naive base, ignorant of what goes on in the rest of the world.

OVERALL COSTS

What with the options open to cycling—either in tourist areas, or in virtual wilderness—chances are that you'll be spending either quite a bit or very little to live in Yugoslavia. It's a cheap country, but not when the only accommodations available are state-run hotels.

You face an anomaly: inexpensive campgrounds and youth hostels are generally located in resorts, which would ordinarily be expensive, while in the hinterlands only hotels will be available for indoor stays.

The examples of two bike tourists illustrate the principle. Ten Hoeve spent $20 a day sleeping in hotels—he didn't bring a tent—and eating only in cafes. Priscilla Logan spent just $5 a day cycling the Adriatic. Logan shared expenses, camped or stayed in private lodgings, and she cooked most meals. Though her trip was taken in 1977, costs since then have not risen enough to surpass that figure by much, if one were to cook all meals and camp. About $6 to $8 should do it. Yugoslavia can be one of the cheapest countries to tour, or you can spend more than in Scandinavia.

Buy some dinars in a Western bank before coming into Yugoslavia. Its currency is on the Western market and you're allowed to bring in $75 worth. The rate in an adjoining country is usually better than in Yugoslavia. There's no black market and you'll do no better in-country. I've been approached by Yugoslavs in Italy, however, who offered to buy money. But I believe that they were just skimming a bit of percentage by offering a little less than the local bank, and then exchanging the money at the same bank for the higher rate.

ACCOMMODATIONS

The range of prices for indoor accommodations is tenfold. Hotels are of four classes. The cheapest will cost $12 a double off-season, and twice as much in summer. You'll find no "small hotel" bargains as you do in France and other Western countries. Prices are standard, set by the state. However, managers can be talked to, and you can often get the prices down.

To pay considerably less, use private lodgings. These are legitimate enterprises and they're often negotiable, if the area isn't overcrowded with tourists, and depending on your charm. A good

303

bet is in a small, off-the-track town, where someone would want to gain some extra dinars.

Hostels are almost all along the Adriatic and in the largest cities. They cost from $2.25 to $5.50 a person. Priority is given to those 27 and under. You can stay as long as you want, so you may have a hard time getting in during the summer or in popular areas. None have kitchens. Hostels aren't a practical accommodation if cycling in remote areas.

Campgrounds are also most common along the coast. You can find some in the interior, too, but only along E94, E5 and other superhighways. There are virtually none away from those. Camps cost on the order of $2.25 a person, the price contingent on offerings. All camps I was in had hot showers, at least a cafe, and good grass on which to tent. Bungalows, at about $8 for two, are also available at the camps.

It's easy to camp in the open. Woods are everywhere, and if you're like me you'll prefer the view from a mountaintop to that of a sea of caravans and tents. There are plenty of streams safe as a water source, and no one will bother you.

304

In any case, open camping is your only alternative in the remote places you'll be going as a cyclist. Unlike conventional bus or train travelers who can pick their nightly destinations, you'll be faced with no other choice probably three-quarters of the time in this backward country. Definitely bring a tent.

FOOD

The Yugoslav cuisine is good, with many savory dishes that are the result of influences from surrounding nations, and from the Turkish past. Costs are low and portions substantial. The customary main meal is at lunchtime.

A moderately priced meal that is well prepared may be hard to find, however. The reason is a lack of independent country inns, such as you find in the West. The usual place that's available is a predominantly state-run or managed restaurant that offers either an unimaginative cafeteria or a posh restaurant catering to well-heeled foreigners. In towns and villages off the tourist roads, cafeterias with steam tables are the rule.

The best bet in a village is a bar. There may be a choice of one or two dishes at noontime, but more usually you can get a sausage, bread and beer. "Buffet" bars are found along the roads occasionally on the outskirts of towns, which serve the same purpose.

Most independently run restaurants are on the Adriatic coast, around the largest cities, and in isolated tourist pockets like Lake Ohrid on the southern border. Relatively affluent Slovenia has more good restaurants than the rest of the country.

YUGOSLAVIA

Those restaurants will charge you as little as $2.75 for a tasty meal, with $4 more usual when complete with some wine and dessert. Cafeteria meals can be good, too, those in large cities, where you pay $1.65 to $2.75.

In large towns and cities, pastry shops, coffee houses and cafes provide pleasant interludes; you can sip plum brandy (slivovic) or wine, and spend a couple of hours writing notes or just lazing. Very civilized.

Wines are excellent and cheap, as are beers. Various fresh fruit juices in cartons of about 10 ounces are sold. Cherry is delicious and almost addictive.

Fruit and vegetables in season are abundant and tree ripened. Salami, pressed ham and other cold cuts are good and reasonable, but the Yugoslav version of a *kielbasa* sausage is inferior to the Czech, Polish or American, to my taste. Bread is dirt cheap. So are various hard rolls, pastries, ice cream and other goodies.

Village stores, and even those in small towns, are very limited in foodstuffs. Variety in packaged goods is confined to a choice between a pasta and rice, for example. Bakeries have one kind of bread, and a kind of cookie with sprinkled sugar. For cakes you have to go to a state general store, where they're packaged, as in the United States. When you're cooking for yourself, make a practice of stocking up in large towns and cities.

305

Shop hours seem to differ, but stores are open well into the evening.

ADDRESSES AND FURTHER READING

Yugoslav National Tourist Office
630 Fifth Avenue
New York, NY 10020

Auto-Moto Savez Jugoslaviye
Ruzveltova 18
11001 Belgrade

David Tornquist, *Look East, Look West: The Socialist Adventure in Yugoslavia* (New York: Macmillan, 1966). Life, economy and politics. Author traveled, lived and worked there. Excellent in all aspects.

Ivo Andric, *The Pasha's Concubine, and Other Tales* (New York: Knopf). Fiction that tells about life in Yugoslavia for three centuries, by a Nobel Prize winner. Good reading.

PART
III
APPENDICES

APPENDIX

A

BIKE TOURISTS' INTERNATIONAL VOCABULARY

English	French	German	Italian	Spanish
ball bearings	billes	Kugeln	cuscinetti a sfera	baleros
bell	clochette	Glocke	campanello	timbre
brake	frein	Bremse	freno	freno
cable	cable	Draht	cavo	cable
carrier	porte-bagage	Gepack-trager	portabagagli	portabultos
chain	chaine	Rollenkette	catena	cadena
cotter pin	clavette	Kurbelkeil	fermadado	chaveta
crank	manivelle	Tretkurbel	manovella	manivela
derailleur	derailleur	Kettenschal-tung	cambio	cambio de marchas
fender (mud-guard)	garde-boue	Schutzblech	parafango	guardabarros
fork	fourche	Vordergabel	forcella	horquilla
freewheel	roue libre	Freilauf	ruota libera	rueda libre
generator	alternateur	Lichtmas-chine	dinamo	generador
handlebar	guidon	Lenker	manubrio	guía
hub	moyeu	Nabe	mozzo	maza
light, rear	lampe de feu arriere	Rucklicht	faro poste-riore	luz trasera

BIKE TOURISTS' INTERNATIONAL VOCABULARY

English	French	German	Italian	Spanish
lock	anti-vol	Schloss	lucchetto (antifurto)	seguro o cerrojo
nut	ecrou	Mutter	dado	tuerca
pedal	pedale	Pedal	pedale	pedal
pump	pompe	Pumpe	pompa	inflador
reflector	reflecteur d'arriere	Ruck-strahler	catarifran-gente	reflector
rim	jante	Felge	cerchione	rim
saddle	selle	Sattel	sella	sillín
spoke	rayon	Speiche	raggio	rayo de rueda
tire	pneu	Reifen	pneumatico	neumático o llanta
valve	valve	Ventil	valvola	válvula
wheel	roue	Rad	ruota	rueda
wheel, front	roue avant	Vorderrad	ruota ante-riore	rueda anterior
wheel, rear	roue arriere	Hinterrad	ruota poste-riore	rueda trasera

APPENDIX
B

AUTHOR'S EQUIPMENT LIST FOR EXTENDED TOURING

Not all these items are taken on every trip. Winter clothes or cooking gear, especially, are omitted often. A trip of a few months in all sorts of weather is the only time a full complement would be needed. The weight of everything listed here is about 50 pounds, without food stores, and without bicycle.

BIKE EQUIPMENT
- Nishiki bicycle, with fenders and bell, Brooks saddle
- components: Avocet crankset 52/47/26; Sun Tour Winner freewheel 13–16–20–26–34; Sun Tour derailleurs, Cyclone front and VGT rear
- Zefal pump, HP
- 3 bottles (one metal for fuel)
- Blackburn carriers, front and back
- rear and front panniers, handlebar bag; no make preferred, all seem to leak
- 5 shock cords
- tools: freewheel remover, spoke wrench, 4-inch adjustable wrench (borrow a larger wrench at gas station to remove freewheel), 2 cone wrenches, set of allen wrenches needed on bike, chain rivet extractor, crank arm removing tool, screwdriver, pliers, bottom bracket adjusting tools (carried only into countries with no 10-speed bikes), Swiss knife
- spares: ball bearings, a few nuts and bolts, front and rear axles, a few pieces of wire, adhesive tape, 15 spokes, 2 brake shoes,

long derailleur cable, long brake cable, a few chain links, 2 extra top-position freewheel cogs (for long trips), rim strip, grease and oil
- tire patch kit
- 3 tire irons
- extra tire (when in countries without them)
- lock and cable
- flasher, attached to rear carrier

CAMPING GEAR

- R.E.I. Ascent tent
- plastic ground sheet, 6 inches smaller in each dimension than floor size of tent
- sleeping bag (Camp 7 Arete, down, or EMS Berkshire, PolarGuard, depending on whether damp or dry weather expected)
- Ensolite pad, half-size (shoulder width, hip length)
- nylon bed sheet, AYH type
- flashlight, Mallory Duracell (AA batteries double with camera's electronic flash)
- French candle lantern
- extra candles
- length of nylon cord

311

COOKING GEAR

- stove (type and size dependent on number in party and availability of fuel)
- asbestos pad, 9-inch diameter
- pots and fry pan (number and type dependent on number in group)
- personal mess kit
- knife, fork, spoon kit
- drinking cup
- cooking glove (optional)
- spatula, nylon (if taking fry pan)
- wooden spoon
- cutting knife, about 6-inch blade
- small, hardwood cutting board
- knife sharpener
- can opener
- measuring cup
- collapsible, plastic water container, 2½ gallon (smaller if only one person)
- soap powder or liquid soap

- long-handled wash brush, nylon
- pot scrubber, nylon mesh
- a few plastic bottles
- a few extra stuff sacks
- assortment of spices in 35mm film cans
- food staples, liquid and solid

CLOTHES

- 3 undershirts, white
- 4 underwear, colored
- Damart lightweight winter underwear, top and bottom
- cycling shorts
- dress pants, light
- riding jeans
- sweat shirt
- knit shirt
- nylon windbreaker
- sweater, light
- 3 pair wool socks, ankle length
- dress socks
- biking shoes, sneaker type
- dress shoes, light
- wool cap
- winter gloves
- pocket handkerchiefs
- large bandanna (has all sorts of uses)
- mosquito head net
- rain gear
- swim trunks

312

PHOTO

- 2 Olympus RD cameras (color and B&W)
- tripod, lightweight
- electronic flash
- film, color and B&W

MISCELLANEOUS

- printed matter: maps, guide, cookbook, passport, personal papers
- writing tablet and pens
- cassette recorder (optional)
- toilet kit, scissors, etc.
- money belt or neck pouch
- sewing kit

EQUIPMENT LIST FOR EXTENDED TOURING

- plastic bags, assortment of about a dozen
- toilet paper
- a few first-aid items
- drugs as needed (Lomotil, Entero-Viaform, malaria pills, vitamin pills, water purification tablets)
- rearview mirror, eyeglass
- sunglasses
- spare reading glasses
- slingshot (when dogs are bad)
- omitted on purpose:
  pillow (put outerwear in a stuff sack instead)
  inflatable mattress (too heavy, punctures eventually, poor insulation)
  warm-up suit (heavy, unneeded)
  riding gloves (don't need them for comfort)

APPENDIX C

USEFUL ORGANIZATIONS

American Automobile Association (AAA)
8111 Gatehouse Road
Falls Church, VA 22042
    Send for application to get an international driver's license.

American Express Company
777 American Express Way
Fort Lauderdale, FL 33336
    Get a directory of international offices, here, or in any local office.

Department of State
Office of Passport Services
Washington, DC 20524
    Send for free leaflet, "Visa Requirements of Foreign Governments."

Esperanto League for North America
PO Box 1129
El Cerrito, CA 94530
    Part of the international Esperanto organization, which promotes the spread of that universal language.

Globetrotters Club
BCM/Roving
London WCI 6XX
England
    International self-help travel club. Membership includes newsletter, "The Globe."

USEFUL ORGANIZATIONS

Harvard Student Agencies
Harvard University, Thayer Hall-B
Cambridge, MA 02138
   Source of international student ID cards, YH and rail passes, student discount flights, as well as the *Let's Go,* guides.

International Association for Medical Assistance to Travellers (IAMAT)
Empire State Building
350 Fifth Avenue, Suite 5620
New York, NY 10001
   An association of English-speaking doctors, world wide, with a unified approach to medical treatment, and with set payments. No membership fee to belong.

National Campers and Hikers Association
7172 Transit Road
Buffalo, NY 14221
   U.S.-based, but you can get an international camping *carnet* from them.

National Council of YMCAs
Office of the International Division
291 Broadway
New York, NY 10007
   Send for Directory of YMCAs in 88 countries. Allow at least a couple of months for a response.

Servas International
11 John Street, Room 406
New York, NY 10038
   Promotes people-to-people contacts and understanding internationally.

Thomas Cook
5 World Trade Center
New York, NY 10017
   Get a directory of international offices here, or in a local office.

Touring Exchange, Bonnie Wong
1320 North Fir Villa Road
Dallas, OR 97338
   Domestic and foreign tour descriptions at a nominal cost.

APPENDIX
D
HOST/GUEST ORGANIZATIONS

Cyclists' Mutual Put-U-Up Scheme
Leigh Howlett, I, New Cottages
Huntham, Stoke St. Gregory
Taunton, Somerset
England

Touring Cyclists' Hospitality Directory
John Mosley
13623 Sylvan
Van Nuys, CA 91401
    Mostly in the U.S., but a few overseas hosts also.

Travel and Friend (Reis en Vriend)
Robert de Bruijne, secretary
Kastanjeweg 10-3
Amsterdam 1092 CG
Netherlands

Travelers' Directory
Tom Linn, Editor
6224 Baynton Street
Philadelphia, PA 19144

APPENDIX
E

BICYCLING ORGANIZATIONS AND PERIODICALS

American Youth Hostels (AYH)
National Campus
Delaplane, VA 22025
     Membership includes periodic bulletins at national and regional levels. Overseas tours.

Bicycling Magazine
33 East Minor Street
Emmaus, PA 18049

Cyclists' Touring Club (CTC)
Cotterell House, 69 Meadrow
Godalming, Surrey GU7 3HS
England
     Membership includes bi-monthly *Cycletouring* magazine, and many free bike travel services. European tours.

League of American Wheelmen (LAW)
PO Box 988
Baltimore, MD 21203
     Membership includes *American Wheelmen* magazine. Occasional articles on foreign touring. No overseas touring service.

APPENDIX F

ORGANIZED GROUP TOURS

Adventure Center
5540 College Avenue
Oakland, CA 94618
    England or Switzerland.

American Youth Hostels
National Campus
Delaplane, VA 22025
    Rhine Valley, British Isles, Western Europe.

Bike Tour France
PO Box 32814
Charlotte, NC 28232
    France.

Biking Expedition, Inc.
Hall Avenue
PO Box 547
Henniker, NH 03242
    Britain, Ireland, France.

Country Cycling Tours
410 West Twenty-fourth Street
New York, NY 10011
    Ireland.

Cycle Touring International
Box 311
Kansas City, MO 64141
    England, Holland, Germany, Austria, Switzerland.

ORGANIZED GROUP TOURS

Directions Unlimited
344 Main Street
Mt. Kisco, NY 10549
    France, Switzerland.

Euro-Bike Tours, Inc.
PO Box 40
DeKalb, IL 60115
    England, Germany, France, Switzerland, Luxembourg, Belgium, Holland.

European Bicycling Adventure
58 Susan Drive
New York, NY 10956
    England, France, Holland.

Gerhard's Bicycle Odysseys
1137 Southwest Yamhill
Portland, OR 97205
    Spain, France, England, Ireland, Germany.

International Bicycle Touring Society (IBTS)
2115 Paseo Doredo
La Jolla, CA 92037
    Western Europe, Balkan countries, Greece.

International Bike Tours
12 Mid Place
Chappaqua, NY 10514
    Holland.

Lucallan Travels, Ltd.
402 Twenty-ninth Street
Des Moines, IA 50312
    France.

Motorless Motion Tours
518 Seventh Street
Rockford, IL 61104
    Ireland, England, Holland, Denmark, Germany.

Out-Spokin'
Box 370
Elkhart, IN 46515
    Europe.

ADVENTURE CYCLING IN EUROPE

Pascal's Bicycle Touring
Box 515
175 Freeman Street
Brookline, MA 02146
   England, France.

Pioneer Travel Service
2 Garden Terrace
Cambridge, MA 02138
   Poland, Hungary, Bulgaria, Czechoslovakia, Austria.

Putney Student Travel, Inc.
Putney, VT 05346
   Holland to either England, France, or to Germany,
Italy, Switzerland, France, or to Scandinavia, Russia.

Small World Adventures
Box 258
Manchester Center, VT 05255
   England, Wales, Scotland.

Student Hosteling Program of New England, Inc.
Maple Hill
Rochester, VT 05767
   Ireland, France, Switzerland, England.

Tamure Study Groups
14613 East Whittier Boulevard
Whittier, CA 90605
   England, France, Switzerland, Germany.

White Tower Travel, Inc.
845 North Michigan Avenue
Suite 946E
Chicago, IL 60611
   Greece.

APPENDIX

G

EQUIPMENT SUPPLIERS

BIKE EQUIPMENT SUPPLIERS

Bikecology Bike Shops
PO Box 66909
Los Angeles, CA 90066

Bike Warehouse
215 Main Street, Box 290
New Middletown, OH 44442

Metropolitan New York Council, AYH
132 Spring Street
New York, NY 10012

Touring Cyclist Shop
PO Box 4009
2639 Spruce Street
Boulder, CO 80306

CAMPING EQUIPMENT SUPPLIERS

Eastern Mountain Sports
Vose Farm Road
Peterborough, NH 03458

R.E.I. Co-op
PO Box C–88125
Seattle, WA 98188

APPENDIX
H
MAP
SOURCES

These sell maps by mail. Send for catalog.
American Map Company
1926 Broadway
New York, NY 10023

The Complete Traveller
199 Madison Avenue
New York, NY 10016

Cyclists' Touring Club
Cotterell House, 69 Meadrow
Godalming, Surrey GU7 3HS
England

B. Dalton
666 Fifth Avenue
New York, NY 10019
    A limited number of Kummerly & Frey and other maps available. Inquire about specific needs.

Michelin
PO Box 5022
New Hyde Park, NY 11042

Send for catalog only.
Bartholomew
Duncan Street
Edinburgh EH4 1TA
Scotland

MAP SOURCES

Geographia Ltd.
63 Fleet Street
London EC4Y 1PE
England

323

APPENDIX
I
FURTHER READING

BIKE TOURING ADVENTURES

Anderson, William C. *The Great Bicycle Expedition.* New York: Crown, 1973.
> Discovery of bike touring by a family of four in Europe. Entertaining family fare.

Logan, Margaret. *Happy Endings.* Boston: Houghton Mifflin, 1979.
> A mother and daughter learn about each other, and about life, through a bicycle tour from France to Italy. Beautifully written, a lot of fun and much substance.

Sumner, Lloyd. *The Long Ride.* Harrisburg, Pa.: Stackpole, 1976.
> Bravura account of an around-the-world tour that reads like Pauline's Perils. Still, it's sustained by Sumner's persistence over initial setbacks and inexperience, and acceptance of come-what-may.

DESCRIPTION AND PEOPLE

Ardagh, John. *A Tale of Five Cities: Life in Europe Today.* New York: Harper & Row, 1979.
> Differences and similarities among France, Italy, West Germany, England and Yugoslavia through comparison of life in each of the five's medium-size cities. Written in an easy anecdotal style, it includes economic, political, cultural and artistic aspects. Well structured, so you can read "Cultural Life," for example, for each city without searching.

Baer, Jean. *Follow Me!* New York: Macmillan, 1975.
> Hints for women on coping with men, wardrobe and travel problems. Breezy, entertaining, and could be useful.

FURTHER READING

Morris, James. *Places.* New York: Harcourt Brace Jovanovich, 1972.
A beautiful prose style in essays about northern Spain, Iceland, Italy, Germany, Ireland, Wales and France. About people in specific places, their attitudes, worries and games.

Pritchett, V. S. *The Offensive Traveller.* New York: Knopf, 1964.
Travels and observations in Eastern Europe, Spain and Turkey by a veteran news commentator, essayist and novelist. A little dated, in fact, but it reflects the intelligence and sharp eye of this critic.

Theroux, Paul. *The Great Railway Bazaar.* Boston: Houghton Mifflin, 1975.
A train ride to India and Siberia, and back through Europe. Amusing and penetrating.

WHY PEOPLE ACT AS THEY DO

Carpenter, Edmund. *Oh, What a Blow that Phantom Gave Me!* New York: Holt, Rinehart & Winston, 1972.
The author tells us about the cultural image we have of ourselves. Emphasis on the electronic media and how they change both civilized and primitive people. Cultural anthropology, but plain, understandable language.

325

Harris, Marvin. *Cows, Pigs, Wars, and Witches: The Riddles of Culture.* New York: Random House, 1974.
An immensely readable description of why some cultures seem so different, yet are understandable when seen in their terms rather than ours.

GUIDES AND FACTS

Carter, James P., and West, E. de Antonia. *Keeping Your Family Healthy Overseas.* New York: Delacorte Press, 1971.
Mostly for State Department and business types living overseas, but a lot of good health information.

Fodor's Worldwide Adventure Guide. New York: David McKay, 1979.
The first 26 pages are useful. Those deal with such details as travel costs, documents, health and various organizations. Forget the rest, Fodor's ideas of adventure and the organized tours. You'll provide your own thrills. Skim through it in the library.

Ford, Norman D. *How to Travel without Being Rich.* New York: Grosset & Dunlap, 1972.
Beating prices. Dated, but principles hold true.

Frommer & Pasmantier. *Frommer's Whole World Handbook.* New York: Simon & Schuster, 1976.
> Travel, work and study abroad, by country. For students and youth, primarily, but older folks can profit from it, too, starting at about page 50, "Touring." Dated but still useful.

Goldstein, Eric, ed. *Let's Go, Europe, 1980-81.* New York: Dutton, 1980.
> The modern Baedeker for cheap travel, it includes a generalized introduction—cutting costs, transportation, formalities, accommodations—and a discussion of each country by city and area. Others in the *Let's Go,* series cover Britain and Ireland, France, and Italy. Revised annually.

Hillman, Robert and Sheilah. *Traveling Healthy: A Complete Guide to Medical Services in 23 Countries.* New York: Penguin Books, 1980.
> The authority, covering 20 European countries. It includes a foreign medical vocabulary, an international list of generic drugs, and first-aid techniques. Paperback but heavy, 559 pages; $7.95.

Michelin Green Guides to Germany, Austria, Italy, Portugal, Spain, Switzerland, and six regions of France. From Michelin Green Guides & Maps in the U.S., about $7 each.

The Official Associated Press Almanac. Maplewood, N.J.: Hammond, Inc., issued yearly.
> All kinds of facts, U.S. and worldwide: history, government, transportation, temperatures, geography, more.

APPENDIX

J

LICENSE PLATES

Do you wonder where those motorists who pass you are from? Here are their plate identifications.

A	Austria	**I**	Italy
AND	Andorra	**IL**	Israel
B	Belgium	**IS**	Iceland
BG	Bulgaria	**L**	Luxembourg
CH	Switzerland	**MC**	Monaco
CS	Czechoslovakia	**N**	Norway
D	West Germany	**NL**	Holland
DDR	East Germany	**P**	Portugal
DK	Denmark	**PL**	Poland
E	Spain	**R**	Romania
EIR	Ireland	**S**	Sweden
F	France	**SF**	Finland
FL	Liechtenstein	**SU**	USSR
GB	United Kingdom	**TR**	Turkey
GR	Greece	**YU**	Yugoslavia
H	Hungary		

APPENDIX
K

EUROPEAN EMBASSIES
IN WASHINGTON, D.C.

Austria
2343 Massachusetts Avenue NW
20008

Belgium
3330 Garfield Street NW
20008

Bulgaria
2100 Sixteenth Street NW
20009

Czechoslovakia
3900 Linnean Avenue NW
20008

Denmark
3200 Whithaven Street NW
20008

Finland
1900 Twenty-fourth Street NW
20008

France
2535 Belmont Road NW
20008

EUROPEAN EMBASSIES IN WASHINGTON, D.C.

German Democratic Republic (East)
1717 Massachusetts Avenue NW
20036

Germany, Federal Republic of (West)
4645 Reservoir Road NW
20007

Great Britain
3100 Massachusetts Avenue NW
20008

Greece
2221 Massachusetts Avenue NW
20008

Hungary
2437 Fifteenth Street NW
20009

Iceland
2022 Connecticut Avenue NW
20008

Ireland
2234 Massachusetts Avenue NW
20008

Italy
1601 Fuller Street NW
20009

Luxembourg
2200 Massachusetts Avenue NW
20008

Netherlands
4200 Linnean Avenue NW
20008

Norway
3401 Massachusetts Avenue
20007

Poland
2640 Sixteenth Street NW
20009

Portugal
2125 Kalorama Road NW
20008

Romania
1607 Twenty-third Street NW
20008

Spain
2700 Fifteenth Street NW
20009

Sweden
Suite 1200
600 New Hampshire Avenue NW
20037

330

Switzerland
2900 Cathedral Avenue NW
20008

Turkey
1606 Twenty-third Street NW
20008

USSR
1125 Sixteenth Street NW
20036

Yugoslavia
2410 California Street NW
20008

APPENDIX

L

UNITED STATES EMBASSIES AND CONSULATES IN EUROPE

The first address, telephone number and telex in each country is for the embassy. Subsequent listings are for consulates. APOs or FPOs are to be used in the address only when mailing from the United States.

Austria: Vienna
IX Boltzmanngasse 16 A-1091
tel (222) 31-55-11 telex 74634

Salzburg
1 Franz Josefs Kai, Room 302
tel 46461

Belgium: Brussels
27 Boulevard du Regent; B-1000
APO NY 09667
tel (02) 513-3830 telex 846-21336

Antwerp
64-68 Frankrijkiel; B-2000
APO NY 09667
tel (031) 321800

Bulgaria: Sofia
1 Stamboliiski Blvd
tel 88-48-01 to 05 telex 22690 BG

Czechoslovakia: Prague
    Trziste 15-12548 Praha
    Amembassy Prague, c/o Amcongen, APO NY 09757
    tel 53 66 41/8 telex 121196 AMEMBC

Denmark: Copenhagen
    Dag Hammarskjold Alle 24
    APO NY 09170
    tel (01) 42 31 44 telex 22216

Finland: Helsinki
    Itainen Puistotie 14A
    APO NY 09664
    tel 171931 telex 121644 USEMB SF

France: Paris
    2 Avenue Gabriel
    Paris Cedex 08, 75382
    APO NY 09777
    tel 296-1202, 261-8075 telex 65-221

    Bordeaux
    No. 4 Rue Esprit des Lois
    33000 Bordeaux
    tel 56/52-65-95

    Lyon
    7 Quai General Sarrall; 69454 Lyon CEDEX 3
    tel 24-68-491

    Marseille
    No. 9 Rue Armeny 13006
    tel 54-92-00

    Nice
    No. 3 Rue Dr. Barety 06000
    tel 88-89-55

    Strasbourg
    15 Ave d'Alcase 67082
    APO NY 09777
    tel (88) 35-31-04/05/06

U.S. EMBASSIES AND CONSULATES IN EUROPE

East Germany: Berlin
108 Berlin, Neustaedtische Kirschstr 4-5
USBER Box E, APO NY 09742
tel 2202741 telex 112479 USEMB DD

West Germany: Bonn
Deichmannsaue
5300 Bonn 2
APO NY 09080
tel (02221) 89, 55 telex 885-452

Bremen
President-Kennedy-Platz 1
2800 Bremen 1
Box 1, APO NY 09355
tel (0421) 32 00 01

Dusseldorf
Cecillenallee 5
4000 Duesseldorf 30
Box 515, APO NY 09080
tel (0211) 49 00 81

Frankfurt Am Main
Siesmayerstr 21
6000 Franfurt
APO NY 09757
tel (0611) 74 0071
After hours: (0611) 74 50 04

Hamburg
Alsterufer 27/28
2000 Hamburg 36
Box 2, APO NY 09069
tel (040) 44 10 61

Munich
Koeniginstr 5
8000 Muenchen 22
APO NY 09108
tel (089) 2 30 11

Stuttgart
Urbanstr 7
7000 Stuttgart
APO NY 09154
tel (0711) 21 02 21

Greece: Athens
91 Vasillissi Sophia Bld
APO NY 09253
tel 712951 or 718401
(area code from US 01130-1)
telex 21-5548

Thessaloniki
59 Vasileos Constantinou St
APO NY 09693
tel 266-121

Hungary: Budapest
V. Szabadsag Ter 12
Am Embassy, APO NY 09757
tel 329-375 telex 224-222

Iceland: Reykjavik
Laufasvegur 21
FPO NY 09571
tel 29100

Ireland: Dublin
42 Elgin Rd, Ballsbridge
tel Dublin 688777 telex 5240

Italy: Rome
Via Veneto 119/A
00187-Rome
APO NY 09794
tel (06) 4674 telex 613425 or 610450

Florence
Lungarmo Amerigo Vespucci 38
APO NY 09019
tel (055) 298-276

Genoa
Banca d'America e d'Italia Bldg
Piazza Portello 6
Box G, APO NY 09794
tel (010) 282-741 thru 5

Milan
Piazza Repubblica 32
20124 Milano
APO NY 09689
tel (02) 652-841 thru 5

Naples
Piazza della Repubblica 80122
Box 18, FPO NY 09521
tel (081) 660966

Palermo
Via Baccarini 1, 90143
tel 291532-35

Trieste
Via Roma 9 (fourth floor)
APO NY 09293
tel (040) 68728/29

Turin
Via Alfieri 17
10121 Torino
Box T, APO NY 09794
tel (011) 543-600, 543-610, 513-367

Luxembourg: Luxembourg
22 Blvd Emmanuel Servais
APO NY 09132
tel 40123 thru 7

Netherlands: The Hague
Lange Voorhout 102
APO NY 09159
tel (070) 62-49-11 telex (044) 31016

Amsterdam
Museumplein 19
APO NY 09159
tel (020) 790321

Rotterdam
Viasmarkt 1
APO NY 09159
tel (010) 117560

Norway: Oslo
Drammensvelen 18
Oslo 1
APO NY 09085
tel 56-68-80 telex 18470

Poland: Warsaw
Aleje Ujazdowskie 29/31
AmConGen, APO NY 09757
tel 283041-9 telex 813304 AMEMB PL

336

Krakow
Ulica Stolarska 9
31043 Krakow
AmConGen, APO NY 09757
tel 29764, 21400

Poznan
Ulica Chopina 4
AmConGen, APO NY 09757
tel 595-86/87, 598-74

Portugal: Lisbon
Avenida Duque de Louie No. 39
1098 Lisboa
APO NY 09678
tel 570102 telex 12528 AMEMB

Oporto
Apartado No 88
Rua Julio Dinis 826-30
tel 6-3094/5/6

U.S. EMBASSIES AND CONSULATES IN EUROPE

Romania: Bucharest
Strada Tudor Arghezi 7-9
AmConGen, (Buch) APO NY 09757
tel 12-40-40 telex 11416

Spain: Madrid
Serrano 75
APO NY 09285
tel 276 3400/3600 telex 27763

Barcelona
Via Layetana 33
APO NY 09285
tel 319-9550

Bilbao
Avenida del Ejercito, 11-3rd floor
Deusto-Bilbao 12
APO NY 09285
tel 435-8308/9

Seville
Paseo de las Delicias No 7
APO NY 09282
tel 23-18-85

Sweden: Stockholm
Strandvagen 101
tel (08) 63.05.20 telex 12060 AMEMB S

Goteborg
Sodra Hamngatan 53, box 428
tel (031) 80.38.60

Switzerland: Bern
Jubilaeumstrasse 93
3005 Bern
tel (031) 437011 telex 32128

Geneva
80 Rue du Lausanne
1200 Geneva
tel (022) 327020

Zurich
Zollikerstrasse 141
8008 Zurich
tel (01) 552566

Turkey: Ankara
110 Ataturk Blvd
APO NY 09254
tel 26 54 70

Adana
Ataturk Caddesi
APO NY 09289
tel 14702/3, 14818

Istanbul
104-108 Mesrutiyet Caddesi, Tepebasi
APO NY 09380
tel 436200/09

338

Izmir
386 Ataturk Caddesi
APO NY 09224
tel 132135/7

USSR: Moscow
Ulitsa Chaykovskogo 19/21/23
APO NY 09862
tel 252-00-11 thru 19 telex 7760 USGSO SU

Leningrad
UL, Petra Lavroya St 15
Box L, APO NY 09664
tel (812) 274-8235

United Kingdom: London
24/31 Grosvenor Sq
W 1A 1AE
Box 40, FPO NY 09510
tel (01) 499-9000 telex 266777

Belfast, Northern Ireland
Queen's House
14 Queen St, BT1 6EQ
tel Belfast (0232) 28239

U.S. EMBASSIES AND CONSULATES IN EUROPE

Edinburgh, Scotland
3 Regent Ter, EH 7 5BW
tel 031-556-8315

Yugoslavia: Belgrade
Kneza Milosa 50
tel 645655 telex 11529

Zagreb
Brace Kavurica 2
tel 444-800

APPENDIX
M

CYCLING IN THE USSR, EAST GERMANY AND ALBANIA

You can bring your bike with you as baggage and use it locally in East Germany and the USSR. Riding it as a bike tourist between towns is prohibited, though. Your itinerary is fixed and your transportation is public, in other words.

Albania accepts only a few foreigners, and those are carefully screened and controlled, and are usually in a group. No bike riding at all.

340

INDEX

INDEX

343

INDEX

346

INDEX